WITHOUT A PRAYER

NORTH AMERICAN RELIGIONS

Series Editors: Tracy Fessenden (Arizona State University), Laura Levitt (Temple University), and David Harrington Watt (Haverford College).

Since its inception, the North American Religions book series has steadily disseminated gracefully written, pathbreaking explorations of religion in North America. Books in the series move among the discourses of ethnographic, textual, and historical analysis and across a range of topics, including sound, story, food, nature, healing, crime, and pilgrimage. In so doing they bring religion into view as a style and form of belonging, a set of tools for living with and in relations of power, a mode of cultural production and reproduction, and a vast repertory of the imagination. Whatever their focus, books in the series remain attentive to the shifting and contingent ways in which religious phenomena are named, organized, and contested. They bring fluency in the best of contemporary theoretical and historical scholarship to bear on the study of religion in North America. The series focuses primarily, but not exclusively, on religion in the United States in the twentieth and twenty-first centuries.

Books in the series

Ava Chamberlain, *The Notorious Elizabeth Tuttle: Marriage, Murder, and Madness in the Family of Jonathan Edwards*

Terry Rey and Alex Stepick, *Crossing the Water and Keeping the Faith: Haitian Religion in Miami*

Isaac Weiner, *Religion Out Loud: Religious Sound, Public Space, and American Pluralism*

Hillary Kaell, *Walking Where Jesus Walked: American Christians and Holy Land Pilgrimage*

Brett Hendrickson, *Border Medicine: A Transcultural History of Mexican American Curanderismo*

Jodi Eichler-Levine, *Suffer the Little Children: Uses of the Past in Jewish and African American Children's Literature*

Annie Blazer, *Playing for God: Evangelical Women and the Unintended Consequences of Sports Ministry*

Elizabeth Pérez, *Religion in the Kitchen: Cooking, Talking, and the Making of Black Atlantic Traditions*

Kerry Mitchell, *Spirituality and the State: Managing Nature and Experience in America's National Parks*

Finbarr Curtis, *The Production of American Religious Freedom*

M. Cooper Harriss, *Ralph Ellison's Invisible Theology*

Ari Y. Kelman, *Shout to the Lord: Making Worship Music in Evangelical America*

Joshua Dubler and Isaac Weiner, *Religion, Law, USA*

Shari Rabin, *Jews on the Frontier: Religion and Mobility in Nineteenth-Century America*

Elizabeth Fenton, *Old Canaan in a New World: Native Americans and the Lost Tribes of Israel*

Alyssa Maldonado-Estrada, *Lifeblood of the Parish: Masculinity and Catholic Devotion in Williamsburg, Brooklyn*

Caleb Iyer Elfenbein, *Fear in Our Hearts: What Islamophobia Tells Us about America*

Rachel B. Gross, *Beyond the Synagogue: Jewish Nostalgia as Religious Practice*

Jenna Supp-Montgomerie, *When the Medium Was the Mission: The Religious Origins of Network Culture*

Philippa Koch, *The Course of God's Providence: Religion, Health, and the Body in Early America*

Jennifer Scheper Hughes, *The Church of the Dead: The Epidemic of 1576 and the Birth of Christianity in the Americas*

Sylvester A. Johnson and Tisa Wenger, *Religion and US Empire: Critical New Histories*

Deborah Dash Moore, *Vernacular Religion: Collected Essays of Leonard Primiano*

Katrina Daly Thompson, *Muslims on the Margins: Creating Queer Religious Community in North America*

Jonathan H. Ebel, *From Dust They Came: Government Camps and the Religion of Reform in New Deal California*

Leslie Beth Ribovich, *Without a Prayer: Religion and Race in New York City Public Schools*

Without a Prayer

Religion and Race in New York City Public Schools

Leslie Beth Ribovich

NEW YORK UNIVERSITY PRESS

New York

NEW YORK UNIVERSITY PRESS
New York
www.nyupress.org

Library of Congress Cataloging-in-Publication Data
Names: Ribovich, Leslie Beth, author.
Title: Without a prayer : religion and race in New York City public / Leslie Beth Ribovich.
Description: New York : New York University Press, [2024] | Series: North American religions |
Includes bibliographical references and index.
Identifiers: LCCN 2023028403 (print) | LCCN 2023028404 (ebook) |
ISBN 9781479817269 (hardback) | ISBN 9781479817276 (paperback) |
ISBN 9781479817290 (ebook) | ISBN 9781479817306 (ebook other)
Subjects: LCSH: Religion in the public schools—New York (State)—History—20th century. |
Race relations—New York (State)—History—20th century. | Education and state—
New York (State)—History—20th century. | Church and state—New York (State)—
History—20th century. | Racism in education—New York (State)—History—
20th century. | Humanism—New York (State)—History—20th century.
Classification: LCC LC112.N7 R53 2024 (print) | LCC LC112.N7 (ebook) |
DDC 379.2/809747—dc23/eng/20230828
LC record available at https://lccn.loc.gov/2023028403
LC ebook record available at https://lccn.loc.gov/2023028404

For my teachers and students

CONTENTS

Introduction

Reframing Religion and Race in Public Education

Educators reading the *Public Schools of New York Staff Bulletin* on September 9, 1963 encountered two pieces of seismic news. On the left side of the bulletin's front page, an article announced that the city would follow the Supreme Court of the United States' *Engel v. Vitale* and *Abington v. Schempp* rulings, which found school prayer and devotional Bible-reading unconstitutional in American public schools. On the right side of the page, a separate article laid out the city's plan for racial integration. The side-by-side layout framed secularization and desegregation as separate stories, each of which related to public schools, but not to the other. However, it was no coincidence that public school secularization and desegregation were happening, and failing, simultaneously. Many of the programs and priorities of this era, from juvenile delinquency prevention to moral and spiritual values curricula and racial integration advocacy, straddled these supposedly distinct issues, tethered by the invented tradition—Judeo-Christianity—and its whiteness.[1] Whiteness undergirded concepts of a "Judeo-Christian" America in areas relating overtly to religion, such as Bible-reading in schools, even as that religious tradition undergirded schools' efforts focused on race, such as integration.

This book offers an as yet untold story about religion's role in shaping twentieth-century American public education. Rather than existing in a separate sphere, religion structured government policies on race and everyday school practices before and after the 1962 and 1963 US Supreme Court decisions holding school prayer and Bible-reading unconstitutional. Using New York City as a window into a national story, I argue that these Supreme Court decisions failed to remove religion from public schools because religion—from the government-endorsed Judeo-Christianity to Pan-African theology—framed how Americans

The Public Schools of New York City

STAFF BULLETIN

VOL. II, NO. 1   SEPTEMBER 9, 1963   WHOLE NO. 12

RULINGS OBEYED, BIBLE READING IN ASSEMBLY ENDS

The Board of Education has amended its practices on Bible reading in the schools to conform to decisions of the U. S. Supreme Court and the State Education Commissioner.

At its meeting on August 21, the Board repealed a by-law requiring school assembly programs to be opened with a reading from the Bible, without comment. The Board also relaxed the requirement of the singing of the fourth stanza of "America" at the beginning of each school day to include any patriotic song. Thus, henceforth, under the Board's vote, the school day will begin with the traditional Pledge of Allegiance by the pupils followed by the singing of a patriotic song in unison. Formerly, the Pledge had been followed by the singing of the fourth stanza of "America" only.

Both actions were recommended to the Board by Superintendent Gross, who said that "the reading of the Bible as a religious exercise has been the only practice of this school system not in

(Continued on page 8)

Barkan Is Sworn In As Member of TRB

Joseph G. Barkan, Member of the Board of Education, was sworn in as a member of the Teachers Retirement Board by Mayor Wagner at City Hall on August 21.

Established in 1917, the TRB administers the retirement funds of over 55,000 present and retired members of the teaching and supervisory staff of the City school system, as well as professional employees of the municipal college system.

The TRB consists of the President of the Board of Education, the City Comptroller, two members appointed by the Mayor, one of whom shall be a member of the Board of Education; and three members elected by direct vote of the pension contributors.

Integration Plan Sets 4 Main Areas

The Plan for Integration, spelling out the school system's approach to improved racial balance, is published below.

It is, in the words of City Superintendent Gross, "the most comprehensive effort to achieve maximum integration, both on the basis of past performance and future commitments, of any city school system in the country." In transmitting the plan to State Education Commissioner James E. Allen, Jr., the Superintendent adds:

"We have planned carefully and thoroughly, using the best advice we could get, to move toward complete ethnic integration to the limit permitted by feasibility and sound educational practice. . . . Our plan represents all possible steps we have been able to devise, short of the compulsory interchange of Negro and white students between distant communities."

The plan had been requested by Commissioner Allen on June 14. It was sent to him on August 23.

Plan for Integration

In the years since the historic 1954 decision of the U. S. Supreme Court, and even earlier, the New York City public schools have pursued earnestly their commitment to the objective of racial integration in the schools. Much has been accomplished. Nevertheless our Midsummer 1963 stocktaking makes it clear that much more has to be done. Our past programs and activities were appropriate for their time, but we now propose to embark on a new series of endeavors which we hope will hasten the day when our City is completely integrated and all of our children will enjoy equal educational opportunity. We believe that school integration is an important part of our pursuit of excellence for all children.

We wish we were able now to provide not only the dates for each new step in our integration plan but also the date by which all our schools will have been desegregated. However, the complicated interrelationships of life in our City require that such a comprehensive program and timetable be developed jointly by all the many agencies whose activities affect integration. The Board of Education will take leadership in urging City-wide participation in the preparation of such a plan and timetable for integration.

In the meantime, we shall move ahead with attacks on four major fronts:

On the *moral* front the professional staff of the school system commits itself to pursue vigorously the unequivocal integration policy established by the Board of Education. We shall establish procedures to enlist a like commitment from civic and community groups in every part of the City.

On the *desegregation* front we shall develop and apply programs which will achieve ethnic integration to the extent permitted by feasibility and sound educational practice.

On the *instructional* front we shall move with imagination and energy to give every child the kind of education which is his birthright especially if he has been denied equal opportunity up until now. By raising children's aspirations and then establishing instructional programs to fulfill them we shall strive to provide a broad and thorough educational background for the new career and academic opportunities which will be opening to them. We shall work towards securing more college opportunities for Negro and Puerto Rican high school graduates.

On the *job* front we shall strengthen our program to prepare students with more precision for the job opportunities which will be offered by New York City industry and commerce. We shall

(Continued on page 4)

Figure I.1. *The Public Schools of New York City*, Vol. II, No. 1, September 9, 1963, Box 3, Series 530, Staff Bulletin, 1962–1972, New York City Board of Education Records at the New York City Municipal Archives.

interacted with public schools far beyond prayer and Bible-reading, and continued to do so, through public education's process of collective moral formation. Intersections of religion and race informed the major conversations about twentieth-century American public education, from school desegregation, youth crime, and multicultural education to government aid to religious schools, community control of education, and prayer and Bible-reading. Both secularization and desegregation in New York City public schools inculcated students into white Christian norms through a repertoire of ideas and practices, as part of their project of shaping students into citizens, at the same time that parents, teachers, and community members drew on, resisted, and reimagined that repertoire to create citizens of a different sort.

The history of race and religion in the urban North is the history of desegregation and secularization of public schools. Collective memory about desegregation and secularization of public schools often focuses on the southern United States.[2] We hear about the rogue school in the "Bible Belt" sponsoring prayer, or we read a sanitized history of Martin Luther King Jr.'s triumph over southern racism. The South shaped American racism and religiosity, but the South alone did not purvey white Christian supremacy. The North did, too, in its own way. Focusing only on the South reinforces stereotypes about Northern innocence, Southern religious fervor, and Black, southern, religious resistance.

Shifting attention to the North requires us to abandon stereotypes and to see how, while the contours differed, Americans revered the public school as a sacred site that produced religious and racial beings through educating the public. Recent decades have seen an influx in scholarship on the Northern Civil Rights Movement, centered in New York City.[3] Reflecting national concerns about school inequality, New York City witnessed the largest school boycott of the American Civil Rights Movement, during which nearly half a million students stayed home. Moreover, a key way to understand racism in the North is to look at desegregation alongside efforts at secularization. Secularization efforts abounded outside the South, which showed that religion existed in public schools there, even as more than half the states had outlawed prayer and Bible-reading by the 1960s. The state-sponsored school prayer case, *Engel*, originated in New York State before landing at the US Supreme Court. The state's governing educational body, the

New York Board of Regents, had written the prayer at issue in *Engel*. The Bible-reading and prayer case, *Schempp*, consolidated cases from Pennsylvania and Maryland, the mid-Atlantic; not the Northeast, but not the South, either. Other significant mid-century Supreme Court religion and school cases began in Illinois and New Jersey.[4] In these contestations over what religion looked like, many Americans throughout the country supported secularization even as they practiced patriotic rituals and an understanding of American history that privileged whiteness. This book asks for a transformation in how we view religion in public schools: as entwined with the history of race in public education. Secularization and desegregation are part of the same story.

As one of the most racially and religiously diverse, and one of the most segregated, cities in the country, New York City sheds light on a national story.[5] The Great Migration of African Americans from the Jim Crow South, migration from Puerto Rico, and immigration from Caribbean countries earlier in the century had altered the city's racial demographics.[6] The racial diversity also contributed to the city's religious diversity, with New Yorkers across racial demographics practicing Catholicism, Judaism, Yoruba traditions, Santería, Protestantism, religio-racial movements, various combinations of these traditions, and much more. Black Liberation Theology and Pan-Africanism also emerged in New York City, and some New Yorkers vibrantly practiced them.[7] Few places had the demographics to test the American ideal of pluralism as New York did. Diversity in and of itself did not solve segregation or religious establishment, but it did shape their terms of engagement.

New York City also had the largest school system in the country, a complex institution where bureaucracy collided with public opinion. In the mid-twentieth century, more than a million students attended New York City public schools. The system included numerous community school districts, but the centralized Board of Education determined hiring, curricula, and more at 110 Livingston Street in downtown Brooklyn. Just as was the case throughout the country, local school boards influenced national policies, and vice versa, making the city's school system a compelling site to study both governance and the people who made and were affected by it.

The common story of desegregation in New York City typically goes something like this: Following the US Supreme Court's 1954 *Brown v.*

Board of Education decision, the New York City Board of Education sponsored a Commission on Integration.[8] The Commission developed ideas for zoning, curricula, hiring, and more, but the Board largely did not fund or actualize the ideas. Instead, the Board proposed insufficient plans to effect change. Black and Puerto Rican New Yorkers organized the 1964 Freedom Day School Boycott for desegregation and school resources. When the Board still failed to make any changes, three districts experimented with controlling their own schools, having community boards responsible for curricula, hiring, and more. Teachers struck, leading to the longest boycott in the school system's history. The strike laid bare existing racial tensions, as many teachers were white and Jewish, while many students were Black or Puerto Rican and not Jewish. To avoid further disruption, the Board decentralized the school system but maintained control over crucial decisions, including zoning districts.[9] The Board remained decentralized until the early 2000s, when the Department of Education formed.

After community control, white teachers still comprised the majority, even in predominantly Black or Puerto Rican schools, and school districts still reflected residential segregation, with Black or Puerto Rican neighborhoods and schools receiving less funding. Community control did not lead to desegregation or more equity across the city, so, until recently, scholars and the public have generally embraced the idea that community control failed.[10]

Yet, whether community control succeeded in New York City depends on how we understand its aims. Community control did not end segregation, but that was not the goal of its proponents; self-determination was. From that perspective, Black and Puerto Rican New Yorkers successfully built grassroots alliances that fueled future social justice advocacy, even though the immediate goal of those groups, community control of public schools, ended.[11] Even less frequently discussed than Black and Puerto Rican New Yorkers' successful coalition-building is that it was their understandings of community and freedom, drawing from Black churches, liberation theology, Pan-Africanism, and more, that helped to fuel the community control movement. While community control may have ended, it showed that another form of public education was possible, one where Black and Puerto Rican religious and racial worldviews were manifest in public education.

Seeing religion as part of New York City desegregation helps us to shift the story from one of failure to one of complex negotiations and possibilities. This book shows that the Board's adoption of what it called "Judeo-Christianity" for teaching American history, preventing juvenile delinquency, and promoting integration as a value contributed to religion's continuing presence in the schools. At the same time, it illuminates that the ongoing struggles around desegregation and community control resisted the schools' Judeo-Christian white moral framework and produced original religious and racial worldviews that sustained educational justice efforts for decades to come. Black and Puerto Rican religious and racial creativity thus also continued in public schools following the early 1960s, Supreme Court cases, and even beyond the late 1960s' community control movement. To understand how religion persisted in public schools without a prayer, let us unpack the historical and enduring intersections of religion and race in public education.

Religion, Race, Public Education

Multiple understandings of religion and race endured through the mid-twentieth century, finding homes in educational policies, practices, and philosophies not normally thought of as having both religious and racial implications. Scholarship on religion and public education and race and public education each complicate straightforward stories about decline or progress.[12] Yet, religion and race are still largely studied separately in the history of education, or if together, understood as two distinct dynamics, primarily because religion is undertheorized.[13] As religion scholar Kristy Slominski shows with regard to sex education, education teaches morality.[14] Our question is then about the texture and content of those morals when it comes to race. Here, scholarship on religion and race helps us to see that religion and race are often co-constructed. Modern understandings of religion and race began in tandem.[15] Beginning with the separation of Christianity from Judaism in the first century and including European colonizers traveling the globe, people, usually Christian people, found those who looked different from them practicing differently from them and created hierarchies based on these differences in appearance and practice, which placed themselves at the top.[16]

Through public schools, ideas about religion and race were perpetuated and transformed. At its foundation, the structure of public schools created American moral norms through a colonial framework of cultural expulsion and assimilation. In everyday school lessons and activities, religious institutions and people embedded within different racial, religious, and ethnic communities and identities influenced what schools taught because teachers, administrators, and parents were also part of such communities. Moreover, constituents from varied backgrounds debated public education's purpose—and, by implication, understandings of citizenship, belonging, and peoplehood—using religious and racial reasoning.

The Court's understanding of religion did not account for the racial dimensions of religion: its colonial structure, its role in both perpetuating and protesting racial injustice. The *Engel* and *Schempp* Court took pains to say that only devotional activities were unconstitutional; teaching about religion and patriotic activities remained permissible. The distinction between devotional exercises and teaching about religion created a strict division between what counted as publicly appropriate religion (teaching about religion) and what was inappropriate (private religion expressing personal beliefs, such as prayer and Bible-reading). The Court framed unconstitutional religion as belief, an understanding hinged on a Protestant interpretation of religion as a personal relationship with a monotheistic God.[17]

Today's lament by conservative evangelicals that religion was removed from the schools when the Supreme Court found devotional exercises unconstitutional *and* frustrations expressed by liberals that students should not be coerced into a particular religion through prayer or Bible-reading both retain the focus on devotional exercises as the most relevant aspect of religion to public education. These arguments privatize religion. In doing so, they frame religion as a discrete entity that can be removed from the public sphere by prohibiting people from expressing their private beliefs in public. Yet, the Court decisions themselves indicate that patriotic exercises (and teaching about religion) were permitted. These public forms of religiosity continued to influence public schools. The privatization of religion reinforces what scholars call a subtraction theory of secularization—the idea that secularization removes religion from the public sphere.[18] Rather than privileging the

Court's understanding of privatized, unconstitutional religion, this book analyzes the public expressions of religiosity that are rarely recognized as religion because they were not at issue in court, charting religiosity's influence on the seemingly nonreligious moral and civic worldviews put forward in New York City's schools.

When we see religion, race, and public education together, the public school emerges as a parenting institution that took mid-century Americans from the Cold War and Civil Rights Movement to the Culture Wars, from the seeming liberation that secularization and desegregation promised to the entrenched political warfare that has marked the late twentieth and early twenty-first centuries.[19] Responding to the dual pressures of secularization and desegregation, New Yorkers developed their repertoire of values and performances on "Judeo-Christianity," democracy, American historical figures as "fathers," racial self-determination, tolerance, and more. This repertoire set the stage for fights ahead on creationism, sex education, sexuality and gender, multiculturalism, and teaching race by establishing the public school as a co-parent with students' families. As co-parent, the public school could authorize behavior, and the contentious home-school relationship became a battleground for America's identity.

A Method of Uncovering

This book places the field of American religions in conversation with new methodologies, disciplines, and sources. I turn from the courtroom to the classroom to understand how people practiced public education religiously. In doing so, I build on recent scholarship in religion and law that aims to understand both categories capaciously.[20] Court decisions only get us so far in analyzing religion in public education, as court decisions often maintain status quo distinctions between religion and nonreligion. Focusing on the national authority distinguishing religion from nonreligion can privilege national religiosities, such as Judeo-Christianity. The book is necessarily interdisciplinary: It draws on the history of education, critical pedagogy studies, law, and critical race theory to make arguments in the study of religion, particularly American religions.

My research began nationwide, and New York City stood out for its connections to national concerns and a uniquely diverse populace. The city's public education archives are vast. While historians of education have studied some sources I analyzed, scholars of religion have not. Many of the sources are previously unexamined in any field. I began by identifying and analyzing references to religion in education policies and programs. I found that references to race and national efforts to educate the public overwhelmingly accompanied references to religion, meaning the word religion, religious traditions, and related concepts such as spirituality. Sometimes the reference was indirect, as in the September 9, 1963 *Staff Bulletin* with its two parallel tracks. Sometimes it was explicit: a program on moral and spiritual values calling for students to live in the US founders' legacy. I also examined programs more overtly dealing with race—desegregation and juvenile delinquency prevention. Sure enough, religion was there, too. A 1963 Board-sponsored one-way transfer program to address school segregation mentioned integration as being in the spirit of "our Judeo-Christian tradition," and delinquency prevention programs showed films broadcasting the message "thou shalt love thy neighbor as thyself" to students who were sent by courts to special "600" public schools for "delinquents." Organizations promoting community control of schools advocated for the seven principles of Blackness as a moral framework separate from Judeo-Christianity. Where there was religion, there was race; where there was race, there was religion.

When I went looking for "religion" in a sea of educational bureaucracy and pedagogical passion, I tracked what people on the ground understood religion to be. For school leadership, religion typically meant both beliefs and practices typically associated with sites of worship, especially churches. The sources also spoke of a "Judeo-Christian tradition" that undergirded American democracy, reflecting a national movement to defeat "godless" Communism in the 1950s.[21] The schools' Judeo-Christianity upheld America's tri-faith (Protestant, Catholic, Jewish) godliness, while protecting a white version of that pluralism. For parents and communities on the ground, religion sometimes meant a particular tradition—Judaism, for example, and the importance of home prayer. I also saw references to Pan-Africanism and liberation that participated in broader projects within African American religions. Following my sources' leads, I situate the religious movements they spoke of in historical context: the nationwide tri-faith movement, also headquartered in New York City, and the role of religious institutions in shaping the Northern Civil Rights Movement.

As I searched through files, I found it became impossible to separate out religion because public schools braided notions of whiteness, morality, and meanings of religion together in colonial projects of creating moral Americans, with "moral" as a category that signaled white purity and innocence. Public schools theoretically accept all students, but their history has been mired in exclusion. Moreover, public schools are just one institution that educates the public. Importantly, public education has aimed to form the character of Americans across a range of institutions, including prisons, Indian boarding schools, and political campaigns. In these examples, religion shapes the terms by which public education aims to create moral Americans.

While the definition of "moral" and "Americans" varies depending on whom you ask, religion influences how people imagine moral Americans. In New York City, school administrators and parents did not use religion to serve a racial project, or race to serve a religious project.[22] Instead, secularization and desegregation were already wound up in public education's process of moral formation. Together, they offered moral narrative arcs and sense-making frameworks for public school participants. Thus, public schools fostered opportunities for imagining the future, with students as redemptive agents.[23] Traditions that people have considered "religions" intertwined with public schools' aims to cultivate upcoming generations.[24] The competing visions of the future engaged racial categories and practices, such as segregation, integration, community control, centralized control, delinquent, dropout, learner-teacher, and more. The categories' racial character reflects the long-standing use of categories of difference to promote cosmologies.

Some scholars have responded to the subtraction secularization thesis by elaborating notions of secularism to talk about the power of state governance over defining categories by which we live our lives. My approach complements a view of secularism as "less . . . restrictive" than reinforcing a secular/religious binary or accepting the Protestant secular as hegemonic.[25] Secularism studies concerns the secular, the frame that distinguishes religion and nonreligion, or good and bad religion, and secularism, the structure of governance that emerges from that frame.[26] I reject the subtraction thesis while retaining the category of religion as historical actors have understood it (even if they sometimes bought into a subtraction thesis) and used it (as their actions often contradicted the subtraction thesis because of religion's intersections with race in public education).

In New York City public schools, religion was malleable, prone to fail at hegemony. I understand religion as an imaginative space where New Yorkers from the Superintendent of Schools to "600" school students played, and in doing so, shaped both the frame and governance of religion.[27] In the American context, secularism studies often reasonably conclude that white Protestantism is hegemonic and all-powerful. And yet, in the case of New York City public schools, we find implicit and explicit challenges in abundance, especially in a city with considerable Catholic and Jewish populations, as well as racial diversity. For instance, Jews who contested the Regents' prayer's Christianity help us to think outside the hegemony because they directly questioned it, and Black Protestants who proposed Freedom Schools offered alternative narratives and spaces to white Protestant hegemony. In short, twentieth-century New Yorkers spoke of and practiced religion as already part of race and public education in American modernity. Public schools naturalized religion, and communities cultivated it toward diverse ends: some dominating, others liberating, and many outside a dominating/liberating binary.

A Structure for Recovering

This book's structure situates whiteness in the narrative of secularization and the Judeo-Christian repertoire in the narrative of desegregation. Part 1 (Secularization | Race) shows how scholarship and inherited public memory typically seen as being about just religion—school prayer and Bible-reading—were also about race. The devotional exercises and the moral and spiritual values programs from which they emerged disciplined Black and Puerto Rican students' behavior while uplifting white behavior as moral. Chapter 1 explores the national uproar over *Engel v. Vitale* (1962) as a response not only to the perceived removal of religion from public schools, but also to the racial disciplining work the Regents' prayer, the prayer at issue in *Engel*, accomplished. In doing so, it introduces the concepts public schools drew on to promote what they called "Judeo-Christianity." Chapter 2 turns to moral and spiritual values programming in New York City, which never adopted the Regents' prayer. Without prayer, but with moral and spiritual values, the Board produced a theological frame that changed the source of moral and spiritual values from God to the Founding Fathers. The change situated students as heirs to a providential and settler colonial American heritage, one where only white men had reigned. Taken together, the chapters show that race was central to the moral and spiritual values movement.

Flipping the focus, part 2 (Desegregation | Religion) shows how public school issues typically considered to be about just race—juvenile delinquency prevention and desegregation—were also about religion. While groups ranging from filmmakers to social scientists framed juvenile delinquency through race and social environment, chapter 3 shows how public schools also cultivated juvenile delinquency as a religious category through a surprising source: the biblical commandment to love your neighbor as yourself. Schools pulled from contemporary social sciences, which identified "high delinquency areas" as areas with large populations of Black and Puerto Rican youth. The schools' commandment to love your neighbor as yourself restructured students' familiarity with the phrase and neighborhoods' physical space to define morally good neighborhoods against neighborhoods in need of reformation. Chapter 4 explores how public school participants employed conflicting religious concepts to advocate for public school integration. While the predominantly white Board of Education saw integration as a value that did not require desegregation, Black and Puerto Rican communities saw integration as a value that did require desegregation to promote equitable schooling. Part 2 shows that the desegregation narrative—even a failed one—conceals religion's role in promoting or challenging the status quo of segregated schools.

Part 3 (Purposes of Public Education) builds on the work of parts 1 and 2 to shift away from narratives about secularization and desegregation. Instead, part 3 reveals that intersections of religion and race in public schools reflected debates about American public education's purpose. In chapter 5, I uncover the debate at the 1967 New York State Constitutional Convention about government aid to Catholic schools. The chapter explores how a dynamic convergence of characters used religious and racial arguments to debate the scope of public education.

Chapter 6 analyzes the debate over community control of New York City schools, focusing on the underlying religious and racial critiques of American public education. Despite often being seen as a failure, community control opened space for Black religious and racial world-making through the public schools, space that reimagined what public education could do and whom it served. Part 3 concludes that public education allowed New Yorkers to imagine different American futures in conversation with theological registers that accounted for histories of colonization and slavery.

Chapter 1 begins around 1950; chapter 6 ends around 1969. I use a chronological structure but resist the assumption that the passing of time promotes progress.[28] Instead, the chronological framing allows us to track change over time *as well as* continuity. This structure allows us to challenge the process-oriented narratives of secularization and de-segregation on their own terms. Through the chronological structure, this book offers a new history of New York City public schools, where, alongside persistent segregation and underfunding, the schools' Judeo-Christian repertoire and Black and Puerto Rican worldviews played an important role in decentralizing the school system.

* * *

Desegregation and secularization may read as incompatible failed processes to pair. Desegregation's failure can be proven through demographics while secularization's is vaguer; people defined the absence of religion differently. Yet, although religion and secularization may more obviously read as contested categories, desegregation is not so straightforward either. Its demographic goals may be well defined, but its moral goals are as amorphous as religion. The possibility of desegregation's tangible demographic shift brought about visions of integration that sought to "de-race" public schools through color-blind racial inclusion much like subtractive secularization aimed to "de-religion" them. For Black and Puerto Rican New Yorkers, the goal of desegregation was equitable resources, not the removal of their cultures and identities. Desegregation was required to access those resources because white people controlled them. Given that not all Black and Puerto Rican New Yorkers desired desegregation, and given that desegregation was a legal process rather than the social-moral ideal that integration was, this conceptual clarity is needed to see how religious and moral ideas bolstered conversations about racial equity, making desegregation as complex as secularization. Unpacking the goals of desegregation, integration, and consequently, today's diversity, equity, and inclusion work, can lead to an understanding of why we are still talking about school inequity and what other ways people might have used, or might still use, to improve conditions for Black and Latinx students' education in public schools. Desegregation and secularization both name processes that assume an end point where participants all too easily forget the past: Racial segregation and subjugation or an explicitly Protestant public square. Whatever moral assumptions undergird the historical processes we study, forgetting is not the answer.

So, to remember. If racial inequity and school prayer in public education seem like perennial issues, it is because the public school's purpose has been to cultivate moral beings through religious and racial categorization, and educators, parents, and teachers have long questioned and reframed this purpose. Religion remains and is essential to understanding the history of race in American public education.[29]

I

Secularization | Race

1

The Racialized Moral and Spiritual Values
of New York State

In 1951, the New York State Board of Regents crafted a prayer. The state's governing educational body, the Regents, included thirteen members, all white, all male except for one woman. Catholic and Jewish members worked alongside Protestants.[1] The Regents worked with rabbis, ministers, and priests to make the prayer nondenominational: "Almighty God, we acknowledge our dependence upon Thee, and we beg Thy blessings upon us, our parents, our teachers and our Country."[2] Nevertheless, in 1962's *Engel v. Vitale*, the Supreme Court of the United States found the Regents' state-sponsored school prayer unconstitutional because it violated the First Amendment of the US Constitution's establishment clause. Following *Engel*, chaos ensued. Many Americans were furious about what they perceived as the removal of religion from public schools. The Court received more negative mail about *Engel* than *Brown v. Board of Education* (1954).[3] The next year, *Abington v. Schempp* added fuel to the fire by finding all public-school-sponsored prayer and devotional Bible-reading unconstitutional. Although more than half the states had already banned prayer and Bible-reading, the national decisions panicked Americans who read the cases as morally corrupting the country's youth, especially in states where courts had not yet outlawed the practices.[4]

Yet, the prayer at the center of *Engel* comprised only one sentence of the Regents' much larger "Moral and Spiritual Values" programs. The programs taught dependence on "the moral and spiritual heritage which is America's" through activities such as the Pledge of Allegiance and patriotic songs.[5] These activities were immersed in whiteness, with anti-Communism as an otherizing strategy to construct a God-sanctioned "American heritage" of white heroes. Prayer was just one facet, while dependence on a white Christian America permeated moral and spiritual values programs' guidelines for the whole school day.

By situating the *Engel* and *Schempp* cases within broader mythologies of whiteness, rather than in the secularization of public schools, we can reorient ourselves to this part of American history and see that race was at its center. Before turning to New York City, we can see that at the state level, the Regents articulated and perpetuated a vision of America as white through their narratives of American identity and history. The broader apparatus around the Regents' prayer shows us how fundamentally inextricable religion was from the project of education in New York State and how fundamentally racializing the project was.

When understood as a primarily religious artifact, the Regents' prayer illuminates Cold War concerns about Communism abroad. Across the country, religion in the public sphere boomed. During President Dwight Eisenhower's tenure, from 1953 to 1961, the US Congress added "Under God" to the Pledge of Allegiance and "In God We Trust" to currency to show that the United States was a religious nation.[6] It was not a godless country that would lead to violent government overthrows, as many American leaders feared the USSR's Communism would encourage.[7] Funding for churches increased and parachurch organizations emerged, as Depression- and World War II–era spending limits were lifted. Churches could more readily spread the government's messages and their own.[8]

The religious boom also amplified domestic concerns about race and gender. Anti-Communists sought to preserve an "American way of life" that precluded advancing civil rights for women, people of color, and people with low income. Conservative white clergy and businessmen coordinated to reverse the New Deal's social spending.[9] Biblical images of the "Ten Commandments" and morality tales about the dangers of an irreligious household, where mothers continued to work outside the home after World War II, populated screens in cinemas and classrooms.[10] Back in New York State, the early chills of the Cold War sent shivers down the Regents' spines. The Regents rejected "godless Communism" by allowing local boards to investigate and fire teachers suspected of current or past participation in a "subversive organization." They feared such teachers would bring Communism into schools. Significantly, affected teachers, many of whom were Jewish, were among those who had advocated for progressive ideals, including civil rights for students of color.[11]

The Regents' prayer evoked the same fear of government subversion as did the moral and spiritual values movement in which it participated. The 1951 "Statement on Moral and Spiritual Training," where the Regents' prayer appeared, recited classic Red Scare religiosity. "We are convinced that this fundamental belief and dependence of the American—always a religious—people is the best security against the dangers of these difficult days," it read, continuing that the prayer and moral and spiritual values could defend "the peace and safety of our country and our State against such dangers."[12] The anti-Communist language created a foreign "other" that could be applied to domestic "others." It provided a new vocabulary for racism at home just as it otherized religious alterity abroad.

While hubbub about the Regents' prayer centered on its constitutionality, moral and spiritual values were not at issue in *Engel*. The Court found, "There can, of course, be no doubt that New York's program of daily classroom invocation of God's blessings as prescribed in the Regents' prayer is a religious activity." Because all respondents agreed that the prayer was religious, the Court argued that it violated the First Amendment's establishment clause, which prohibits any law "respecting an establishment of religion."[13] According to the Court, the problem was that the Regents' prayer was a prayer, "a solemn avowal of divine faith and supplication for the blessings of the Almighty." While the decision clarifies that the prayer was not exempt from religious status "because it is based on our spiritual heritage," it tacitly encouraged patriotic activities and history lessons. Because the Court did not have to decide whether these activities and lessons were constitutional, they could continue.

Yet, the Regents' prayer's pedagogical origins in moral and spiritual values training warrants further scrutiny.[14] This context brings into relief how subtracting religion from public schools could not be as simple as removing a prayer because it was a part of a structure that wove together religion and race in a prescribed American subjectivity. Following the 1951 statement that included the prayer, the Regents kept developing a moral and spiritual values program. On March 25, 1955, they unanimously adopted "The Regents Recommendations for School Programs on America's Moral and Spiritual Heritage."[15] Four days after the 1962 decision, the Regents issued a press release acknowledging that, although the state recognized *Engel's* legal authority, "The Regents have long had and continue to have a deep and abiding concern for the teaching of moral and spiritual values in the schools," citing their 1951 and 1955 statements. The release expressed "confiden[ce]" that public schools "will continue to give strong emphasis to those fundamental values so clearly set forth in the basic documents and pronouncements which are America's heritage."[16]

This heritage discouraged not only Communist dissent among students and teachers, but other dissent, too. Some took the form of vocal, formal dissent; some dissented merely by existing in bodies that were not white and male.[17] New York's moral and spiritual values programming thus responded to national conversations about civil rights and immigration while establishing a sense that white Americans had become influential because they had God's favor. The Regents' larger project signaled that white, male students belonged in and controlled the United States, while students of color, who represented increasing demographic populations, would need to revere white, male history or get lost.

Moral and Spiritual Values

The foundation for widespread moral and spiritual values programs was the 474-word "Regents' Statement on Moral and Spiritual Training in the Schools," issued in 1951. This was the Regents' prayer's birthplace. Although the prayer sparked nationwide controversy, only 10 percent of districts in New York State had ever adopted it.[18] By contrast, moral and spiritual values programs flourished throughout the state and country. In New York State, all "city, village, and district superintendents" received notice of the Regents' 1951 statement and follow-up 1955 recommendations from the state's Commissioner of Education. The recommendations "reemphasize[d] one of education's oldest and most fundamental responsibilities," which the Regents claimed was to "build [. . .] in youth character deeply rooted in the moral and spiritual values underlying America's cultural heritage."[19] Beyond the state, the National Education Association (NEA)'s Educational Policies Commission published and widely distributed a 1951 report on "Moral and Spiritual Values in the Public Schools." The American Association of School Administrators' 19,000 educators approved a resolution stating that "the teaching of moral and spiritual values in public schools is "'indispensable to the perpetuation of the American way of life.'"[20] Educators across the country discussed moral and spiritual values at conferences held at Teachers College and Union Theological Seminary in New York City. At the Teachers College conference, educators prepared to present a case for moral and spiritual values education to the White House because "the 'intangibles' of present-day living, such as training for citizenship, cannot be overlooked."[21] Public schools from Florida to California developed guidebooks and curricula on moral and spiritual values.[22] Moral and spiritual values programs were among the most influential educational programs in 1950s America, but what were "moral and spiritual values"?

The NEA report's definition of "moral and spiritual values" was so open-ended that it appeared almost meaningless: "By moral and spiritual values we mean those values which, when applied to human behavior, exalt and refine life and bring it into accord with the standards of conduct that are approved in our democratic culture."[23] Yet, the contrast between the impossibly general ("human behavior," "life," and "culture") and moments of specificity ("democratic culture," "brotherhood," and "spiritual enrichment") subtly built consensus around particular values.[24] Within the NEA's framing of democratic culture, the goal was to promote specific, unnamed standards that a public consensus "approved." The report created this consensus through the way it framed institutions. "Institutions as the servants of men" and "common consent" to the norms institutions set were especially important values for consensus-building. Therefore, the NEA implied that public schools enacted American democracy by establishing how people treated each other.

One critique of the NEA's definition of "moral and spiritual values" pushed back against the assertion that moral and spiritual values built consensus. Secretary of Education for the Catholic Archdiocese of New York Rt. Rev. John J. Voight suggested that in God's absence, who or what approved human conduct was unclear. He distinguished moral from spiritual values, arguing that moral values related to "human judgment regarding what is right and wrong in accordance with God's law" and spiritual values "related to the supernatural."[25] Under Voight's definition, God still approved all values, but with moral values, human judgment came into play. Voight argued that without God or a Christian context, the NEA's definition "become[s] vague and pragmatic."[26] To collapse the two terms, Voight argued, was essentially secularization, which for him meant removing God.

In New York State, the Regents landed somewhere different, where the ultimate source of approval was still understood as God, via American leaders. As the NEA did, the Regents explained "moral and spiritual values" generally to convey a specific vision of American values. However, the Regents more visibly employed God language to uplift a white America. An undated early draft of the Regents' follow-up to the 1951 statement most directly explained: "A moral value is a guide to conduct based on an understanding of life. A spiritual value embraces a knowledge of life, worthy standards of conduct and an emotional and religious attitude or impulse."[27] At this draft stage, the Regents identified that "a moral value" related to conduct and "a spiritual value" operated in the emotive or religious realm, echoing Voight's Catholic contrast, except the Regents were opaque about the source of the spiritual values. The vagueness allowed the Regents to appear open to varied interpretations at the same time it indicated that behavior was less religious than feeling, which was a distinctly Protestant view.

By the publication of the 1955 recommendations, no such definition remained. Instead, references to God's influence on America implied the terms' meanings. The recommendations supplement's first section cited the Declaration of Independence, the New York State Constitution, the American Seal, the recently added "In God We Trust" to currency, George Washington and Benjamin Franklin at the Constitutional Convention, Abraham Lincoln at Gettysburg, Woodrow Wilson, and Dwight Eisenhower to connect freedom to God.[28] The section concluded, "these Fundamental Beliefs have been our moral and spiritual ideals." To the Regents, moral and spiritual values signified that God gave Americans freedom. The final section on "Stressing Moral & Spiritual Values" concluded that children "will renew in their daily lives America's Moral and Spiritual Heritage: Liberty under God, Respect for the Dignity and Rights of Each Individual," and "Devotion to Freedom," each item a main section of the publication.[29] In the Regents' final recommendations, their implicit morality and spirituality came into focus: a sense that God had ordained the freedoms American schoolchildren were afforded.

The focus on white figures and a providential American heritage took place against a backdrop of demographic changes in American public life sparked by desegregation, migration, and immigration. Public schools, especially in New York City, had become increasingly religiously and racially diverse in previous decades due first to Jewish and Catholic immigration from Eastern Europe, followed by immigration and migration from the Caribbean, particularly Puerto Rico, and Black American migration from the US South during the Great Migration. Moreover, major legal decisions on desegregation came down amid the moral and spiritual values phenomenon. Future US Supreme Court Justice Thurgood Marshall and the NAACP strategized to end school segregation. The Court had already heard school segregation cases *Sipuel v. Board of Regents of University of Oklahoma* (1948), *Sweatt v. Painter* (1950), *McLaurin v. Oklahoma State Regents* (1951), and *Bolling v. Sharpe* (1954). Attorneys filed *Brown v. Board of Education* in federal court in February 1951, the same year the Regents' first statement, the one including the prayer, and the NEA's pamphlet emerged. Though they did not name it, moral and spiritual values programs aimed to protect against how commingling children of different racial, ethnic, and religious backgrounds would affect American public schools and culture.

The Regents also identified a supposedly malignant "foreign" "other" in the form of potential "subversives." In its January 1952 "Platform" issue on "new crises for education," *Newsweek* laid the groundwork for why Americans needed moral and spiritual values education during "some of the sharpest controversies in its [education's] history," namely "the ideological conflicts which divide the world."[30] The issue listed "controversies" from California, New Jersey, Indiana, Ohio, and other states to stress what it identified as a widespread Communist influence.[31] Controversies included: "subversive" textbook content; phonograph records in nursery schools with performers whose political affiliations troubled the publication and a record company producer that "had been cited as a Communist front by the House Un-American Activities Committee"; and professors who refused to sign loyalty oaths. The article lobbed criticism at schools, including that "they neglect moral and spiritual values,"[32] faculty declined to "deflate[]" "evil and foolish values,"[33] and faculty ignored that "Education shouldn't be propaganda."[34] *Newsweek* framed progressive educators as maliciously failing to teach a required set of pro-American values. With words like "neglect," "evil," and "propaganda" on the table, the stakes were high.

In opposition to the subversive, foreign Communist template, the Regents cultivated the template of a white, God-fearing, obedient American. In the "Report of Special Committee of the Board of Regents in the Inquiry Relative to Subversive Organizations" from September 24, 1953, the Regents employed heritage and ancestor language in opposition to Communists. With the caveat that free speech was America's heritage, the Regents continued that "such advocacy must be based upon those lawful, constitutional processes which likewise are part of such heritage."[35] Loyalty to an idealized image of the Constitution superseded practicing its guaranteed rights. Although "The philosophy of dictatorship, violence, brutality and fear may not be strange to a people who have never known liberty," the Regents argued, "in our country with its heritage that all men are born equal, that they are endowed by their Creator with the inalienable right of liberty," "it is both tragic and wicked that a misguided few should not value that priceless inheritance but should seek to destroy it by force and violence."[36] To the Regents, because it came from God, the heritage opposed Communists, whose support for evil originated outside the United States.

By creating an evil other, the Regents aimed to cure people they had otherized or who might be tempted by the Communism and Progressivism they had otherized. The cure? Moral and spiritual values. In November 1952, the New York State Teachers Association announced a revised code of ethics that affirmed the pledge of loyalty to the state and federal governments that teachers already took at the time of employment. The new code wrapped moral and spiritual values into its support for the pledge by adding that "The teacher believes in . . . moral and spiritual values as fundamental to education."[37] Moral and spiritual values' appearance in a teachers' loyalty code reiterated the contrast between moral and spiritual values and Communism for teachers, who undoubtedly already feared for their livelihoods. The binary between foreign, immoral Communists who would infiltrate schools and democratic, moral, and spiritual white Americans who would not had become common sense in the Regents' lexicon.

This binary of foreign and American could easily be applied to anyone who did not match the American gold standard because of race, ethnicity, or religion. Given the demographic changes and existing racism, Black and Puerto Rican students could become easy targets for failing to meet the standard simply because of who they were. For example, a promotion for the NEA moral and spiritual values report elided foreign and domestic threats. The promotion critiqued Communism and war abroad—"Moral values have been shaken in our generation by two world wars, by a wasteful economic depression, by a resurgence of barbarism among supposedly civilized peoples, by social disasters following technological triumphs"—alongside domestic social unrest: "The changing patterns of home and family life seriously complicate the problem of developing moral and spiritual values in young people."[38] "Changing patterns" likely referred to immigration, migration, and desegregation's influence on demographics. The reference also evoked changes in women's work patterns during World War II. The *Newsweek* issue put it more bluntly in a reprinted cartoon from a National Council for American Education pamphlet cover. The cartoon pictures a bespectacled and skirted figure with a hairline down to her brow and bugged out eyes. Her rage has fashioned her almost monstrous. She chops down a tree, the trunk of which reads "American Way of Life," with branches for "Truth," "Honor," "Justice," "Loyalty," and "Order." The caption reads: "Progressive Education Increases Delinquency."[39] Here, progressivism disfigured the matronly teacher and provoked her to destroy American values. And, those values were racialized: New York City and State disproportionately charged Black and Brown children with delinquency.[40]

New York State drove moral and spiritual values education throughout the country. For example, Regent Roger Williams Straus Sr. traveled in influential state and national circles. A Jewish financier and activist for religious freedom, Straus Sr. was the son of religious liberty activist and Roger Williams biographer Oscar Straus, husband of heiress and nutrition expert Gladys Guggenheim Straus, and father of Farrar, Straus, and Giroux publisher, Roger Williams Straus Jr.[41] Straus Sr. straddled state education and national religious freedom endeavors, as he cochaired the National Conference of Christians and Jews alongside his Regent duties. The largest national interfaith organization in the mid-twentieth century, the NCCJ organized educational awareness-raising campaigns to promote positive relations between Protestants, Catholics, and Jews. The group also instrumentally promoted America as a tri-faith nation, albeit one that often adopted Protestant supersessionist views—i.e., where Christianity superseded Judaism and Protestantism superseded Catholicism.[42] In a May 19, 1953 address to the New York Academy of Public Education, Straus named the NCCJ's goal in the title, "Strengthening the Moral and Spiritual Forces of the Nation Through Education." He combined his NCCJ work with his Regents work when he said he was "proud to have been associated with" the Regents' 1951 statement on moral and spiritual values that included the prayer, because it "admirably summed up" the aims of his speech.[43]

Straus's theological solution to the "the problems of working for unity within diversity" amplified whiteness even as he recognized diversity's importance. Straus staunchly supported "the brotherhood of all men under the fatherhood of God," which he saw as "a dynamic force in shaping Western civilization, drawing its strength from the great stream of religious tradition." He also endorsed that "the founding fathers" articulated that rights were "God-given," because if the state bestowed rights, the state could take rights away without moral redress.[44] He explained that New York City was the ideal place to test his theories because "Few if any other parts of the country exhibit such a spectrum of religious belief—of national cultures—of racial backgrounds."[45] He claimed to see the city's diversity as "heartwarming" and not "threatening," even as he used racialized language of "Western Civilization" and promoted only white men as moral exemplars.

The tectonic moment around the Regents' prayer crucially promoted moral and spiritual values as building a white America. Focusing on the 1951 statement, with reference to the 1955 recommendations, further exemplifies race's significance to the Regents' prayer.

Establishing a White Judeo-Christian Repertoire Through the Regents' 1951 Statement

The Regents joined the NEA and schools throughout the country in producing a school-specific repertoire of terms that put white American heritage at the center of moral education. The repertoire participated in nationwide tri-faith America efforts, i.e., the idea that America was a Protestant, Catholic, and Jewish nation where belief in any tradition was better than no belief.[46] The tri-faith model tied American heritage to a recent tradition politicians and interfaith leaders alike called "Judeo-Christian heritage" or "Judeo-Christianity." As scholars such as K. Healan Gaston have shown, this framework privileged (white) Protestant voices in the name of pluralism.[47] Pieces in the repertoire included "covering" the three traditions of the tri-faith, extolling the Founding Fathers, forming commitment to democracy, and emphasizing moral and spiritual values. Such pieces produced binary sets: brotherhood, human relations, love of neighbor fell on the good side; suppressive behavior, intolerance, and bigotry on the bad. Public school participants performed a liberal subjectivity that did not require challenging its own underlying assumptions.[48] Moreover, the power dynamics were malleable; its players could contribute individual experiences, historical moments, current politics, and more to it.

A father–male child relationship exemplified the kinship between "our pioneering ancestors," "our Founding Fathers," and God. The Regents praised that "our pioneering ancestors" held "an abiding belief" "in the universal brotherhood of man based upon their acknowledgment of the fatherhood of their Creator, Almighty God." The phrase "Brotherhood of Man under the Fatherhood of God" unsurprisingly became a slogan for the NCCJ, given Straus's role on the Regents and NCCJ as well as the far reach of ideas about Judeo-Christianity. Brotherhood of man and fatherhood of God signaled a male inheritance theology, while the Regents remained quiet regarding whether men of color could be brothers. Although the Regents claimed anyone could access brotherhood, the portrait of the ancestors suggested otherwise.

In the Regents' view, America owed its "way of life" to a reverent, dependent father son relationship, as their statement opened. "Belief in and dependence upon Almighty God was the very cornerstone upon which our Founding Fathers builded [sic]." The statement emphasized the supplicatory nature of this relationship, noting that the "pioneering ancestors" acknowledged their Father God parentage because "they loved and reverenced" God "in diverse ways." While "diverse ways" nods to many religious traditions, God remains singular, as does the loving and reverential dependence on God.

The Regents used the term Founding Fathers as though it had always existed. In fact, it was relatively new. Just a few decades earlier, then-Senator Warren Harding had coined "Founding Fathers" to describe men like Thomas Jefferson, James Madison, and Alexander Hamilton. Harding used the phrase to support his own agenda, suggesting that the Founding Fathers would support his candidacy for president.[49] So did the Regents.

In the Regents' imagination, schools reared devoted sons who would become exemplary fathers. Schools could teach children how to excel as reverent and dependent white sons of God by facing "the basic truth of their existence and inspired by the example of their ancestors," i.e., through the prayer but also through "specific programs stressing the moral and spiritual heritage which is America's" at the day's beginning. Through such activities, "our children . . . will be properly prepared to follow the faith of his or her father, as he or she receives the same at mother's knee, by father's side, and as such faith is expounded and strengthened for them by his or her religious leaders." In the Regents' rendering, because God blessed America and public schools educated it, schools became parents who had "a high function of supplementing the training of the home, ever intensifying in the child that love for God, for parents and for home." As parents, schools taught children that revering authority figures mirrored how the men they called Founding Fathers had revered their Father God.

The Regents produced many drafts of the recommendations publication between 1953 and 1955, experimenting with different framings of American exceptionalism.[50] For example, earlier versions aimed for a tri-faith vision of America, as they contained sections excluded from the final version on "Protestantism and American Culture," "Protestant Sanctions for Moral Conduct," "Catholic Contributions to American Democracy," "Hebraic Ideals in American Democracy," "The Role of Jews in American History," and "Jews in America Today." These sections spun a narrative of American values beginning with ancient Greece, stopping in first-century Judea and landing with the Pilgrims.[51] Yet, they left readers wondering about Catholics' and Jews' roles in American culture, with passages such as: "Many groups contributed to the building of America. The Jews had no special role but with others made a significant contribution."[52] The erasure of Jews from early American history gave the impression that Christians, especially Protestants, were solely responsible for a laudable American morality and spirituality.[53] The statement also omitted any reference to white, Christian violence against Native Americans and Black Americans. With selective examples in place, the draft presented white Protestants as the standard bearer American citizens. In this framing, other groups might influence ideas about American values, but they contributed to an established model, not one they created.

Therefore, tri-faith appeared to mean writing Judaism and Catholicism into a Protestant American narrative. For example, the "Hebraic Ideals in American Democracy" section began with John Adams and the Pilgrims, not with Jews. The Protestant section paid homage to a Jewish and Catholic past when it claimed, "Protestant concern for others, especially the exploited and the under-privileged, has a venerable rootage in the Hebrew-Christian tradition."[54] Yet, only scripture from what the document calls the "Old Testament" supports the claim—no Jewish or Catholic interpretation of that scripture. Personnel developing the recommendations also exemplified the Protestant focus. Arthur Kendall Getman worked part time to develop materials for the Regents on teaching moral and spiritual values in the schools.[55] A retired Assistant Commissioner of Education and chief of the agricultural education bureau, and former Vice President for the State Council of Churches, Getman took a distinctly Protestant angle on the materials, despite consulting with a rabbi, a minister, and a priest.[56] In 1959 and 1960, state officials contacted presses to publish a version of Getman's work on teaching moral and spiritual values. Nonsectarian presses declined the manuscript because the work read as "specifically Christian in orientation," as one publisher put it.[57]

Some earlier versions of the recommendations referred to biblical or ancient stories of governmental overreach to elevate America as the freest place on earth. One November 1953 progress report lamented, "Today mankind lives under a menace like that of Sodom." The Regents proceeded to quote Augustine on the fall of the Roman Empire, and asked students if they saw connections between Rome and America today.[58] In doing so, the Regents placed contemporary schoolchildren into a biblical history where they held responsibility for redeeming a free and pure nation from tyranny. The Regents explicitly named Communism as the source of that tyranny, writing that while democracy promoted moral and spiritual values, "Communism utterly abhors such values."[59] They therefore used moral and spiritual values to differentiate good and evil.

Anti-Communism was in the water the Regents drank. When a concerned citizen, Mrs. Irving (Bella) Crown in Mamaroneck, New York, wrote to State Commissioner of Education Lewis A. Wilson that the Regents' prayer poorly defended against Communism, Wilson responded, "I do not believe that this statement of the Board of Regents was in any way an effort to fight Communism."[60] Scholars today would likely disagree, as the last decades of scholarship have declared Cold War religion a nation-building tool against the USSR.[61] Nevertheless, Wilson responded that the prayer "was directed primarily to encourage our schools to place greater stress on abiding moral and spiritual values."[62] The story of an "abiding" good fighting evils had become so commonplace that Wilson could deny that the Regents had Communism in mind.

The final Regents' 1955 supplement to the 1951 statement and prayer further established the supremacy of white American heritage by doubling down on the 1951 statement and drawing on other resources in the repertoire. Compared to the earlier drafts, the published recommendations were much shorter, organized into three concise sections: Brotherhood of Man under Fatherhood of God; Devotion to Freedom; and Stressing Moral and Spiritual Values.[63] Whiteness especially appears in its limited definition of freedom. The Regents offered Thomas Jefferson's September 23, 1800 letter to Benjamin Rush: "I have sworn upon the altar of God eternal hostility against every form of tyranny over the mind of man" as an example of "Devotion to Freedom."[64] Jefferson originally wrote this line about tyranny against sectarianism, which could seem ironic, given the Protestant dimensions of the Regents' work, but in fact exemplified how Protestant anti-sectarianism often worked.[65] The Regents emphasized "Our freedom of speech and worship and the press, and to do all things which do not harm others" which "must constantly be defended and cared for lest we lose it." While the first clause refers to Jefferson's First Amendment, Jefferson hardly exemplifies nonviolence. An enslaver who fathered children through a relationship that could never be consensual, Jefferson was only devoted to a freedom that does "not harm others" if Black people, especially Black women, are not included in the social contract that regulates "human."

While the *Engel* Court found the prayer itself to violate the establishment clause, Justice Hugo Black, writing for the majority, acknowledged in a footnote that: "There is of course nothing in the decision reached here that is inconsistent with the fact that school children and others are officially encouraged to express love for our country by reciting historical documents such as the Declaration of Independence which contain references to the Deity or by singing officially espoused anthems which include the composers' professions of faith in a Supreme Being, or with the fact that there are many manifestations in our public life of belief in God." Black, a former Ku Klux Klan member who expressed ardently anti-Catholic views, continued that "Such patriotic or ceremonial occasions bear no true resemblance to the unquestioned religious exercise that the State of New York has sponsored in this instance."[66] Though Black framed schools leading prayer as an unconstitutional expression of religion, he encouraged schools to develop an exclusive Judeo-Christian tradition. The Regents' prayer's impact is a result of the lessons and ceremonies as much as the Court's controversial decision.

Solidifying "The Other"

Moral and spiritual values programs' attacks on Communism participated in a more protracted story of anti-Communism in the city. Communism had long existed in the New York City Teachers Union. From the 1920s to 1940s, the TU collaborated with the American Communist Party and included Communist members who fought for unionism inclusive of social justice. Organizations deemed "subversive," such as the TU, often advocated for civil rights. As historian Clarence Taylor has argued, among teachers' unions in the city, the TU had ties to the Communist Party and uniquely "fought diligently to end racial discrimination."[67] As the Red Scare increasingly frightened the country in the late 1940s, the Regents aimed to root out Communism in New York schools. In 1949, the New York State legislature passed the Feinberg Law, which allowed the state to investigate teachers presumed to belong to, or to have belonged to, "subversive" organizations.

The Regents defined "subversive organization" in relationship to a non-American entity. A Special Committee of the Regents focusing on the inquiry wrote in their September 24, 1953 report that an organization was subversive if inquirers found it to: "advocate, advise, teach or embrace the doctrine that the government of the United States or of any state or of any political subdivision thereof shall be overthrown or over-turned by force, violence or any unlawful means," or "advocate, advise, teach or embrace the duty, necessity or propriety of adopting any such doctrine."[68] Subsequent inquiries into TU teachers led to mass firings, especially in New York City. The law allowed the Board to investigate more than 1,100 teachers whom they suspected of being Communist spies in the early 1950s. Over a few years, the New York City Board of Education dismissed hundreds of teachers in a reflection of the Board's anti-Communism and a systematic eradication of anti-racist peda-gogy.[69] Through their inquiries, the Regents solidified Communists as a foreign other, not just because of possible connections abroad, but be-cause at home, "subversives" focused on race. Agitating for racial justice labeled teachers as un-American, as the Special Committee's 1953 report adopted a narrow understanding of "American," one where "Freedom to advocate changing our form of government into a communistic state, repugnant as it is to the overwhelming majority of the American people, is part of the American heritage of free speech," while "such advocacy must be based upon those lawful, constitutional processes which like-wise are part of such heritage."[70] Free speech was limited.

The firing or dismissal of many Jewish teachers marginalized Jew-ish voices in the Regents' Judeo-Christian American heritage, as well as Black voices the teachers lifted up. As one news article titled "More Bias-Fighting Teachers Fired in N.Y." put it, "all were school system veterans (15–25 years) with no complaint of their classroom conduct; all officers or members of the Teachers Union; all active in community work against jim-crow [sic] or anti-Semitism; all Jewish."[71] In "An Ap-peal to the Jewish People of New York from Eight Teachers Suspended from the Schools by Superintendent Jansen,"[72] a group of suspended teachers called out New York City Superintendent of Schools William Jansen's implicit anti-Semitism and anti-Black racism. Historians of edu-cation have documented Jansen's racism well.[73] Even as Jansen worked in interfaith groups and received support from the Jewish Teachers As-sociation, this cohort of suspended teachers questioned coincidences in their stories.[74] While all had clean teaching records, each had also "been active in efforts to secure the removal of bigoted teachers and to eliminate anti-Semitic and other biased materials from textbooks." Suspiciously, teachers who had called "the immigrants to America after

1880"—i.e., many Jews and Catholics—"'the scum of Europe'" or "against whom charges of anti-Semitism and anti-Negro bias had been made" remained employed.[75] The teachers cited the Black newspaper the *New York Age* to emphasize that not only did "the ax appear[] directed primarily at Jews," but "most of these teachers have been active in fighting against discrimination, and for school improvements among minority groups."[76] The teachers maintained that Jansen sought to eliminate them because of their socially progressive views on race. Even if one plays devil's advocate to say it was coincidental that Communist and social justice values aligned in these teachers' cases, the result was the same. Their suspension further marginalized attempts to eliminate bias against Jewish and Black Americans and to improve school conditions for Black Americans.

Some Jews found themselves on the sidelines of dominant American narratives because they supported civil rights and nondiscrimination; others landed there because of their religion. In March 1955, the Board, in conversation with Jansen, proposed that teachers who knew of other teachers' ties to "subversive" organizations ought to turn in those teachers to protect American democracy and religious freedom.[77] However, Jewish organizations responded to the Board proposal by invoking the authority of the Babylonian Talmud, specifically the principle of *mesirah*, meaning "to turn over" to secular authorities. The New York Board of Rabbis, an organization "representing all branches of Judaism,"[78] implored the Board on April 21, 1955 "not to exact any ruling requiring former Communist teachers to inform on their past associates." The rabbis reached their position by "applying the long and honored ethical tradition of Judaism which condemns slander as an offense as serious as idolatry and murder, and denies the informer a share even in the world to come."[79] Some Jews considered *mesirah* irrelevant in the United States because "the application of the law of Mosor" required "The gentile government concerned" to be "one which acts 'violently'" and "Our government does not act violently."[80] Yet by drawing attention to *mesirah*, the NYBR reasoned that the city and state's approach to creating an America free of Communism excluded Judaism, which drew attention to what many saw as an abhorrent practice. The government supported religion, but only religion that viewed Communism as a threat to American heritage, one Americans needed to fight at all costs.

The New York City Council of the American Jewish Congress simultaneously objected to the informant proposal *and* Communism. The Council warned that no "real necessity for such a rule" existed since "Communists have been eliminated from the New York City school system with dispatch and thoroughness."[81] On their view, after the previous years' teacher raids, the city now stepped too far: "Informing was the practice in Nazi Germany. Today it is required in Soviet Russia. . . . Shall the United States adopt this hallmark of a prison society?"[82] By comparing New York City and State to the totalitarian regimes the governments sought to fight, the council found solidarity with Jews across the world.[83]

Because school-specific Judeo-Christianity at once perpetuated white, Protestant supremacy while New Yorkers from an array of religious and racial backgrounds cultivated it, it represented a flexible repertoire rather than a hegemonic, well-oiled machine. In secularism studies, "the secular" is the mechanistic framework for determining religion versus not religion or good versus bad religion, while "secularism" is the form of governance that promises freedom through supposedly separating church from state.[84] Here, no framework was set in stone—it mutated depending on who employed it and why. People on the ground improvised new ideas and rehearsed old ones. Both the AJC Council and the NYBR argued that the informant rule was anti-American because it highlighted a disjuncture with Judaism. As the repertoire changed, the form of governance, too, destabilized. There was no single, knowable secularism, rather, a rotating set of government scripts that fresh players influenced over time. In New York City, the diversity of players and perspectives made the show.

The Regents' Prayer Goes to New York City

Throughout the state, each city school system contended with how to implement the Regents' statement. While cities like New Rochelle, just north of the Bronx, heartily adopted all the Regents' 1951 Statement's components, in New York City, the situation was more complicated.[85] Few city dwellers took issue with the Regents' vision of American history, but many contested the role of God and formal prayer in the Regents' statement. Organizations including the TU, the United Parents Associations, and the NYBR strongly opposed the prayer. To the NYBR, prayer conveyed a connection with God, which required mediation unavailable in public schools. The NYBR worried that the prayer violated the sanctity of specifications about prayer in Jewish law and practice, including that Jews pray at home or the synagogue, and that some Jews required specific clothing for prayer.[86] Nevertheless, the NYBR supported "the motives of the New York State Board of Regents in seeking to develop the moral and spiritual fibre of our children."[87] In short, as many opponents did, the NYBR could abide some activities to develop children's moral and spiritual compasses, but not prayer.

Eventually, following many challenges and much controversy, on March 6, 1952, President of the Board of Education Andrew G. Clauson Jr. announced that New York City public schools would not begin the day with the Regents' prayer.[88] Nevertheless, the question remained: How would New York City address the Regents' call to incorporate moral and spiritual values in the curriculum, if at all?[89]

The answer was bureaucratic. The Board of Education adopted two resolutions. One included singing the song "America" and reciting the Pledge of Allegiance. The second introduced the city's statement on moral and spiritual values, which spoke directly to the Regents' broader moral and spiritual vision for public schools. In the early days following their adoption, the first resolution had New Yorkers abuzz; the second seemed like an afterthought.

The first resolution came from Jewish Board member Colonel Arthur Levitt, whose idea for how to teach students values promoted reverence to country. Levitt, writing for the Jewish Teachers Association Bulletin in May 1953, argued that no Jewish teacher could truly be Communist because of Judaism's ethical tradition. He anointed Judaism "the mother of Christianity and of Mohammedanism" who "gave to the world the Judeo-Christian tradition."[90] In doing so, he played into the Judeo-Christian repertoire to uphold the Regents' American heritage perspective: "I propose no compromise with the wholesome objectives of the Regents. My purpose, indeed, is to achieve their very aims."[91] Simultaneously, Levitt aligned Judaism with American democracy over Christianity (which likely would have upset the Regents) and Islam (which the Regents all but ignored). He improvised that American values were ultimately Jewish values.[92] From his dual position as Judeo-Christian and an American Jew, he suggested that instead of the Regents' prayer, New

York City schools ought to open the day with the Pledge of Allegiance and the singing of the first and fourth stanzas of "America," also known as "My Country, 'Tis of Thee." Levitt argued that singing the two stanzas and reciting the pledge would fulfill the Regents' statement's objectives, "emphasizing the need for strengthening adherence to the moral and spiritual values upon which our democracy is founded."[93] Continuing the Regents' focus on God, Levitt understood the singing to revere a higher power, calling it "an Act of Reverence to God."[94]

The song's lyrics also narrated dedication to the country, especially by the European settlers in New England—"Land where my fathers died/ Land of the pilgrims' pride." Through the shared vocalization of the two verses, Levitt claimed students would cultivate the perspective the Regents wished for them: "Let us reflect upon its singular poetic beauty and upon its soul-stirring appeal, at once religious and patriotic. Who has not derived inspiration from hearing the first and fourth stanzas sung? Who, indeed, has not felt a surge of emotion and fervor in joining in its singing?"[95] To Levitt, singing could shape students' behavior by creating a swell of emotion. Through singing, students would become the anti-Communist Americans the Regents wanted—devoted to God and to a legacy of white New England settlers.

Levitt's proposal found more support than the Regents' Prayer in New York City, but the fourth stanza proved contentious because Levitt sought for the stanza to cultivate not only reverence to country—which most critics accepted—but also reverence to God, which many city organizations did not. The lyrics read:

> Our Fathers' God, to Thee,
> Author of liberty,
> To Thee we sing:
> Long may our land be bright
> With freedom's holy light;
> Protect us by Thy might,
> Great God, our King.[96]

Reflecting on the stanza's structure and lyrics, the January 10, 1953 edition of the *New York Teacher News*, the publication of the TU, called the fourth stanza itself "a prayer" and referred to this as a "'compromise'" in quotation marks, mocking the idea that a new prayer could appease all parties.[97] While fine with the first stanza, the *NYTN* found reverence to God in the fourth too specific.

Five days after the *NYTN* publication, despite uproar over the Levitt proposal from additional organizations such as the UPA, the Board adopted a version of Levitt's proposal with the controversial fourth stanza but *not* the first.[98] God became the center of patriotism, much like in the Regents' 1951 statement. Clauson responded to the UPA's "deep shock" about the adoption of the Levitt proposal by emphasizing the good that the patriotic rituals would do for students: "By their action, the Board members indicated that they do consider the proposal to be in the best interests of the City's children and, after all, the final decision is in their hands."[99] The action effectively quashed dissent.

But there was also the second resolution, which took devotion to white American ancestors beyond prayer to the content of school lessons. It called for review of how the curriculum addressed values throughout the entire school day, not just at the beginning of the day. Perhaps because the resolution did not mention God nor offer guidance as to how moral and spiritual values would be taught, the second resolution seemed like it would do what groups such as the NYBR, TU, and UPA who had rejected the prayer or "America" nevertheless thought that public schools should do—shape children's moral behavior through examples. Yet when the Board released the guidelines that emerged from this resolution two and a half years later, the second resolution became anything but an afterthought.

2

New York City and the Deification of the Founding Fathers

Following the New York State Board of Regents' initial short 1951 statement, including the prayer, New York City sought to fulfill the Regents' call for moral and spiritual values in public schools, since the Regents governed state policy. Like 90 percent of the state, New York City did not adopt the Regents' prayer, the prayer at issue in *Engel v. Vitale*.[1] However, that did not mean that the city did not teach moral and spiritual values. Far from it; the New York City Board of Education had its own extensive history of developing moral and spiritual values programs. As the Regents were preparing the detailed suggestions for teaching moral and spiritual values beyond prayer that we have already seen, the question for the Board was this: How, in a diverse and massive public education system like the city's, could schools teach moral and spiritual values? The sheer number of people from different religious and racial backgrounds living so close together heightened the potential for debate. As a result, more people called out the moral and spiritual values programs for privileging a Christian view of God. Ironically, in responding to criticism, the city solidified a new theology. Where the Regents laid the groundwork for the theology by claiming that God favored white Americans, the Board deified the figureheads of white American heritage: the Founding Fathers.

As we have seen, to replace the controversial prayer, the Board adopted two resolutions in 1953. The first required students to recite the Pledge of Allegiance and the fourth stanza of "America" ("My Country, 'Tis of Thee") at the beginning of each school day.[2] Similar to the prayer, the recitations set apart moral and spiritual values instruction and patriotic reverence in the day's routine. In the second resolution, by contrast, the whole school day was dedicated to teaching love of God and country. The Board resolved that the Superintendent of Schools would review the entire curriculum to ensure that it was "emphasizing the spiritual interest and patriotic motivations of our pioneering ancestors, the devotion and self-sacrifice of the Founding Fathers and their abiding belief in the principles of democracy."[3] The Board interpreted patriotism as spiritual, but the path toward that understanding was a winding one. The Board and Superintendents eventually developed a curriculum that embedded ideas about moral and spiritual values in the legacy of the Founding Fathers throughout the school day without the Regents' emphasis on God.

The second resolution's story involves many characters and two drafts of the moral and spiritual values statement. The original draft was issued on June 14, 1955. After more than a year of debate, a revision was produced the following October. The Office of the Superintendent of Schools, run by William Jansen, who as noted earlier was known to hold racist views, authored the initial statement.[4] Protestant and Catholic groups supported the draft. The Teachers Union, the Teachers Guild, the United Parents Association, and the New York Board of Rabbis opposed it. The Board—which was intentionally religiously diverse (with equal numbers of Protestant, Jewish, and Catholic representatives) but overwhelmingly white and male—requested and approved the revised statement.[5]

Interpretations of God's role in public schools guided the debate. Opponents rejected the draft's positioning God as the source of moral and spiritual values, as the Regents suggested, because it claimed that these values "presuppose the existence of a Supreme Being."[6] They argued that this presumption violated the separation of church and state. In response to the opposition, the Board crafted a revision, a sixteen-page booklet with a blue cover. On the surface, the revision put forth a secularized view about God. It no longer assumed that values, which it claimed were essential to all school subjects, emerged from belief in God: "Even those who may question the validity of the concept that God is the source of the inalienable rights of the individual admit that this ideal was basic in the thinking of our forebears," i.e., the Founding Fathers and historical figures in their wake.[7] Although studying school subjects no longer required belief in God, the revision embedded God in assumptions about right and wrong through "forebears."

The revision produced a theological change: The Founding Fathers replaced God as the source of moral and spiritual values.[8] This change was made possible by the deification of the Founding Fathers, which was itself a theology of whiteness. The linguistic shift between references to

God in the draft and revision expanded ways to access God by making white historical figures God-like, elevating white people as moral exemplars in God's image.

The debate over moral and spiritual values in public schools never went to court, which is generally where scholars have looked to examine contestations over religion and public education.[9] Comfortable with constitutional language, Board members, parents, teachers, and concerned community members navigated theology—which might seem to violate the establishment clause—by foregrounding theology in American history. In making the case that theology was embedded in American history, I build on emerging claims that mid-century Judeo-Christianity ran on whiteness by showing that the deification of the Founding Fathers produced a theology of whiteness.[10] The theology combined elements of Judaism, Catholicism, and Protestantism and became a set piece in the school-specific Judeo-Christian repertoire. Judeo-Christianity in New York City public schools developed theological claims, not merely civic ones, by making understandings of God central to the American history curriculum's tale of white conquest.[11]

The Draft and the Debate

Like the Regents, the city's moral and spiritual values statement draft assumed that Americans believed in a Protestant God. Before the draft's already-quoted line that moral and spiritual values "presuppose the existence of a Supreme Being," the draft drew from one of the Cold War religious boom's central ideas: "The American people are, characteristically, a religious people who derive their accepted moral and spiritual values from religion." The draft further situated this religiosity in a particular tradition by arguing that "These values are inherent in the Hebraic-Christian tradition."[12] "Hebraic-Christian" positioned the statement within early twentieth-century liberal Protestant Supersessionism, a theology in which Judaism existed only to birth Christianity.[13] The term "Supreme Being" built on the 1948 Draft Act's definition of religious belief, which also prioritized a Protestant understanding of religion.[14] Within liberal Protestant and state trends, the draft lauded values including "the importance of individual worth and of individual and group obligations in organized society" and "learning to assume responsibility for the consequences of one's own conduct and recognizing the validity of equal justice and consideration for all men."[15] By focusing on individual worth, the draft lent divine authority to God-given values from a particular Christian tradition, rendered universal. And, the public school became the vehicle for promulgating that tradition in organized society.

Criticism abounded. Without going to court, the critics developed their own "lived constitutionalism" or "lay constitutionalism," meaning interpretations of the US Constitution created by "lay" people rather than courts.[16] They argued that the draft's framing of God as the source of moral and spiritual values violated the separation of church and state. In their view, the principle dictated that religion and public schools should remain separate. For example, the United Parents Association claimed that the draft "is flagrantly violative of the Constitution and of one of the most sacred principles of our democracy—the separation of church and state" because of "its assumption that moral and spiritual values must, *in the schools*, be anchored in the area of religion."[17] Here, the UPA suggested that morality and religion *could* be separated.

The UPA's lived constitutionalism framed religion as the backdrop to the country, while claiming that patriotic religion differed from the statement's particular religion. Even in arguing for the separation of religion and schools, the UPA referred to "separation of church and state" as a "sacred principle[]," suggesting that respecting America had religious dimensions. The claim echoed Thomas Jefferson's argument in the Virginia Statute for Religious Freedom. Jefferson offered a theological justification for the separation of church and state; because "Almighty God hath created the mind free," the state should not impose religion.[18] Since the Virginia Statute inspired Jefferson's contributions to the US Constitution, the UPA also offered a Jeffersonian constitutional approach. For example, the UPA used the phrase "separation of church and state," which does not appear in the US Constitution, but which Thomas Jefferson did use in a letter to describe his intentions for the Constitution, and the Court later supported Jefferson's aims.[19] By calling "the separation and church of state" sacred, the UPA evoked a rich history of Americans transferring God's divinity onto American leaders and documents, even as the organization criticized the Board for doing the same.

Like the UPA, the New York Board of Rabbis understood the draft to support a particular religion. The NYBR "registered its 'vigorous opposition'" to the draft by arguing that it represented an "intrusion of the state—through the public school," because "religious education and training are the exclusive responsibility of the home, church, and synagogue." The "intrusion" was "clearly neither desirable nor welcome."[20] Although the UPA and NYBR were on the same side of the debate, their arguments differed. While the UPA prioritized American democracy's sacredness, the NYBR highlighted the home's, church's, and synagogue's sacredness. Nevertheless, each group identified that the draft imposed religion, which they argued violated the Constitution.

Critics defined "religion" through references to God. In November 1955, following criticism of the draft, Board President Andrew Clauson, himself likely a Methodist, sent a memo to "interested organizations."[21] He claimed the draft was "not a new Course of Study, Syllabus or program of studies."[22] Instead, he wrote, it "reaffirms the goals of education which refer to character training and the American Heritage, and makes explicit the moral and spiritual values which have always been implicit in the curriculum." Clauson's omission of God implied that he thought all accepted the draft's articulation of divine authority. He avoided discussing religion in a public institution, following the recent Supreme Court cases holding that the First Amendment of the US Constitution applied to the states.[23] Yet, the UPA objected to a number of the memo's assertions: that "children be 'led' to appreciate the references to God in some of our historical speeches and documents," literature "owes its greatness to its allusion to Providence and the religious motivations of its characters," science and math "lead 'to humbleness before God's handiwork,'" industrial arts makes the student "speculate about 'the marvelous working of a Supreme Power' from his observation of the wonders of the compositions of metals, wood and electricity," and the "religious motif" was most important in music.[24] Through these examples, the UPA showed that Clauson had indicated that God already undergirded the curriculum. In their view, this assumption was both untrue and unconstitutional.

Many of the same critics who saw God as the sticking point argued that moral and spiritual values could be detached from sectarian understandings of religion and endorsed the general idea of teaching moral and spiritual values. These critics offered alternative visions of moral and spiritual values, based on something other than God. For example, the UPA said that "Some of these suggestions are all the more deplorable because they are interspersed among some excellent proposals for building moral and spiritual values—and because their manner of introduction into the curriculum is furtive and indirect."[25] The "excellent" proposals' content remained unclear. The Teachers Guild provided more context. In their framing, moral and spiritual values arose from rationality: "We, of the New York Teachers Guild believe, as do right thinking citizens, in stressing moral and spiritual values in our teaching."[26] In opposing the initial Regents' prayer, the NYBR "applaud[ed] the motives of the New York State Board of Regents in seeking to develop the moral and spiritual fibre of our children," referring to the Board's goal "to fulfill the objectives of the Regents in seeking to nurture the moral and spiritual fiber of our children."[27] As a metaphor, "fiber" implied that educational programming shaped children's behavior and belief from within their physical bodies—the fibers of which children were made. The organizations were open to moral and spiritual values, separate from God, that shaped children's internal beliefs and external behavior to cultivate rational citizens.

Yet, the lack of specificity about the non-God source opened the door for the Office of the Superintendent's perspective. For example, the Teachers Guild, one of multiple teachers' unions in the city, explained that religion could be part of public schools in three ways: (1) teaching religion, (2) teaching about religion, and (3) teaching human-centered moral and spiritual values. The Guild argued that the latter two, which they supported, were distinctly different from the first. Like the UPA and NYBR, Teachers Guild Legislative Representative Abraham Lefkowitz, himself Jewish, found the draft "a dangerous unconstitutional experiment which violates the separation of church and state," even as the longtime union leader sympathized with anti-Communism.[28] Lefkowitz's reasoning, however, diverged from the UPA's and NYBR's. Lefkowitz argued that the draft's framing of God as the source of moral and spiritual values represented teaching religion rather than teaching about religion. Eight years before *Abington v. Schempp* articulated the distinction in its concurrence,[29] Lefkowitz asked: "How can we teach about religion without an examination of tradition and interpretation?" With religion as object of study rather than object of devotion, the Guild's objections to the "handiwork" claims took on new meaning. The Guild objected because the claims suggested that students should learn science not for its own sake but to submit to a creator.[30]

Lefkowitz intimated that, apart from God's immanence, moral and spiritual values could be humanistic. In doing so, he participated in a much larger international conversation about religion and politics in a post–World War II world concerned with human rights.[31] He wrote: "We challenge the assumption that spirituality is a matter of knowing scripture rather than service to one's colleagues and fellow men," framing the practice of human engagement as what schools ought to teach. He continued, "Those who do not accept your basic and unwarranted assumption resent the implication that they cannot be good, moral citizens." Here, the "basic" and "unwarranted assumption" contrasted God and religion with spirituality, which Lefkowitz defined through human engagement. Although Lefkowitz rejected what he called "a religious qualification for teaching," the Guild nevertheless supported serving other people, much like the patriotism in the Board's resolution.

Christian organizations also employed a universalizing, human rights language, but they did so to support the draft rather than to reject it. The Roman Catholic Archdiocese of New York sang the draft's praises. The archdiocesan secretary for education, Msgr. John J. Voight, who had opposed the National Educational Association's vague definition of moral and spiritual values, lauded that "the use of this guide in the classrooms of our schools will do much to provide an atmosphere and environment friendly and favorable to religion without in any way indoctrinating the pupils in the tenets of any particular religion." Voight addressed the constitutional issue by claiming that the draft was not sectarian. As a result, he argued, it could "reflect the spirit of America by recognizing God's existence—Father, Creator and Lawgiver—as the only sound and generally recognized basis on which to build convictions and habits essential to moral living," especially "in a nation which even from the constitutional and legal point of view is a nation under God."[32] In Voight's framing, the draft taught religious truth about God's influence on the nation. Unlike the critics, Voight celebrated what he saw as the draft's constitutionality, while simultaneously suggesting that Catholic and American values were one and the same. God was truth, in his view, and thus the draft reflected the Catholic theology of universalism.[33] Connecting God to America allowed Catholics to place themselves in the American story, out of which they had often been written.

Protestant officials tentatively supported the draft because they thought students could choose the source of moral and spiritual values. The Protestant Council of the City of New York's Department of Christian Education chairman Sidney G. Menk emphasized *belief* in God, rather than a recognition of God's existence, as the Catholic Voight had. Instead of God as the "only" source for achieving moral and spiritual values, Menk argued that "these moral values find their most meaningful sanction and motivation in belief in and dependence upon Almighty God."[34] "Most meaningful" suggested that belief in God was a personal, private choice, but the right choice. The Protestant Council said it would more thoroughly review the draft before fully approving, again suggesting the possibility for choice but offering no clear alternative to a private belief in God. The tentative approval and the framing of belief as "most meaningful" rendered choice illusory.

Prior to the revision, a silencing mechanism structured the debate about religion in public schools. After a long summer of debate, the Board scheduled a meeting to discuss revisions to the statement over the 1956 Labor Day weekend. UPA Executive Secretary Harold Siegel called this timing an "outrageous breach of faith" because many would be unable to attend.[35] The Board received "Twenty-eight requests from individuals and organizations" for postponement.[36] With Rosh Hashanah beginning two days after Labor Day, several Jewish groups in the city met on August 1 and "it was the unanimous feeling that the August 30 hearing date was unfortunate in that it came on the eve of Labor Day as well as the Jewish holidays," thus many were out of town or otherwise busy.[37] As late as August 13, the date remained unchanged.[38] On August 23, a week before the scheduled meeting, the Board changed the public hearing to Monday, September 17, at the Board of Education offices in Brooklyn.[39] Although members of the public were ultimately able to express their views, they expended labor to change the initial meeting schedule and expressed concern as the Board delayed taking steps to rectify the schedule. Without so many groups protesting, the Board's original plan had been poised to shut out potential dissent over the draft's God language, especially because Jewish organizations were among its largest critics.

Though religious organizations' voices fill the historical record, they were not the only ones affected. Black silence on the draft, and the whole debate, does not represent consent to the values articulated, but rather meaningful neglect or resistance. Just two years after the initial *Brown* decision came down, New York City public schools remained as segregated as ever. No evidence indicates that Black organizations responded to the statement. The only Black member of either the Board of Education or Superintendents, the Rev. Dr. John M. Coleman, commented, "I vote for the statement" at the October 4 meeting.[40] That was all he said. Coleman, the first Black member in the Board's history, was the rector at St. Philip's Protestant Episcopal Church in Brooklyn. By December 1957, he would miss three months of meetings due to illness and ultimately send his resignation letter.[41] Coleman's lack of commentary leaves a gap in the archive. He might have supported the revision unreservedly. Or, he might have felt that he could not oppose it, or perhaps he did not feel comfortable raising concerns or saying more. Whatever Coleman's reasoning, his approval reveals nothing about other Black New Yorkers' views.

There are many possible explanations for why Black people did not comment on the statement. As public historian Rodney Carter argues, archival silences reflect power. Silence marks the absence of voice. Silence often obscures the oppressed. Yet, the oppressed can also choose silence, to comment by saying nothing.[42]

Black communities might have been otherwise occupied, prioritizing other instances of racism in schools, such as Superintendent Jansen's geography textbook series with Nellie Allen, the Jansen and Allen Textbooks. One of Jansen's textbooks asserted that Africans "are backward and of mixed races," perpetuating the racist idea that African cultures were less advanced than white ones.[43] In 1950–1951, the Teachers Union released "Texts on the 1950–1951 Board of Education Approved Textbook List Containing Objectionable Material against Minority Groups," which included Jansen's geography textbooks.[44] Though his books had been written years earlier, Jansen never backed off his claims. Instead, he redoubled when parents requested the firing of Mary Quinn, a teacher who told a class, "Negroes were happy before they knew about racial discrimination." He refused to fire her.[45] Black New Yorkers had long criticized Jansen's book, as newspaper coverage suggests that R. Francis Bey, a member of the Moorish Science Temple of America, petitioned against the textbook in the 1930s.[46] While the statement remained un-published, textbooks already clearly affected students' learning and thus may have seemed a more urgent focus.

Or, their silence could suggest that Black New Yorkers knew little about the statement. With Coleman as the only Black Board member, few community ties existed. Or, through silence, they may have asserted that the Boards needed to work out racist history themselves. Or, the silences may be archival; Black New Yorkers may have talked about what they thought of the statement but may not have written it down, or perhaps the municipal archives never followed up on what they did write down. Perhaps the silence meant something else, now lost to time. Whatever the specific meaning, the silences reflect the racial power dynamics in both the draft's and revision's narratives of American history.

Reframing God

The debate over the city's moral and spiritual values statement opened the door for instituting an American tradition, distant from God. Arguing for a stricter church-state separation and declaring explicit God-talk as unconstitutional, the statement's critics had helped make possible a less God-centric, more humanistic and nonspecific articulation of American moral and spiritual values. The debate changed the statement's relationship to God and moved away from the state's comfort with God language.

The theological change appears in a linguistic shift that embedded God in textual references. A simultaneously Protestant, Catholic, and Jewish vision of America emerged, one that participated in the national tri-faith Judeo-Christian movement while also complicating its assumed Protestantism. The Protestant universalism remained, but the revision depicted a more Catholic and Jewish relationship to God than the draft provided. The relationship to God was no longer through individual belief. The revision preserved texts that referred to God, and teachers mediated between students and God by interpreting texts that uplifted historical figures' interpretations. The preservation of texts reflected a relationship to God more typical of Judaism than Protestantism, as Protestantism prioritized individual access to God through the text alone. Framing the teacher as interpreter of text mirrored the rabbinical tradition of interpretation, *and* the Catholic theology of priest or object as mediator between individual and God.[47] The theology and practices created a hybrid Protestant-Catholic-Jewish document.

The revision retained a typical Protestant universality, while changing specific references to God in Jewish and Catholic fashions. When the Board approved the revision on October 26, 1956, some sections deleted reference to God altogether. For example, the section on Language Arts now claimed "Good literature owes its greatness to the fact that it inevitably deals with matters of good and evil, life and death. Through literature pupils have access to the spiritual experience of their race."[48] The sentence's general audience suggests that "race" refers to the "human race" rather than the "white race." Nevertheless, white people often conflated the two, leading to the erasure of people of color in the "human race." The universalizing move preserved assumptions about values and whiteness, even as it removed reference to God. Where the Board no longer explicitly talked about God, it could still convey that white people inherited God's good favor because the language of race had absorbed the language of religion. Similarly, the revision claimed that Industrial Arts "give rise to speculation about the planning and the orderliness of the natural world."[49] Yet, it cut the explicit clause: "and the marvelous working of a Supreme Power."[50] The revision removed the most recognizably "religious" piece, "a Supreme Power," which followed the courts' language about what counted as religion. Nevertheless, the values the draft attributed to God stayed.

Other changes conveyed the draft's theological position through omission. For instance, the revised Science and Mathematics section still claimed that "the concept of infinity cannot do other than lead to humbleness before God's handiwork,"[51] but the draft's quotation from Psalm 8—"One can only say 'When I consider the Heavens, the work of Thy Hands'"—was gone.[52] The change reflected the view that a direct biblical citation was sectarian and religious. Being "led" to God, though, was not necessarily problematically religious to the Board, because anyone could cultivate a personal relationship with God. Objecting organizations disagreed because they saw any reference to God as sectarian. They lost the battle over that sentence.

The theological change also involved a different engagement with Judaism. The statement universalized Protestantism by replacing Jews' covenant with God with the Protestant notion of choice to love God. The statement continued by turning to the Decalogue as an example of the values: "They find their expression in the Ten Commandments, which are succinctly summarized: 'Thou shalt love the Lord, thy God, with all thy heart, and with all thy soul, and with all thy might—, and thou shalt love thy neighbor as thyself.'" This quotation combines Deuteronomy 6:5 and Leviticus 19:18 as Jesus combines the two in the synoptic gospels, Mark, Matthew, and Luke. The revision thus presented the Deuteronomy and Leviticus quotations—first presented in the context of Israel's covenant with God—through the lens of the Christian New Testament. Then, the revision claimed that Jesus's words represented "the very heart of our culture," which the revision identified as "Western civilization."[53] By highlighting a New Testament reading of the scripture as universal, rather than discussing the varied interpretations of the commandment, the statement implied that Judaism as represented in Deuteronomy and Leviticus only mattered insofar as it set the scene for Jesus. On this view, Jesus developed Christianity and "the West," which incorrectly implied that Jesus was white and ushered his whiteness into Europe and the Americas.

The references mirrored other supersessionist school-sponsored activities about "Hebrew culture." Starting in 1945, shortly after World War II ended, and as American conversations about the State of Israel began, the Board sponsored a "Hebrew Culture Contest" and ceremony where winners read their essays aloud. As Jansen explained to students, parents, and educators at the Board of Education headquarters during the 1952 ceremony, the contest illuminated "how a Jewish thread runs through American history."[54] Underscoring Jansen's point, student prize winners narrated Judaism into a Protestant American history. A student from Montauk Jr. High School in Brooklyn read from his essay, "The pilgrims spoke of their journey to America as the exodus from Egypt to the Promised Land." He offered "the pilgrim fathers" as an example of Judaism in America, even though "pilgrims" were generally Protestants who occupied indigenous land. The student continued this line of thinking by repeating Board member Arthur J. Levitt's and Jansen's claims that all students, regardless of religion, could participate in the contest.[55] The notion that Judaism belonged to all Americans allowed a Protestant narrative to co-opt Judaism.

The Hebrew Culture Contest represented America as democratic because of its diversity, which positioned Judaism and the newly formed State of Israel as important for America's project of conquest. Opening the 1950 contest ceremony, Levitt praised the contest's participation in "the democratic rebirth and the spiritual and everyday life of the new Israeli nation." Levitt framed America as birthing freedom throughout the world by occupying land. Building on this thread, the contest participants employed the language of democracy to describe Israel and America, suggesting that the contest organizers valued Judaism for the way it supported America's image in foreign policy as a spreader of democracy. For example, another student prizewinner supported the teaching of Hebrew in thirty-nine city schools, saying, "Having a knowledge of Hebrew culture helps us to understand our Jewish fellow citizens and thereby to make our living together more harmonious. This is true democracy." In short, the speech praised assimilation for being democratic. Levitt celebrated the "American Way of Life" as "A force which is not ashamed to learn from and feed upon other established cultures."[56] Levitt's phrase "feeding upon" Judaism encapsulated the contest's understanding of Judaism's role in the American project—as fortifying an American diversity from which dominant groups could selectively extract value.

The revision indicated that even if one did not relate to a Christian or Jewish God, a Christian interpretation of love of neighbor could still foster moral and spiritual values. According to the statement, love of neighbor could be separated from the initial commandment's source, because the commandment had influenced so much else that consensus existed: "Even those who reject the idea of obligation to God, and love of God, accept as a prime moral and spiritual ideal the love of neighbor, and they seek to find a philosophic base for their acceptance of this ideal apart from God." The phrase "obligation to God" likely referred to Jewish theologies of covenant, and "love of God" to Christianity. God remained the only source of moral and spiritual values mentioned explicitly, though the possibility for other sources emerged through reference to "a philosophic base." Although the statement moves to frame God as optional, since "the ideal the love of neighbor" emerged from a Christian interpretation of scripture, its introduction of nontheistic sources of moral and spiritual values rendered nonbelief inconsequential because believers had already so influenced "Western civilization."

Attempting pluralism, the revision explicitly included Asian traditions by assimilating them into the ideal of love of neighbor. The revision called Asian practices "religions," which it defined in relation to a Christian reading of loving thy neighbor. In doing so, the revision indicated that non-Christian practices could only become legible by comparison to Christianity. The revision claimed: "Other great religious systems give expression to the same ideal. Thus, for example, 'Minister to friends and families by treating them as one treats himself.' (*Buddhism*); 'What you do not like when done to yourself, do not do to others.' (*Confucianism*); 'Let no man do to another what would be repugnant to himself.' (*Hinduism*)."[57] This pluralistic universalizing echoed the "World's Great Religions" concept, popularized by *Life Magazine* between the draft's and revision's publication.[58] The revision even quoted the same abridged Confucius saying that *Life*'s "Religion in the Land of Confucius" issue did. Both likened the saying to the Golden Rule.[59] Yet, the move to make the traditions parallel obscured differences. For instance, some formulations commanded what to do, and some, what not to do. Thus, the revision insinuated that the Judeo-Christian tradition was the root of both the public school's values and the "great"-ness of the world's religions. In an Orientalist move that noticeably ignored Islam, the revision framed Buddhism, Confucianism, and Hinduism as "other" traditions, differentiated from mainstream American society. The Board implied that it valued all religions; yet, by omitting Islam and assimilating Asian traditions, the Board indicated that religious "others" could become more American by finding consonance with Christianity.

The explicit references to Judaism prioritized a Protestant interpretation of Judaism, but much of the textual work reflected Jewish reading practices. To embed God into tradition, the revision quoted other texts, creating cross-references and commentary, not unlike midrash, the ancient commentary on Hebrew scripture. The revision's theology used quotations to absorb and transform tradition. In doing so, the revision mirrored what Daniel Boyarin describes as midrashic intertextuality. Midrash is deeply intertextual, which means that it refers to other texts indirectly throughout. Rather than citing scripture as a "prooftext," "in support of previously determined conclusions," Boyarin argues that "the textual system both establishes continuity with the past and renews itself for the future."[60] The revision absorbed the values about God granting individualism in the draft and renewed it with a focus on American history. It made the new through the old, "striking (and strange)."[61] The revision operated within diverse religious modes with which New Yorkers were familiar. Although exact contributions to the theological change remain unknown, Jews and Catholics were involved, given the Board of Education's and Superintendents' religious makeup.[62]

The revision employed Jewish intertextuality to preserve a God who reflected Protestant principles. Although the number of references to God minimally differed (twenty-one in the original, eighteen in the revision), the nature of references to God metamorphosed between the versions. Only four mentions of God in the draft cited the Regents' or Board's policies, the Bible, or American documents. The revision attributed seven references to God to such sources. Nineteen percent of the draft's references to God were in quotations, compared to 39 percent in the revision. For instance, the revision cited the Regents' recommendation that "at the commencement of every school day the Pledge of Allegiance be joined with an act of reverence to God." It also cited the Board's own previous resolutions, on "'stimulating thereby that love of God and country which springs from a wholesome home environment.'" And, it cited well-known American documents: the Fourth Stanza of "America," which referred to "Our Fathers' God," and Abraham Lincoln's Gettysburg Address, which aligned Black freedom with a providential American one by claiming "that this nation, under God, shall have a new birth of freedom." Such quotations delegated authority to the American tradition in which public school administrators took the public schools to participate, a tradition based on Protestant individuality. The shift in proportion of direct versus quoted references to God distanced the schools from making claims about God. The revision transformed the tradition by changing the students' proximity to God, if not the nature of God. Simultaneously, the revision absorbed the authority of the Protestant interpretation of God represented in those statements.

From draft to revision, God went from direct source to precedential, reappropriated source.[63] The draft concluded without quotation, in the Superintendent's and Board's voice: "The public schools encourage the belief in God, recognizing the simple fact that ours is a religious nation, but they leave and even refer to the home and to the church the interpretation of God and of revelation." In its own voice, the draft had claimed that public schools "teach the moral code and identify God as the ultimate source of natural and moral law." By contrast, the revision shifted the authority from New York City officials to the Regents. It concluded by quoting the Regents' Statement on Moral and Spiritual Training in the Schools about schools "ever intensifying in the child that love of God, for parents and for home." The revision omitted declarative statements about God's role, which turned past state articulations of God's existence in policy into precedent. In doing so, the revision did not directly establish God's existence. Rather, it established God's authority through the Regents' authority.

The quoted references to God extended beyond citing policies to embedding God in history. On multiple occasions, the revised statement recited something akin to: "the religious underpinning of our moral and spiritual ideals, our Western culture, and our American democracy." Words such as "underpinning," "permeat[ing]," and "underlying" described the relationship between American life and God or the Bible. The revision articulated an inseparability between Christianity and moral and spiritual values. It indicated that religion underpinned America and "the West." Instead of claiming God's influence, the revision pointed to the "religious" and "the Judeo-Christian ethic." The formulation highlighted the inseparability of Christianity and public schools. "Religious underpinning" of "our moral and spiritual ideals" suggested that religion created moral and spiritual ideals. The source was no longer a specific God, but because "moral and spiritual ideals" still belonged to America, which owed its formation to God, the "religious underpinning" still referred to God.

Although the revision specified that teachers were to demonstrate "friendliness" toward but not endorse religion, teachers nevertheless mediated between students and God, almost as a Catholic leader would. The draft positioned the teacher as "exemplify[ing] moral and spiritual values" and "find[ing] many opportunities to affect the lives, character and attitudes of pupils" because "It is an incontrovertible fact that as a rule the American teacher is religious in character, in action, and in belief."[64] The draft missionized the teacher, so the teacher could in turn missionize students. The Teachers Guild resisted this characterization of teachers. They argued that "the adoption of a religious qualification for teaching" would be inevitable in such a framing. In response, the revised version deleted lines about teachers' beliefs, and it clarified that "The teacher may not use his position in the school to become a missionary for his own religious beliefs."[65] While the revision retained reference to "the example of the teacher," i.e., the teacher as model for behavior, it shifted focus to the teachers' actions: "The methods used by the teacher, the materials of instruction available, and the activities in which children engage," which, it claimed, "provide many opportunities for fostering desirable moral and spiritual attitudes." Methods, materials, and activities introduced mediators to moral and spiritual values through the teacher's presence.

Because the statement called on teachers to mediate between students and the divine, it reflected understandings of God beyond belief alone. Mediation is central to Catholic theology.[66] Anthropologist of religion Birgit Meyer frames media "as a broad array of authorized material forms that are to bring about and sustain links between humans and what, for lack of a better term, I call the 'transcendental,'"[67] a definition that illuminates that teachers and the guide were mediators. The statement's materiality produced its own kind of imagined ritual, where teachers would turn to this resource on moral instruction for guidance. The revision came in booklet form, a road map of sorts for teachers to study and reproduce.

The Board's and Superintendents' theological language managed racial power dynamics at home through Cold War anti-Communism, as the Regents' statement and suggestions had done. The revised Social Studies section instructed teachers to denounce totalitarianism: "They learn that this American ideal of the supremacy of the individual has been challenged as an 'illusion and a dream,'" by "the theory of the supremacy of the State." According to the revision, Marx's view on religion supported the theory, which it called "the fundamental sources of the great ideological conflict of our age." The revision selectively quoted Marx, "'Religion is the opium of the people,'" omitting the previous sentence, "Religion is the sigh of the oppressed creature, the heart of a heartless world, and the soul of soulless conditions." Marx said that religion made people sleepy, but he also articulated religion's importance for the oppressed. Religion was heart and soul where none existed. The revision continued: "They understand the reasons for totalitarian hostility to religion, and for the totalitarian doctrine of the exaltation, almost deification, of the state contained in the slogan, 'Nothing above the state, nothing outside the state, nothing against the state.'" The revision articulated its position in the ideological conflict by aligning the quotations of Marx with Mussolini, a dictator. It represented Marx as religion's enemy because he glorified the state yet participated in its own deifying of national figures.

The revision's Red Scare, pro-religion language naturalized what Frederick Douglass might call "slaveholding religion" and James Baldwin might call "not Christian." The revision focused on the conflict between totalitarianism and democracy. It overlooked critiques of America as "illusion" in Black political and religious traditions. Schools' omission of such critiques would be among the reasons Black New Yorkers would mobilize to change public schools in the 1960s. Baldwin offered a critique of public schools' logic. "What passes for identity in America," Baldwin told an in-service training session of about 250 primarily white teachers at the predominantly Black and Puerto Rican PS 180 in Harlem on October 26, 1963, "is a series of myths about one's heroic ancestors. It's astounding to me, for example, that so many people really appear to believe that the country was founded by a band of heroes who wanted to be free."[68] Baldwin sounded like he could have been responding to the 1956 revision. Here, the "illusion" was America's promise of freedom for all. Echoing Douglass's famous distinction between the "Christianity of Christ" and the "slaveholding religion," which was not Christianity, Baldwin argued that Black Americans understood Christianity, and white Americans failed: "My ancestors and I were very well trained. We understood very early that this was not a Christian nation. It didn't matter what you said or how often you went to church. My father and my mother and my grandfather and my grandmother knew that Christians didn't act this way."[69] The Board's statement erased violence wrought by white Americans, and, instead, looked outward, to "totalitarianism," for an enemy. The Boards avoided their sins, on their own religious framework, by depicting America as God's chosen nation contrasted with "Godless" totalitarianism.

In the Board's final vote of overwhelming approval, there were a few minor remaining sticking points, as critics argued that some part of the statement still equated religion with a Protestant God. Board Member Charles J. Bensley noted that the UPA, NYBR, and Citizens' Committee on Children continued to oppose three specific sections of the revision. The sections included the notion that practices such as reciting the Pledge of Allegiance and reading the Bible "are meaningless unless pupils are deeply conscious of the religious underpinning of our moral and spiritual ideals, our western culture, and our American democracy"; the section about being "led to humbleness before God's handiwork"; and school assemblies as "rich in the possibilities for moral and spiritual guidance" and for "the discussion of issues whose resolution becomes a matter of common consent."[70] While disagreement about the approved statement remained, the first and third complaint no longer fit the Protestant definition of religion that courts used, as Jewish and Catholic textual practices had come into play.

Protestant, Catholic, and Jewish bureaucrats who faced secularizing legal apparatuses and community opposition took up a hybrid Protestant-Catholic-Jewish vision of God in the service of Protestant values. The revision enacted temporal distancing: By shifting religion to past documents and events, it indicated that students could only understand America through understanding "Western culture and civilization" and the "Judeo-Christian ethic." It manipulated the logic of secularization. The revision retained God's influence by valorizing historical references to God. Due to criticism from the community and the legal landscape around religion in public schools, the schools could not talk openly about God. Instead, the revision turned to American history.

Founders as Father-Gods in the American Family

The "religious underpinnings" especially emerged in the revision's Social Studies curriculum section, which highlighted how the statement embedded religion into the country's history and heritage. Social Studies comprised "history, government, geography, economics, civics." History and government were among the subjects the statement indicated "present richer opportunities for strengthening moral and spiritual values than others." "Literature, music, art" remained intact, except previously mentioned changes about explicit God language. However, the Social Studies section more than quintupled in length, from 289 words in the initial draft to 1,561 in the revision. The expanded section developed a vision of the public school as an incubator for producing "good citizens and patriots dedicated to the task of preserving and enriching their country's heritage" through the concept of family.

As we have seen, the Regents' 1951 statement initiated the discussion of family for the state by making God central to how students would understand themselves as inheritors of a white, male America.[71] The city had access to the Regents' 1951 statement and possibly the Regents' 1955 suggestions. In the Regents' logic, historical figures became exemplary through their commitment to God. In the city, the historical figures became gods.

As father-gods, they created. God created "man"; the Founders created the United States. Although the city's draft statement referred to "our illustrious men" and "great men," and included documents by the traditional Founding Fathers and those adjacent, "such as the Mayflower Compact, the Declaration of Independence, the Gettysburg Address, Lincoln's Second Inaugural Address, the Constitution of the State of New York," the term Founding Fathers appears nowhere in the draft. The language of "our" implied that students might participate in the history, but the American family theology was less present in the draft, which more explicitly named religion and God.

By contrast to the state's "brotherhood of man, Fatherhood of God" theology, the city's revised statement replaced God with the Founding Fathers. The revised Social Studies section now used the language of "Founding Fathers," "our forefathers," and "our forebears" to situate students in their legacy. For example, the revised Social Studies section recommended a selective teaching of history: "A guiding principle in the teaching of American history has always been to emphasize anew for each generation of pupils the highlights of our country's history" with the discussion of certain parts of the history. On their view, history was inspirational, "to instill in pupils a wholesome sentiment and idealism for our traditions"; inherited, "to kindle in them that spark of patriotism which carried our forefathers through deprivations, hard work and suffering to glorious achievement"; and aspirational, "to inspire them to become good citizens and patriots dedicated to the task of preserving and enriching their country's heritage." The goal of history lessons thus became prescriptive, teaching students about the sort of Americans they ought to become as they "learn these ideals of the Founding Fathers." The statement named the exact ideals: "The underlying philosophy of

American Democracy is based upon the premise that the individual possesses God-given rights which the state can neither give nor take away." Through obedience to the father figure, students gained religious knowledge about "God-given rights."

Teaching obedience disciplined students into behavioral norms. At the meeting to approve the revised statement, Board member Vito Lanza, who was Catholic, echoed contemporary conversations about the dangerous effects of comic books and television on children's morality.[72] In by far the meeting's longest speech, Lanza expounded that the Board had a responsibility "to step in with a positive and effective course of action combatting the present malignant situation with regard to juvenile delinquency. Surely the salvation of the minds, the hearts and the souls of our youth, is a dire emergency of a most serious nature."[73] By framing delinquency as a "dire emergency" and "malignant situation," Lanza positioned the school as parental disciplinarian. With the addition of "salvation," Lanza's paternalism imagined American history curriculum's heroes as saving, deified fathers.

Deviant students disobeyed a Christian God, in Lanza's view. He continued, "Our entire moral code is taken directly from the Ten Commandments given to us by God." He, too, universalized Christianity by saying that "All of the major religious faiths in this country recognize God." He then went one step further to implicate all religions in the fatherhood theology: "All of these faiths believe in the brotherhood of man, which brotherhood is a meaningless term unless the relationship of brothers is understood to be that of sons of a common Father."[74] Lanza's explication of a "common Father" nevertheless echoed the revision's language of the moral example-setting Founding Fathers.

Lanza was not alone in his concerns about delinquency. In fact, the revision explicitly mentioned delinquency whereas the initial draft had not. The revision stated: "Community indifference to vice, lawlessness, low standards of recreation, health, morality, family life, and general welfare is bound to produce higher incidence of anti-social behavior and attitudes than is found in a community consciously striving to maintain an environment which supports and encourages the highest moral and spiritual aspiration."[75] Here, "anti-social behavior and attitudes" violated moral and spiritual values. Explicit references to vice and euphemisms for sex and drugs such as "low standards of recreation" carried theological significance. Although the specific quotation does not name God, God's moral commandments linger in "family" and "community" because of the theology of the Father God who expects obedience.

The Father theology now signaled God without needing to name God; instead, ideas about God emerged from examples of human moral excellence. The revised Social Studies section extended the framework of the Founding Fathers to a roll call of "ancestors" on whom students could model their behavior. On the statement's reasoning, these "ancestors" stood in the Founding Fathers' lineage, as did the students. The list included a surprising combination of figures: Roger Williams, Peter Zenger, Hayne and Webster, Robert E. Lee, Daniel Boone, Meriwether Lewis and William Clark, Robert Peary, Charles Lindbergh, Richard Byrd, Thomas Jefferson, Andrew Jackson, Horace Mann, Dorothea Dix, Carl Schurz, William Lloyd Garrison, Booker T. Washington, Susan B. Anthony, Jacob Riis, and Jane Addams. All these figures were supposed "to stir the imagination of our boys and girls and arouse their faith and devotion to our great ideals," as though Lee and Garrison, on opposite sides of the Civil War and slavery, were devoted to the same ideals. Lee's appearance in a New York City document reflected the Lost Cause Movement's broad influence. As historian of education Jonathan Zimmerman has argued, changes to American history curricula have often "concerned the roster of eligible patriots, not the patriotism itself."[76] The revision's list now included white women and one Black man alongside white men. However, the list was just the beginning of the lesson.

Inheriting Settler Colonialism

Settler colonialism was implicit in the father figure theology. The statement described the following as examples of the behavior students ought to emulate: "exploration and settlement of the New World"; "the daring trail blazing of Boone, Lewis, Clark, Peary, Lindbergh and Byrd"; and "the conquest of the prairie." Explore, settle, blaze, conquer: The actions exemplify what historian Patrick Wolfe calls the "logic of elimination" that characterizes settler colonialism as "a system, not a historical event."[77] As actions to eliminate land and people, the examples above reinforce settler colonialism as "destr[uction of] indigenous peoples and cultures in order to replace them and establish themselves as the new rightful inhabitants."[78] Settler colonialism extends far beyond the historical moment of colonial contact and formal colonial occupation because it is a structure of thought and action. New York City's statement demonstrated colonial ideology to celebrate religiosity against Soviet Communism and discipline dissent against civil rights. In teaching students whom to emulate, the Boards instructed students to become settler colonizers.

The statement's characterization of various social progressives' works as "humanitarian striving" implied that humans, like land, could be blazed, conquered, explored, and settled. The figures listed offered visions with end goals that were distinct from each other. For instance, Horace Mann's vision of schooling "everyone" into moral American Christians differed from Jane Addams's efforts toward universal housing security, which was reflected in New York City settlement houses.[79] The list included elites such as Mann, who promoted phrenology, the study of how brain size and shape determined ability, and excluded Black, indigenous, or low-income peoples from his approach.[80] While Mann's America may have appealed to the state, Addams and others challenged the state. The pairing flattened distinctions among the "humanitarian" efforts and indicated that human problems could be eliminated through "striving."

The statement's racial ideology follows from its authorship. After all, the Board's second resolution made Jansen, whose textbooks had referred to Africans as "backward and of mixed races," responsible for morality and spirituality in New York City public schools. In 1957, the Black newspaper the *New York Amsterdam News* collected a list of "derogatory adjectives" cited in school textbooks to describe Black Americans, such as "ignorant," "illiterate," "easily led," "foolish," "superstitious," "shiftless," "backward," "evil," and "irresponsible."[81] The list included Jansen's book.

Jansen codified racist stereotypes as expressions of good behavior and belief. The language of "easily led" implied that Black people could not think for themselves. It also echoed the moral and spiritual values draft statement, which conveyed that students were manipulable. A major critique of the draft was its claim that curriculum could "lead" students to God. Opponents critiqued such "leading" for church-state reasons. However, the phrasing also framed students as gullible embodiments of racist stereotypes. Similar language in Jansen's 1931 geography textbook and the revised values statement reveal the school system's persistent settler colonial mentality. Jansen co-authored at least nine textbooks, written with Nellie B. Allen, mostly on the United States and Europe, for students between grades four and eight. Even the seventh-grade textbooks, which focused on Africa, Asia, Australia, and New Zealand, centered the United States and Europe. The front cover depicts New York City and a bridge over the Hudson River with an airplane hovering above, transporting students to the title's *Distant Lands*. Both the textbook and statement use the language of Euro-American "settlement," "discovery," and "exploration" to describe occupation of Native American and African land. *Distant Lands* emphasized the difference between white men and "the native people of Africa, most of whom belong to the Negro race, [and] are very backward." Jansen and Allen referred to Africa as "the Dark continent," whose "various handicaps to development have been and are being overcome" since "the greater part of the continent has come under the control of European nations."[82] The "pioneering ancestors" and "Western man," just as in Jansen's and Allen's textbooks, were figured as moral and spiritual exemplars.

To communicate the logic of elimination to students, the statement framed the teacher as the narrator of settler colonial American history. As described earlier in reference to mediation, teachers were key to the statement's overarching plan: "the teacher, as a person, has a profound influence in building the character of children." The portrayal of teachers as good examples made them the most immediate inheritors of students' "ancestors." In the statement's portrait, they ought to inculcate the "moral and spiritual growth" so students could inherit the tradition. The statement encouraged teachers "to exemplify such qualities as justice, love, kindness, idealism, humility, reverence, and a sincere respect for the religious and moral beliefs and practices of all pupils," thus modeling their inheritance. As US imperialism does, the statement conveyed a tension between the settler-colonial logic of elimination and purported kindness.

The degree to which teachers implemented the statement's guidelines remains unclear. The statement described itself as "this statement of policy," but omitted repercussions for failure to implement its contents. Perhaps because enforcement was difficult, the statement described the teacher's importance to appeal to teachers' moral, rather than legal, duty. Yet, multiple teachers' unions disputed the revision. The TU claimed that "introduction of the teaching of religion in public schools" remained the revision's "basic defect." Lefkowitz's Teachers Guild similarly criticized the revision, calling it "indoctrination of religious beliefs."[83] Their continued disapproval indicates that teachers might not have widely implemented the statement's specifics. However, that the Superintendents and Board approved the revision nevertheless reflected administrative paternalism in pedagogy. Moreover, the unions' silence on race and colonialism implies that the organization rejected overt religion, not its racialized assumptions.

Those racialized assumptions were key to the revision's moral formation goals. The revision rendered American history something for students to absorb to become "loyal and intelligent citizens." In his influential 1970 work *Pedagogy of the Oppressed*, Paulo Freire critiqued the "piggybank" education model, where teachers insert a narrative into receiving students. A piggybank has only one hole—it must spew forth information. Freire writes that the banking concept of education involves "projecting an absolute ignorance onto others, a characteristic of the ideology of oppression," which "negates education and knowledge as processes of inquiry."[84] The statement cultivated a relationship where the Father God became a knowledgeable authority because he created humans. The statement imagined students as "containers" of "narrated content," designed for students to later re-narrate and regurgitate for the next generation—a cycle that allowed the Founding Fathers to succeed God, not just obey God.[85] Women's and Gender Studies scholar M. Jacqui Alexander has written, "Pedagogic projects are not simple mechanistic projects for they derive from theoretical claims about the world and assumptions about how history is made, in other words, pedagogy and theory are mutually related."[86] The statement's assumptions about history as divine model expanded white American heritage and eliminated everything else.

The linguistic shift from the draft's "moral and spiritual values" to the revision's "moral and spiritual ideals" represented nonconsensual consensus-making. The revision's use of "ideals" rather than "values" as the noun that "moral and spiritual" modified at once expanded the concept and eliminated the possibility for other concepts in the public schools. Lanza offered the only explanation: "Presumably, the term 'Spiritual Ideals' was substituted for 'Spiritual Values' because we recognized that ideals are goals to be sought after."[87] The internal explanation reflected the expansion's colonial, mediated pedagogy. The term "ideals" allowed for agreement around action, as the statement read: "Although there may be differences of opinion concerning the precise terms in which moral and spiritual ideals may be defined, and the application of these ideals to specific acts, there is fortunately agreement concerning the substance of what is meant by the phrase moral and spiritual ideals." The pedagogy ran on false consensus.

* * *

The debates about moral and spiritual values were about race as well as religion, and they illustrate how religion and race intersected in telling a narrative about American history. The embedded racial logics that uphold white Protestant supremacy—such as the father theology's paternalism and the logic of elimination inherited through belief in the Founding Fathers as father-gods—shaped New York City's alternative to the Regents' prayer. A strict secularization narrative prevents us from seeing how Protestant, Catholic, and Jewish understandings of God perpetuated an American white supremacist pedagogy in response to a changing constitutional landscape. In the next two chapters, the script flips, as topics that have largely been described with a focus on race—juvenile delinquency and integration—also were plotted within the public school–specific Judeo-Christianity.

II

Desegregation | Religion

3

Juvenile Delinquency and the Love of Neighbor

In the 1950s, the American public feared a full-fledged attack at the hands of juvenile delinquents. Films such as 1955's *Rebel Without a Cause* captured the popular imagination. A drunken Jim Stark, played by quintessential "bad boy" James Dean, represented the juvenile delinquent. In the principal's office for drinking alcohol at school, Stark cried out to his bickering parents, "You're tearing me apart!"[1] Paired with anti-delinquency instructional films that carried titles such as "Boy with a Knife," and the US Congress's censorship of comic books because psychologists argued they threatened children's moral purity, juvenile delinquency appeared to the American public as an illness targeting white youth, especially white boys—the country's presumed future. Family structures were changing beyond the stereotypical heteronormative, two-parent, white Christian household. And, according to governmental media campaigns, including instructional films, a host of corrupting influences put white boys at high risk.[2] After World War II, women who had worked outside the home during the war came back, and men wrestled with the aftermath of brutal battles. These adjustments to civilian life and the return to the domestic sphere gave way to moral panic: Could juvenile delinquency end nuclear families and "traditional" religious values?[3] White men were in danger, Dean's Stark screamed to audiences. With Dean as the archetypical delinquent, badness allured. Dean's blond hair, blue eyes, defined jawline, and assertive presence painted him so close to the country's ideal citizen—and yet, lost.

While popular culture portrayed delinquents as the fallen white male, law and the social sciences criminalized Black children. Pop culture's emphasis on white delinquency obscured Black punishment. Recent scholarship has shown that early-twentieth-century social sciences pathologized Black environments.[4] Years before the 1965 Moynihan Report lambasted single Black mothers for crime and poverty in Black neighborhoods, social scientists claimed that Black neighborhoods and culture produced crime. Moreover, courts frequently charged Black children with truancy and theft, even when Black children might have missed school or stolen food because they lacked basic resources.[5]

As institutions that engaged with youth on a daily basis, schools frequently addressed students' transgressions before other institutions. In doing so, they helped invent delinquency as a criminalized category. Concerns about race have shaped scholarship about the cultural, legal, and social scientific aspects of delinquency.[6] In an effectively segregated city, schools played a crucial role in unequally doling out punishments for white students and students of color. Moreover, in New York City, the public schools' approach to delinquency, an already racialized issue, had everything to do with religion. As the Regents' and New York City Boards of Education and Superintendents' conversations about moral and spiritual values showed, where there was religion, there was race. With juvenile delinquency, where there was race, there was also religion. Excavating seemingly invisible religious influences reveals that religion was inseparable from public schools because public schools were sites for understanding race in the United States.

Schools criminalized Black students through race *and* religion. In September 1957, after a Black student threw a bottle of lye in class and nearly blinded a white student in a Brooklyn school in a "transition neighborhood," i.e., a neighborhood beginning to desegregate, the New York City Board of Education claimed religion and morality could solve delinquency: "The problem, and its solution, are the joint responsibility of the entire community: the family, the churches, the school, the government at all levels, the social agencies and of every individual citizen," before turning to religion: "Together these can solve the problem provided there is full recognition by the whole community *that there is no substitute for the principles of religion and morality*."[7] Not only could religion and morality save delinquents, but their absence had created them, according to the Board.

While the Board referred to the Black student as an example of the "less than 1 percent of our total school population" who "constitute a hard core of young people who require special attention, guidance, treatment, and in some cases, custodial and corrective care," the case became "a focusing event."[8] Newspapers pointed out that nearly 1 percent of New York City's one-million-student system added up to almost

10,000 "hard core" delinquents. A judge known for "severity" toward youth crime, as well as anti-immigration and anti–Puerto Rican positions, proclaimed that "We should get tough with these young thugs." He called a grand jury on the incident.[9] The boy who threw the lye landed in a psychiatric institution, and once a legal adult, in prison.[10] After the school's principal testified twice, the principal committed suicide, leading to speculation about how the jury treated him. The grand jury recommended having a police presence in all schools, which frustrated the Board.[11] Even Superintendent William Jansen, who wrote racist textbooks, called the proposal "unthinkable" and brought up painful recent memories: "We do not want a Little Rock in New York City."[12] In response to the upheaval, the Board reversed a policy that was viewed as "pampering delinquents," immediately suspending 644 students deemed "hard core delinquents" from traditional elementary and high schools.[13] Yet, a facility shortage left schools scrambling to place the suspended students.[14]

News coverage framed the event and its aftermath as products of "the streets," a "crowded rat-infested slum which breeds crime and delinquency," "the law of the jungle," "depressed areas" that "breed[] lawlessness, hatred and ignorance," are "marked by slum blight and human blight," and rife with "racial tensions."[15] The press pathologized neighborhoods based on their inhabitants' races. Articles lamented the white boy "whose face was seared" as a victim of "a vengeful boy."[16] The Board and media positioned Black and Puerto Rican neighborhoods, or Black and Puerto Rican students in predominantly white neighborhoods, as the problem. Although films staged fallen white boys as the delinquents, the lye incident delivered the same message: A changing culture victimized white boys. In *Rebel Without a Cause*, the problem was broken homes; Stark's delinquency was caused, or exacerbated, by parents' fighting. In the controversies over delinquency in schools, the issue was not simply individual parenting failure but neighborhood racial change due to (im)migration and the promise of desegregation. Why did the Board turn to religion and morality as a solution?

The trope of the "Judeo-Christian tradition" in the United States helps us answer this question. The notion that Americans had always shared, and continued to share, common moral and religious values despite sectarian differences emerged among civic leaders to present a unified national front to totalitarian forces abroad.[17] However, the "tradition" also had local iterations at home. The New York City public schools echoed the call from the National Conference on Christians and Jews in materials, distributed in churches and synagogues for Brotherhood Week in 1955, for Americans to "love thy neighbor as thyself."[18] Moreover, the tradition was preoccupied with juvenile delinquency: For instance, one Minnesota judge inspired controversy by posting paper copies of the Ten Commandments in juvenile courts to promote moral behavior.[19]

The focus on preventing delinquency intersected with racial exclusion. The Judeo-Christian tradition notably excluded religions largely practiced by people of color, including Islam, Hinduism, Buddhism, or Yoruba traditions. While the NCCJ differentiated between brotherhood appropriate for religious and public school contexts, the schools nevertheless embodied the religious idea, too. Social scientific studies conducted by the Board and others racialized "high delinquency" neighborhoods as Black and Puerto Rican. These studies laid the groundwork for school programming to target Black and Puerto Rican students in instructional films on loving neighbors, as well as anti-vandalism cleanup efforts in "high delinquency" neighborhoods, as seen in related memoranda and photographs. Although "love thy neighbor" may sound benign, the schools implemented the slogan as a regime for dealing with delinquency at a particular moment when social scientists had racialized the concept of neighborhood.

The Commandment Reconsidered: From Neighbors to Neighborhoods

The Board and Superintendents commanded students to "love thy neighbor as thyself." As they did with the city's moral and spiritual values statement, the Board and Superintendents folded all traditions' formulations of "thou shall love thy neighbor as thyself" into the synoptic gospels' prescriptive formulation of the commandment. They assumed Judaism, Confucianism, and other traditions shared the New Testament's interpretation of the phrase. In the statement, the Board and the Superintendents then assimilated the Golden Rule into the teaching about loving thy neighbor. They argued that "the ideal of love of neighbor finds expression in the golden rule: 'As you would that men should do to you, do you also to them.'"[20] They indicated that the love of neighbor and the Golden Rule meant the same thing.

The Board's assimilative work framed the neighbor as an enemy by using the commandment to love thy neighbor in a Christian register. The commandment in the Torah/Old Testament to love thy neighbor positioned the neighbor as a friend, someone like you, someone nearby. However, when Jesus instructed Christians to love their enemies as well as their neighbors, religious studies theorist Gil Anidjar reasons, Jesus, "having made the neighbor and the object of Christian love into an enemy . . . may have failed to abolish the distinction between self and other, may have failed to put an end to enmity" because enemies still existed. Instead, he made the neighbor and enemy interchangeable; love of neighbor as enemy reinforces the fact that one is not the same as their neighbor, creating a distinction between self and other.[21] To love the enemy in a way that ended enmity would mean no one would ever have to love their enemy again. In the context of the Board's work, loving one's neighbor preserved their status as someone in need of salvation, like the enemy. It dramatized the differences between the person loving and the person they loved, creating a pitying structure of exchange.

Sources from Judaism and Confucianism emphasized not hurting others, but loving and forgiving the enemy were distinctly Christian concepts. Rabbi Hillel reportedly said something like the New Testament teaching, though framed as a prohibition rather than prescription. In Confucianism, the framing has also been read as prohibitive, and is at the least ambiguous given the contexts in which the saying appears.[22] Although similarities exist, the notion that the traditions share a principle called the "Golden Rule" misrepresents each original text by assuming that all traditions are the same. However, deliberately treating everyone as yourself and not directly harming others differ conceptually. The Board's history of collapsing religious differences for a universal Christian interpretation presages the schools using "love thy neighbor" and the "Golden Rule" to name agreed-upon values and condemn delinquent behavior.

Assimilation operated at many levels—traditions into Christianity, love of neighbor into the Golden Rule, and the enemy into the neighbor. In the world of segregation and rival neighborhood gangs, the commandment to love the enemy implied another space—a rival territory.

Since loving the neighbor required seeing the neighbor as outside of the self, as in need of love, just as loving the enemy reinforced the enemy's enemy status, neighbor applied broadly throughout the city, beyond the person who lived next door.

A Framework Where Neighborhoods Imply Race

Mid-century social scientists understood race in two particularly relevant ways for public schools: through racial liberalism and racial conservatism.[23] Racial liberals saw environmental circumstances as causing behavioral differences between racial groups, whereas racial conservatives theorized that biological predisposition caused crime, i.e., certain races passed down crime. Even as racial liberals distanced themselves from a biological understanding of race, they still generally approached crime unsympathetically. As historian Khalil Gibran Muhammad argues, white racial liberals sounded more like white supremacists "when it came to discussing black crime, vice, and immorality."[24] White racial liberals developed a social science of "black pathology" rooted in an environmental understanding of race that "in effect . . . incriminated black culture."[25] Racial conservatives outwardly opposed racial change, whereas racial liberals claimed to support racial change while expecting Black people to do all the changing.

Against the backdrop of the burgeoning Civil Rights Movement, New York City funded racially liberal and racially conservative social science to understand delinquency. Two examples in particular show how social scientists' interpretations of neighborhoods and delinquency helped public schools connect neighborhood and race. The first example took place before the lye incident: when the New York City Youth Board, a city agency separate from the Board, replicated husband and wife criminology team Sheldon and Eleanor Glueck's controversial delinquency prediction method. The second example began before the lye incident and continued after it: the Board's Juvenile Delinquency Evaluation Project. Although the two projects' methodologies differed, together, they cultivated the city's attitudes that neighborhoods caused delinquency, and that neighborhood was a racial category.

The Glueck Social Prediction Tables from the Gluecks' 1950 book *Unraveling Juvenile Delinquency* exemplified both environmental and biological racism. Originally conducted in Massachusetts with 1,000 white boys,[26] the Glueck Social Prediction Tables predicted that biology and environment could both lead to delinquency. In 1952 and 1954, the New York City Youth Board applied the tables to New York City students. The Youth Board studied and served youth after World War II, so it sat squarely in conversations about delinquency and the city's changing racial landscape.

The data did not support the Gluecks' assumptions about race. Scholars hotly debated the Glueck Social Prediction Tables because they implied a causal link between the backgrounds of youth and delinquency without sufficient evidence to prove causation.[27] The Glueck Tables resulted from a ten-year study of 500 delinquent white boys in Massachusetts training schools and 500 nondelinquent white boys in Boston public schools. The initial study paired delinquents and nondelinquents with the same general age, ethnicity, neighborhood type, body type, and intelligence. The Gluecks began their work with a question they said remained unanswered in the literature: Why did most children living in high delinquency areas not "succumb to the evil and disruptive neighborhood influence"?[28] To answer the question, the Gluecks examined factors from church attendance to number of household occupants. Even though they tried to show that individuals could withstand neighborhood influences, their premise that neighborhoods could be "evil and disruptive" reified a moral pathology of neighborhoods by reverting to prejudicial understandings of crime.

The Gluecks racialized the study's variables by testing for biological causes of delinquency on the assumption that physical traits could dictate behavior. Given their premise that biology and delinquency were correlated, the Gluecks' conclusions are unsurprising. They argued, among other things, that certain physical characteristics, such as body build, predicted delinquency. To do so, they drew on somatotype and constitutional psychologist William H. Sheldon's disputed work. Eleanor Glueck concluded "twice the proportion of delinquents as of nondelinquents were of predominantly mesomorphic physique," which, according to Sheldon, "means relative predominance of muscle, bone and connective tissue."[29] Many scholars have criticized Sheldon's work as racially prejudicial, as well as unethical, since he used photos of naked students from different research without their consent. Sheldon was "a staunch biological determinist" who supported eugenics and saw himself as a "psychologist and religious philosopher" akin to William James.[30] As the Gluecks drew from Sheldon, the Youth Board drew from the Gluecks. The Youth Board judged students' behavior based on racist understandings of physique.

The Gluecks also pathologized religion. Although the Gluecks claimed that the tables worked for sample sizes with different religious distributions in subsequent studies (including one on Jewish boys and that carried out by the Youth Board), prediction suggested a causal link between religion and delinquency. Given the original sample, future applications related their findings to the findings in a Massachusetts-based study, where most boys were Catholic. Playing into media fears about fallen white adolescents, the racial categories the original Glueck study employed primarily focused on white racial groups: "English (including English-Canadian, Scotch); Italian; Irish; American; Slavic (including Polish, Lithuanian, Russian); French (including French-Canadian); Near Eastern (including Greek, Syrian, Turkish, Armenian); Portuguese, Spanish; Scandinavian, German, Dutch; Jewish; and Chinese."[31] Furthermore, the Gluecks explained, "Since religion is very largely related to ethnic origins, our findings concerning the religion of the boys and their parents are presented here as a matter of interest. . . . As for the boys themselves, 81.2% of the delinquents and 71.6% of the non-delinquents were Roman Catholic; 15.9% and 23.6%, respectively, were Protestant; 2% of each group were Hebrew; and 1% and 2.8%, respectively, were of other faiths."[32] The Gluecks had identified delinquents as predominantly white ethnic Catholics whose religious identity did not positively affect their moral actions. They did not go as far as to say Catholicism negatively affected their moral actions, though one could read such an implication into the findings. However, nondelinquents in the original study were also predominantly Catholic—Catholicism was simply a major religion among white people in and around Boston in the mid-twentieth century. Yet, by considering religion a potential cause for delinquency that could be replicated elsewhere, the Gluecks made Catholicism into a potential predictor of delinquency.[33]

According to Executive Director Ralph E. Whelan, the Youth Board intentionally selected neighborhoods for the study based on race: "In choice of schools and neighborhood, the study group, by design, includes high proportions of Negro and Puerto Rican children."[34] The Youth Board constructed the New York City delinquent as nonwhite and from particular neighborhoods. Moreover, Whelan held a long-standing interest in researching delinquency and religion: He had written a thirty-eight-page publication on juvenile delinquency called "God's Rascals" that the National Conference of Catholic Charities published in 1943.[35] As the Glueck study had done in its assessment of white ethnic Catholics, the Youth Board positioned delinquents as potentially deficient of religious values.

While Eleanor Glueck responded to criticism by simply claiming "it works,"[36] the tables amplified stereotypes of Black and Puerto Rican students, whose environments had already been criminalized and who had historically faced biological racism.[37] Ten years after the initial study, Sheldon Glueck claimed the tables were neutral. He defended his study's focus on white and predominantly Catholic boys by writing "our social prediction table based on certain sociocultural factors of family life has proved to have very high prognostic force when applied to samples of Jewish, Negro, French and Japanese delinquents." However, the critique and Sheldon Glueck's response did not unsettle the study's initial premise. The study had assumed that race and ethnicity predicted delinquency, as did "sociocultural factors of family life," including neighborhood and parental behavior. So, when the schools invoked neighbors and neighborhood, these were already racial and religious categories that some argued caused delinquency.

Mayor Robert Wagner cemented neighborhood as a racial category that could signal criminality by creating the Juvenile Delinquency Evaluation Project. In 1956, Wagner hired former Columbia University professor and past president of the American Sociological Association Robert MacIver to run the JDEP.[38] MacIver rejected the day's popular positivism for analyzing how diverse environmental factors affected delinquency.[39] To collect data, the JDEP reported delinquency and other factors by geographical districts designated by the Health Department.[40] Most significantly, the report ranked each district 1–30 by rates of "Delinquency 6–20 Years 1958" in the first column. The JDEP tracked arrest rates and cases in Health Department–designated districts, using Children's Court cases (ages 6–15), referrals to the Youth Division of the Police Department (ages 6–20), and Police Arrests (ages 16–20). Because geographical districts organized the analysis, the JDEP took an environmental approach to neighborhood and race, rather than a biological one.

The JDEP relied on the concepts of "slum" and "high delinquency area," reinforcing the association between neighborhood and criminality to evaluate the causes of delinquency. MacIver's project suggested that "slum" and "high delinquency area" technically meant different things. "Slum" referred specifically to the housing and living conditions in a concentrated area, such as "dilapidated dwelling units, high population density, old buildings, and insufficient park and playground facilities, and termed 'substandard and unsanitary.'"[41] The word "slum" connoted moral uncleanliness and insufficiency based on physical conditions. By contrast, a "high delinquency area" was where a high concentration of youth crime occurred. Although the two categories' technical meanings differed, the JDEP reports identified the same neighborhoods as both "slums" and "high delinquency areas"—Central Harlem, East Harlem, Fort Greene, Bedford-Stuyvesant, the South Bronx, and the Lower East Side. Uncoincidentally, these areas also housed large populations of people of color and immigrants.

Thus, neighborhood signaled race. Some districts scored high in all three areas—delinquency, characteristics associated with slums, and nonwhite births. For instance, Central Harlem ranked first in each index on each table, except one. Other generally high-ranking districts in delinquency, health problems, economic problems, and nonwhite ethnic origins included East Harlem, Mott Haven and Morrisania in the South Bronx, and Bedford and Fort Greene in Brooklyn, neighborhoods that were also "high delinquency" and "slums." By merging racial population, geographic frequency of delinquent acts, and the characteristics of "slums," the JDEP implied that race and delinquency inherently connected. The analysis moralized "slum" and "high delinquency area," while mapping the categories onto physical places. Then, the JDEP applied the moral judgment of "slum" and "high delinquency area" to the neighborhood's inhabitants. This racially liberal approach looked for causes of delinquency in places rather than people. Yet, the JDEP accused of delinquency the same children whom eugenicists might have accused of delinquency due to biology because of where they lived.

The city also racialized delinquency through redlining. The city classified each "high delinquency area" and "slum" as a "Class D: Hazardous" redlined neighborhood, except for Fort Greene, which it labeled as "Class C: Declining." Redlining segregated the city and prevented resources from going to low-income neighborhoods with high percentages of people of color.[42] By neglecting to mention the city's redlining practice, MacIver further associated crime and race in his JDEP classification.

Beyond naming areas with large Black and Hispanic populations as both high delinquency areas and slums, the JDEP racialized behavioral problems that it claimed were not inborn, but a feature of being reared in a high delinquency, slum, redlined neighborhood.[43] The reports intimated that these areas passed on immoral values and behavior to new children in each generation, almost as a person passes on genetic traits. As the JDEP's final report concluded, "The constant factor was the nature of the slums themselves, not the ethnic origin of the people living there."[44] Although the final report claimed that ethnic origin was not a factor, it framed the neighborhoods as having innate features. The reports thus racialized the neighborhoods by describing their pervasive negative features as inevitably producing crime.

To make this claim, the JDEP framed delinquency spatially, employing theories about "mass society," specifically "social disorganization" and "cultural transmission." In the first half of the twentieth century, sociologists grappled with changing values—religious and otherwise—in what they called a "mass society." "Mass society" constituted a structural change after the Industrial Revolution, which brought together previously separate groups through migration and urbanization.[45] In the report's discussion of "slums," MacIver built on Clifford Shaw and Henry McKay, who had expanded Edwin Sutherland's theory of "social disorganization." Shaw and McKay argued that a lack of clear social structure could cause crime. They went further to describe "cultural transmission," where people living in the same "disorganized" area would pass down the area's norms to the next occupants.[46] Cultural transmission theorists therefore promoted the concept that whoever lived in high delinquency areas would be more likely to engage in delinquency and adopt the area's negative values.

Drawing on social disorganization and cultural transmission theories, MacIver framed behavior as inherited from a place. In the JDEP's analysis, delinquency arose from spatial arrangements. As terrain, the JDEP indicated that neighborhoods bred "the still increasing volume of juvenile delinquency," "a great evil the City has so far failed to over-come."[47] The word "evil" invoked Christian ideals, as well as the city's concern that delinquency could overpower their efforts because of its monumental force. The JDEP understood delinquency as a spatial and contagious moral threat because it could spread—more reason for the city to continue redlining and school segregation.

MacIver had theorized evil before. In a 1947 piece in *American Weekly* titled "My Religion," MacIver prioritized the universal as the most im-portant moral premise, writing, "Religion seeks the universal, and I found the enemy of religion, the first denial of the universal that leads to all other denials, in the wrathful divisions we set between man and man, between nation and nation."[48] He used the same word he did fourteen years later in the JDEP—evil—to describe a denial of the universal when he continued, "The source of evil lies not in death, not in destruction, not in folly, not in waste, not in what the theologian often called sin, but in the separation of my good from yours, of our good from theirs, in the malevolence that springs from the false separation of good from good."[49] Here, MacIver defined "evil" as divisive acts. However, the JDEP report created the very division among neighborhoods he claimed de-linquents perpetuated. MacIver presumed that some divisions cured evil (i.e., sociological investigation of neighborhood conditions), while oth-ers produced it. His definition required acquiescence to his premise that inherently good and bad spaces endured.

The Glueck study and the JDEP identified neighborhood as a cate-gory of difference that drew from racially liberal and conservative ideas, sprinkled with some religiously liberal universalism. The Youth Board's extension of the Glueck study enforced environment and biology as po-tential causes of delinquency, with race and religion as parts of each. The JDEP racialized and moralized the neighborhoods by characterizing neighborhood spaces as good or bad and rationalizing how neighbor-hood values influenced residents. Because, in the city's view, neighbor-hood was a racial category and neighborhoods caused delinquency, race undergirded school programs on delinquency, even those that taught the seemingly innocuous commandment to love thy neighbor.

Biblical Metaphors and Patriotic Rituals of Neighborhood Against Delinquency

The city's studies, conducted and supported by social scientists, led to a clear conclusion: Religion could cure delinquency. Since neighborhood conditions caused delinquency, and neighborhoods with larger percentages of people of color had among the highest delinquency rates in the city, school administrators and teachers imbued delinquency prevention and treatment with religious pluralism. Two concepts especially took hold: "thou shalt love thy neighbor as thyself" and the Golden Rule to "do unto others as you would have done unto you." The schools had assimilated the love of neighbor commandment into the Golden Rule to universalize the Golden Rule. The school programming taught biblical rules by asking students to embody the lessons. From jingles that named the Golden Rule to effervescent anti-vandalism parades that could instill a love of neighborhood, a delinquency-specific form of Judeo-Christianity undergirded the schools' delinquency prevention. Despite emphasizing love and treating others well, this Judeo-Christianity enlisted teachers and administrators to separate, control, and reform students. By inviting students and parents into their Judeo-Christian repertoire, schools taught that certain neighborhoods and students, not the schools, needed to change. They ignored a thriving Black religious metropolis by seeing Black students as lacking in religion.[50]

The citywide 1953 Clean-Up Campaign celebrated the Golden Rule and love of neighbor as antidotes to school vandalism. The campaign included all districts in the school system in a thorough reporting system. Each district informed the Board about the activities its schools had programmed. The Board of Education, the Superintendent of Schools William Jansen, and the Department of Sanitation jointly sponsored the campaign. As we have seen, Jansen was a controversial figure who had tried to root out Communist teachers early in his tenure and wrote a geography textbook describing the "backward" "native people of Africa."[51] The city founded the Department of Sanitation in 1881 to rid New York City not only of odor, but of vice.[52] With the campaign, the department again targeted vice, and Jansen again targeted people of color and the places they called home. As a value, cleanliness conveyed the moral weight of whiteness and sacredness.[53]

Publicity materials sent to the schools included the Golden Rule in a jingle that warned and scolded students as they recited it. The tone of the jingle portrayed a one-way relationship from schools to students. It placed the onus on students to change, thus fixing a limited understanding of reform:

> Boys and girls don't be a vandal
> Such deeds are just a social scandal.
> You know you are wrong
> In the things you have done.
> Do you really and truthfully think
>   They've been fun?
> So live more closely to the
>   Golden Rule
> And take more pride in your
> community and school.[54]

The jingle taught shame through rhyme and associated the rhyming ideas with each other. For instance, "Golden Rule" and "school" affirmatively suggested that students follow the "Golden Rule" at "school." A vandal would cause scandal, i.e., bring shame to the community. The middle rhyme's guilt tripping ("you know you are wrong") and pointed questions ("really and truthfully") challenged the association between "things you have done" and "fun." By its end, the jingle communicated that the Golden Rule could counteract students' vandalism by commanding students to care for their communities and schools. In an unstated rhyme, the Golden Rule was a *tool* to connect students to their neighborhoods.

One school used "loving thy neighbor" to decrease aggression. PS 27 in Queens at 122nd Street and 14th Avenue sent original poems home with children. One poem included the lines: "Teach him to really understand his neighbor he must love/And when is bewildered to ask help from God," and concluded, "Create within your very home an atmosphere of love/Ask God to help you in your task; He sees all from above."[55] Even in this "low delinquency area," the poems proposed that God surveyed parents' behavior. Here, parents ought to love because God was watching. Before the Clean-Up Campaign officially began, Superintendent Jansen tracked school vandalism throughout the city.[56] Years before social scientists James Q. Wilson and George L. Kelling introduced the "broken window theory" in a 1982 article, arguing that keeping up the appearance of buildings could prevent more severe crimes in urban areas, the Board counted the broken glass incidents in each city school.[57] The Office of the Superintendent of Schools sent each district a form to track the "Location of Broken Glass" ("Outside Windows, Stairwell, Other Inside Windows"), when it happened ("School Hrs., Other Times, Weekends") and "Cause of Breakage" ("Unknown, Accident, Malicious").[58] Like this earlier anti-vandalism effort, the Clean-Up Campaign operated in a spirit of surveillance, with God as lookout.

PS 27 also proposed that religion could have an antidotal effect. At a parents' meeting, school officials asked: "Do you set the example in the home of going to church, and then in turn of teaching them the word of God and making them go to church at least on occasion?"[59] The phrase "at least on occasion" hinted that a little religion was better than no religion, because religion could help prevent delinquency. The school officials strategically used religion to invoke accountability to a higher power. Without teaching children about God at school, which could have stirred controversy, the school recommended parents take their children to church to reverse their behavior.

In 1957–1958, a few years after the Clean-Up Campaign, the all-boys PS 614 in Manhattan showed a curated film series to "delinquent" boys that highlighted how "loving thy neighbor" cultivated geographical pride as a cure for animosity toward peers. The Board's "600" program and New York University's Film Library organized the viewing "to determine whether" PS 614 students "could relate to and identify with the content of mental hygiene oriented films, whether attitudes could be restructured and behavior changed."[60] A five-story walk-up, with a "depressing exterior" and an interior "generally kept in good condition," PS 614 housed teachers who reportedly stayed in their classrooms until after school because they feared further interactions with students.[61] When PS 614 showed the films, the city lacked ideal treatment options for "600" school students. These schools operated on separation, as the Assistant Superintendent sent students to "600" schools after they had been suspended.

PS 614 was one of five "600" day schools: two in Manhattan and one each in the Bronx, Queens, and Brooklyn. Three of the schools were in "substandard residential areas," while the Queens school rested in a "modest residential neighborhood" and one Manhattan school (PS 612, not 614) in a "superior neighborhood." Students whom school authorities or courts determined were "delinquent," "socially maladjusted," or generally "problem children" attended the "600" schools.[62] The Board-supported JDEP report on "600" schools did not specify student racial demographics.[63] The schools were well-established as they had existed since the late nineteenth century.[64] Since the 1930s, the "600" schools had theoretically been treatment programs, but they had few resources to address students' needs, as many had "emotional" issues.[65] The "600" schools report recommended further attention to students' treatment needs and learning development, as well as recruitment of teachers and principals the report framed as more qualified than those currently there.[66] However, in the meantime, the resource deficit shaped students' experience of separation in "600" schools.

The PS 614 film study strived to reform students, but it ended up shaming the students in the process, as the jingle had. The series began with the eight-minute 1952 film *Neighbours* and continued with other films about mountain goat hostility, nomad families in Malaya, jewel thieves, beaver and bear family habitats, and the Polish foster system, all topics relating to antagonism, lawfulness, and home and community environments.[67] According to principal researcher Carol Cordes Smith, the project began by showing films that displayed "aggressive, hostile behavior—to be followed by films which would increasingly emphasize cooperation and consideration of others."[68] The researchers hoped that showing the films would teach the students how to calmly cooperate with their neighbors. However, the film series' structure criticized the students by comparing the aggression on screen to the boys' behavior.

Neighbours, the first film the students viewed, established the boys' behavior geographically by implying that location shaped aggression. The film showcased violent interaction between two male neighbors staking their own turf. Canadian director Norman McLaren intended for the Academy Award–winning film to deliver a strong anti-war message, influenced by his visit to China during the Korean War.[69] Using pixilation, a technique that employs live actors as objects of animation

Figure 3.1. "Love Your Neighbour" screenshot from *Neighbours*. *Neighbours*, film, directed by Norman McLaren (1952; Montreal: National Film Board of Canada).

to produce a fast-paced effect, the film opens with both men seated on their lawns, reading newspapers, one with the headline "Peace Certain if No War"; the other, "War Certain if No Peace." Shortly after sitting down to read, both men notice a flower growing between their houses. Each indicates that the flower belongs to him. Then, the men build fences to symbolize that the flower grows on his property. Next, the fighting begins. Each man tears the other's house down and kicks his wife and child out of the screen, killing them. In the end, each man dies from the fighting, and the fences they built rearrange to form crosses over their graves. A saying flashes in many languages, landing on the English: "Love Your Neighbour."[70]

In the context of the PS 614 screening, this anti-war film implied that juvenile delinquency meant war. On this view, the students who had been deemed delinquent were waging war against their schools, communities, and each other. The film pictured the characters' fight as a rivalry between neighbors. The characters' nasty demise imparted to students the message that they should not fight with their peers. Large conflicts often emerged from small ones, such as the scuffle over the flower. If students gave in to these fights with their peers, they could lose their home and family; or worse, they could die. Rejecting the Korean War and keeping soldiers alive, according to director McLaren, required loving thy neighbor. To reject the delinquency war at PS 614 also demanded loving thy neighbor.

The study's goal to reform the students' behavior thus relied on the pluralistic, yet threatening, message of *Neighbours*, encapsulated in the versions of "Love Your Neighbour" in the final shots of the short film. Smith concluded that showing the films would minimize strife, as doing so "can and will induce the initial discharge of conflict necessary as a beginning point in the rehabilitation of emotionally disturbed, socially maladjusted boys."[71] Specifically, it could rehabilitate the boys through the message of loving their neighbor, which the film, by displaying the saying in so many languages, framed as a universal value.

The researchers and teachers placed the burden on students to change. According to Smith's report on the film activity, the students adopted the view that the film represented territorial conflict: "Their main reactions to this film were: the actions of the characters were all out of proportion to the provocation; in a 'grudge' fight no one really 'wins'; the needless cruelty to the mothers and babies was the result of loss of self-control."[72] The reactions echoed territorial conflicts the students had experienced: fights in their neighborhoods, the Cold War, battles for Black rights. The students had internalized the message that the researchers aimed to instill—that fighting with neighbors harmed the greater good. Smith showed that students already felt the weight of reform. Students sensed that adults expected them to amend their wrongs, for themselves, but also for others.

The delinquency-specific iteration of the Judeo-Christian repertoire in New York City public schools also took embodied forms. The embodied expressions of loving thy neighbor and following the Golden Rule added ritual dimensions to delinquency prevention. For instance, the Board's 1953 Clean-Up Campaign uplifted cleanliness as vandalism's enemy. The campaign conceived of vandalism and dirt as characteristics of the same problem: neighborhood immorality. Because city officials understood dirt to signify "slum" neighborhood conditions that produced delinquency, the campaign equated litter with vandalism. As cleanliness conveyed a sacred whiteness, litter signaled a Black and Puerto Rican neighborhood. While fewer city resources likely were allocated for Black and Puerto Rican neighborhoods to clean litter given redlining practices, the moral symbolism persisted.[73]

The city's parades rendered cleanliness patriotic—to keep land and property clean expressed love of country. At least two parades took place in the city in May 1953, one in Harlem and one on the Lower East Side. The city classified both neighborhoods as relatively "high delinquency." At the Lower East Side parade, students embodied patriotic cleanliness through the symbol of the American flag. A photograph captures students wearing white tops and dark slacks or skirts, marching from PS 110, an elementary school on Delancey Street. They carried signs reading "THIS IS YOUR CITY PLEASE TRY TO KEEP IT CLEAN!," "P.S. 110 KEEP N.Y. CLEAN," and "CLEAN UP OUR CITY!," a sign with a picture of a garbage can labeled "D.S." for Department of Sanitation, and a cut-out of the New York City skyline.[74] Other children held brooms and mops from the bottom up, the cleaning tools at least doubling the children's heights. In front of the sign- and broom-wavers a student held an American flag, mirroring the smaller children behind her lifting cleaning items. The cleaning items and flag took on similar visual roles in the picture, though she stood ahead of the others, marking the flag's domain over their mops, brooms, and D.S. signs. Marching students enacted good American citizenship in school officials' eyes by associating cleanliness and vandalism prevention with American patriotism. The flag sacralized the mops and brooms with the schools' portrait of American values.

Some cleanup programs even more explicitly emphasized that America valued cleanliness and rejected vandalism. For instance, PS 138 at 253rd Street and Weller Avenue in Rosedale, Queens showed films on citizenship. The school also hosted "Know Your America" and "Flag Day" Programs, where the Mothers' Club awarded prizes to fifth and sixth graders for an essay on vandalism "because vandalism and lack of respect for the property of others are un-American and are the mark of the poor citizen."[75] At PS 23, another elementary school in Queens, students engaged in school plays on "How To Be a Good Citizen."[76] The schools reaffirmed that values associated with the flag contrasted with vandalism.

The parades transformed love of country into love of neighborhood through shared participation in the ritual. They aimed to ensure loyalty to the neighborhood by involving the students and adults in the parades. On the Lower East Side, three thousand children from neigh-

Figure 3.2. Students carried mops, brooms, and an American flag at the May 1953 Anti-Vandalism Clean-Up Parade through the Lower East Side. "Photo Book, J.H.S. 188, May 1953," Folder 4, Box 3, Series 521, NYCBER.

boring schools marched from Houston to 13th Street "to publicize the city campaign"[77] to clean up the city. A float from the city's Department of Sanitation traveled the streets, reading "Pull Together for a Cleaner New York." The float held cardboard drawings of four people dressed in clothes ranging from a suit to an apron pulling a broom away from a cut-out of the city. At the broom's end a collection of thistles dripped down with "DIRT" written atop it. Behind the float, junior high schoolers, wearing ties, looked ahead. Led by the band of Junior High School 188 on Houston Street in Manhattan's East Village, "This activity involved the school Art groups and the special music classes as well as the general school population. Classes developed costumes, posters, slogans and songs. Preparations resulted in intense discussions of cleanliness as pupils worked to get the message across to the 'public.'"[78] The Harlem parade also involved people throughout the community in the ritual:

Rollicking music, colorful floats, gracefully gyrating drum majorettes thrilled laughing, cheering throngs on May 27. The parade delighted hundreds of spectators from 109 St. to 96 St. south on Columbus Avenue and north on Amsterdam. The Joan of Arc Junior High School Band under police escort led the way followed by Sanitation Department floats. Children wearing caps and aprons marched along carrying mops and brooms. Gay striking posters created by our junior citizens accented the spirit of the parade. Twenty-five children each from P.S. 179, 166, 165, 118, 93, 54, 75, 9 and the band and drum majorette of J.H. 118 formed the colorful line of the march.[79]

The parades cultivated belonging to the white, "Judeo-Christian" country, and to the neighborhood, by involving students in preparations for the spectacle. With city departments and students gathering for music, marching, and celebration, the parade assembled the community to share in preventing delinquency through cleanliness.

Figure 3.3. Department of Sanitation float at the May 1953 Anti-Vandalism Clean-Up Parade through the Lower East Side. "Photo Book, J.H.S. 188, May 1953," Folder 4, Box 3, Series 521, NYCBER.

The Clean-Up Campaign directed students and parents to commit to the neighborhood. Other disciplinary mechanisms for creating student neighborhood loyalty joined patriotism. For instance, one school developed pledges to encourage students to commit to cleaning their neighborhoods. Students and a block committee from near PS 72 on 104th Street at Lexington Avenue in (lower) East Harlem cleaned a "badly littered vacant lot adjoining the school." The school sent commitment pledges to the neighborhood stating, "[I swear] that I will help clean up the empty lot on 104th Street near Public School 72." ["Yo juro que ayudare a limpiar el lote vacio en la calle 104 cerca de la escuela 72."] Volunteers could check two boxes: "I will work [Yo trabajare]" and "I will bring a shovel or rake [Traere pala y rastrillo]."[80] By including English and Spanish versions of the pledge, the campaign could reach Spanish-speaking families who might otherwise be excluded from the schools' plans. The commitment pledge framed students and parents as being responsible for cleanliness while also helping organizers determine how many people would show up. By pledging allegiance to neighborhood cleanliness, families transferred love of country (pledging allegiance to the flag) to love of neighborhood.

As the 104th Street efforts demonstrated, schools used the campaign to direct adults' behavior, as well as children's. In a campaign summary report, PS 72's principal outlined six essential steps to success: "Interest was aroused," "Good will was created," "The block has become litter-conscious," "Parents have won the increased respect of the school," "Campaign has carried over into the school," and "Many groups cooperated in the campaign."[81] In each step, parents played important roles. They learned from the schools, then joined the school program to teach students about the dangers of litter. In the first two steps, the passive voice conveyed an omniscient school, controlling parents' actions behind the scenes. In the later steps, the parents, block, campaign, and groups became subjects. They had taken steps to assimilate into the all-knowing school's values by participating in the Clean-Up Campaign.

Parent and student involvement produced intergenerational accountability. At PS 34 in the Bronx, students wrote a letter addressed "Dear Neighbors," with a list of action steps, including "Train your children (that is us) to do the same [Put all litter (papers, wrappers, and other odds and ends), into the wire baskets provided by the Department of

Sanitation or into your own cans.] The school is doing a grand job, but the school can't do it alone."[82] Students became messengers for the city to teach care for neighborhoods. Students' letters showed off their commitment to the neighborhood to inspire adult neighbors. Then, this active pedagogical approach asked the adult neighbors to play the role of teacher for other children, enforcing an intergenerational bond.

The school system's anti-delinquency programming invited students to take ownership of their own transformation and that of their surroundings. For instance, at PS 4B in Brooklyn, "The School Garden Boys" guarded an embodiment of school reform, the school garden. They "were supplied with belts and Clean City League buttons," which, coupled with their posture to "st[and] on guard at the garden during entrance and dismissal time," visually signaled the importance of their role. To protect the garden, "They assisted the Custodian in keeping the garden free of litter, and the plants and bushes watered. They took pride in their work."[83] The students protected the garden from vandalism. As the garden physically demonstrated a transition from dirty to clean, from littered to beautiful, the boys actively supported the school's disciplinary program against delinquency.

The campaign taught students and adults to improve neighborhood conditions through embodied lessons about transformation from dirty/ vandalized to clean/patriotic. In particular, the campaign taught students to "love thy neighbor" and follow the Golden Rule, both directly, as a lesson from God, and in tending to neighborhood litter and parading American flags and brooms. A distilled, universalized religion operated as control, separation, surveillance, reform, and celebration. The schools drew attention to what neighborhoods and children needed to change but left their own responsibilities relatively untouched.

Reciprocity as an Alternative Mode of Delinquency Prevention and Treatment

By contrast to the schools, religious leaders taught the concept of love of neighbor in delinquency prevention as an effort that required communities to identify how they might have contributed to delinquency, rather than primarily blaming delinquents. Across Christian and Jewish traditions, religious leaders emphasized their community's responsibility to love their neighbors, including delinquents. In New York City, religious leaders claimed that their institutions could model good citizenship for delinquents by treating them with love. Unlike the schools, they strove to meet the children partway. White Union Theological Seminary theologian Arthur L. Swift Jr. wrote in a *Union Seminary Quarterly* article called "Gangs and the Churches" that "to bring church to gang or gang to church is to perform a miracle in the conjunction of opposites. So it seems to many."[84] Swift argued that churches were meant to help youth in need so such a perception "ought not and need not be so," and that delinquents may benefit from the church. Robert Lee, another liberal Protestant, argued that the church should reflect on its own mission. In an article titled "Delinquent Youth in a Normless Time" for *The Christian Century*, Lee wrote that "We must confess that we are indeed a delinquent church," because to become "so respectable" as to neglect youth signaled failing in their function.[85] Like the schools' racial liberals, Lee argued that communities, not individual actors, caused delinquency: "The fact is that 'doing something about delinquency' means that the community at large must do something about itself."[86] Unlike the racial liberals, though, Lee placed responsibility on the community. As churches sat within the community, Lee suggested that churches ought to model their values by treating delinquents respectfully. Rather than perpetuate a culture of poverty, he prioritized reciprocity.

J. Archie Hargraves took the argument that churches should and could help delinquency in communities further, claiming that churches were ideally located to help solve delinquency because they operated in the same environments that fostered delinquency. By changing the environment through religious care, churches could minimize delinquency. Founder of the East Harlem Protestant Parish and the West Side Christian Parish in Chicago, and pastor of the Nazarene Congregational Church in Brooklyn, Hargraves, who was Black, wrote: "Juvenile delinquency is a neighborhood problem because it involves flesh-and-blood people who live next door or across the street. Ideally, the local church can be the decisive instrument in combatting delinquency on the neighborhood level."[87] He described the theological significance of the church's involvement: "[The local church] has to seek a new community orientation that implies it will cease existing for itself and will come to share its particular concerns, techniques and love with the whole neighborhood so that all may advance together."[88] As Hargraves also developed racially inclusive school curricula based on the reciprocal model of loving thy neighbor, his framing of delinquency participated in his overall approach to racial justice.

Like Hargraves, other religious leaders postulated that if delinquency was an environmental problem, the solutions also lay in the environment. These religious leaders offered guidelines as much for themselves as for the children, a key difference between their approach and the schools' approach. For example, Rabbi Milton Matz mused in *The Reconstructionist: A Journal of Contemporary Jewish Thought*: "Churches and synagogues can perform vital services in combating delinquency," because "unlike most other social institutions, they deal with individuals as family units. The membership unit is the family, not the individual."[89] As school authorities argued that schools needed to guide families, Matz claimed that religious institutions could address environmental delinquency because they could access children's home lives. Matz reinforced that religious institutions could be actively involved in delinquency prevention because delinquency arose in communities.

On a national scale, the best-selling New York City adventure tale *The Cross and the Switchblade* recounted reciprocal religious transformation from an evangelical perspective. The book details white evangelical pastor David Wilkerson's journey from rural Pennsylvania to serve Harlem's youth upon receiving a calling from God. In Wilkerson's descriptions of young people and himself, he positioned Christianity and delinquents as having opposing values, which created the opportunity for salvation. He described young people with foul mouths, active sex lives, and unrelenting violence. For instance, he depicted Nicky Cruz, affiliated with the MauMaus, with his "rock-hard gaze," "sixteen stabbings to his record," and reputation "as a vicious knife-fighter not only to the Brooklyn kids but to the gangs in Manhattan and the Bronx as well."[90] By contrast, Wilkerson presented himself as "a country preacher," who found meeting Nicky "the worst two minutes of my life."[91] After Wilkerson's initial resistance, Nicky became one of his most successful converts, eventually gathering his own following.[92] Wilkerson used Nicky's example to convey that religion could cure even the most severe delinquents. Wilkerson devoted himself to Nicky and the other Harlem children, albeit exploitatively. Yet, he claimed that guidance, care, and attention could address their behavior, and when enough people changed, the community could transform. By opening himself up to the teenagers, he demonstrated that he, too, needed to change to solve delinquency.

* * *

The version of religion in New York City public school delinquency prevention upheld the schools' goals in a Judeo-Christian repertoire, not necessarily institutionally religious communities' principles. In the 1950s, courts were beginning to consider whether there was a violation of the establishment clause by determining whether a practice's purpose was religious or secular.[93] Perhaps because they served a perceived greater good—ending delinquency—the jingles, parades, and films never saw the light of day in court. Whether the practices ought to have gone to court is not the issue, though. Rather, religion clause case law has so shaped the framing of religion in public schools that other religious concepts and work in public schools often remain invisible.

Rhetorical and embodied religious pluralism prevailed in New York City public school delinquency prevention and treatment. In addition to never being taken to court, these iterations of human kinship created neighborhood as a category of racialized and moral difference, where students were supposed to feel ashamed about failing to perfect values attributed to white communities. Through ritual, the shame became internalized. The schools used the rhetoric of love and community to control, survey, separate, and reform the students and parents in neighborhoods where they perceived delinquency to threaten social stability. A religious understanding of students' moral geographies racialized school discipline.

The schools' project against delinquency used religion, specifically the command to love thy neighbor, to differentiate racial others and selectively assimilate them into a white, Christian norm. The approach prepared schools to articulate integration on assimilationist grounds. Judeo-Christianity gave the schools language to differentiate moral and immoral places. The tension between the language of love and the disdain for or indifference to purportedly love-lacking neighborhoods also appeared in programs on racial integration in schools. As we turn to school activities on brotherhood and racial integration, it becomes clear that the call for racial and religious unity took place during the battle over desegregating the very redlined neighborhoods the city identified as "high delinquency" and "slums."

Simultaneously, the same neighborhoods modeled the integration to which the Board aspired. A front page 1950 *New York Amsterdam News* article by Randolph White titled "Harlemites Help Puerto Ricans Battle Slums" affirmed that "cops call the neighborhood 'hot' meaning that something is always happening" and "naturally, juvenile delinquency and crime rates are high as they are in any slum area."[94] One in a three-part series on "uniting Harlem," the article continued: "Puerto Ricans and American-born Negroes live side by side to support the theory that Harlem is capable of uniting to fight its common enemies." Moreover, citing Lillian Smith, a "noted Southern liberal and writer," White continued that "One of the finest examples of what can be done in this regard is found in the public schools . . . where all races are represented," and Smith noted "'the children are growing out of trouble.'" "Common enemies" referred to the schools, the city, and the state—any entity of power failing to provide resources for Black and Puerto Rican New Yorkers. The article presented a narrative of solidarity and progress within Black and Puerto Rican neighborhoods that contrasted with the city's depictions of public schools in "high delinquency areas." The tension between how the Board and communities viewed neighborhoods such as Harlem shaped understandings of integration as a moral value.

4

Conflicting Religious Visions of Integration

Although both desegregation and secularization were supposedly occur-ring in the 1950s and 1960s, neither process succeeded, because of the other. Schools could not be "de-religionized" by removing prayer, nor could they be "de-raced" by claiming all children of God were broth-ers. As in juvenile delinquency prevention, where the phrase "love thy neighbor as thyself" was aimed at controlling youth crime in Black and Puerto Rican neighborhoods, religion played a significant role in deseg-regation efforts in New York City public schools by shaping the concept of integration. Whereas desegregation was the act of white students and students of color moving schools to avoid racially separate institutions, for some, integration was the idealized vision of everyone getting along.[1] However, integration was a contested moral value. Diverse religious resources influenced New Yorkers' understandings of integration, and these understandings helped determine where and with whom children attended school.

While schools were supposed to be both desegregating and secular-izing, administrators embedded a version of Judeo-Christian pluralism, designed for public schools, through the value of integration. For the Board, integration did not require desegregation. Instead, integration involved coordinating with the National Conference of Christians and Jews on rituals such as Brotherhood Week and describing a one-way transfer program, sending Black or Puerto Rican students to white schools, as "a natural consequence of the morality of our American heri-tage and of our Judaeo-Christian tradition."[2] The Board envisioned in-tegration religiously at the same time as it was supposed to be removing religion from public schools. Its vision never resulted in desegregation.

Black and Puerto Rican New Yorkers, however, demanded equal educational resources for their children and argued that integration re-quired desegregation. They drew from diverse religious resources, such as local churches, ancestors, Pan-Africanism, ideas about freedom, and occasionally the schools' Judeo-Christian repertoire, to advocate for better resourced schools. The persistent "FAILURE OF PUBLIC EDU-CATION" to adequately educate Black and Puerto Rican students or desegregate schools put integration, the value, under scrutiny for Black and Puerto Rican New Yorkers.[3] By the late 1960s, many Black and Puerto Rican parents prioritized not desegregation but educational re-sources and the creation of spaces where students felt welcome and able to learn, which might have been separate from white people.

Identifying integration as a value allows us to draw a parallel be-tween diversity/desegregation and pluralism/integration to highlight the religious forms that influenced desegregation/integration debates. In the study of religion, religious diversity refers to various religions co-existing; pluralism means that "this great diversity is not simply toler-ated but becomes the very source of our strength."[4] The desegregation/integration parallel to religious diversity/pluralism is more than coinci-dence. In the 1950s and 1960s, as the NCCJ and US government articu-lated a Judeo-Christian American pluralism involving primarily white Protestants, Catholics, and Jews, public schools performed integration through their own vision of that pluralism.[5] Judeo-Christian American pluralism shaped the Board's understanding that integration was a value that did not require desegregating.

Because Judeo-Christian pluralism and desegregation intersect in the primary sources, it is useful to examine two relevant literatures—on pluralism and on school desegregation—together. Doing so allows us to see intersecting patterns of political urgency and stalling tactics. While the broader pluralism literature has shown that tolerance rhetoric de-politicizes freedom struggles by universalizing Christianity, the litera-ture specifically on Judeo-Christianity has only recently invited further exploration of race.[6] Analyzing public schools and race together in the context of mid-century pluralism responds to such calls in one signifi-cant effort for racial liberation.

The rich scholarship on school desegregation has focused on attempts to contain the movement for racial justice in education. Some schol-ars have shown that the 1964 New York City boycott—the Civil Rights Movement's largest school boycott, when nearly half a million students stayed home—led to community control.[7] Other scholars have critiqued *Brown*'s influence in defining racism because it focused on individual psychology rather than white economic advantage or residential segre-gation.[8] Religion plays a small but important role in this desegregation literature.[9] For instance, religious figures mobilized for the cause: Rev. Milton Galamison organized the boycott with activists Bayard Rustin and Thelma Hamilton and the Parents Workshop for Equality. Critical race theorist Derrick Bell also uses a religious register to name *Brown* a "racial sacrifice covenant" where Black people were required to sacrifice their own rights for white people's interests.[10] Above all, the desegrega-tion literature's emphasis on the inertia to desegregate exemplifies plu-ralism's reach in public schools.

Following the Supreme Court's 1954 *Brown v. Board of Education* de-cision, the Board's Commission on Integration framed integration as a long-standing value in a Judeo-Christian tradition, even as some mem-bers of the Commission sought systemic changes. Rather than codes for one another, as religion and race in the South are often framed, religion and race coalesced to narrate northern virtue through pervasive rituals of assimilation into white Christian norms that cultivated everyday hab-its. This was integration. For example, the NCCJ's Brotherhood Week performed a temporary expression of family to symbolize integration in a school festival, a break from the normal behavior of segregation. The Board also established a program to assimilate Puerto Rican students into American norms. In the wake of *Brown*, the Board claimed that they had always supported the ideals represented in *Brown*, even though they practiced desegregation as a one-way street where Black and Puerto Rican students were supposed to be the only ones who moved schools.

Integration rituals extended beyond the Board's and highlighted differing perspectives on its meaning. For instance, Black and Puerto Rican communities associated integration with "quality education in a de-segregated school system" during the 1964 school boycott, a different take on integration from that of the Board.[11] The boycott's slogan was "Integration is an Education," insisting on the pedagogical value of in-tegration. Some Black and Puerto Rican New Yorkers retained the idea of integration as a value to promote quality education, but reimagined it as largely about improving education for communities of color rather than maintaining the status quo, where the city claimed to value every-one but demonstrated otherwise. Others found new spaces, including churches, which had long fulfilled social needs, to educate students of

color in spaces free from the white gaze.[12] In Freedom Schools and summer reading programs, regardless of whether integration was the value,
quality education and equal educational resources for Black and Puerto
Rican students were the desired actions. Some Black and Puerto Rican
parents concluded that because religion shaped public schools' racism,
it could help to undo it.[13]

Integration as Long-Standing Value

When the Board resolved to appoint a Commission on Integration on
December 23, 1954, it called *Brown* "a legal and moral reaffirmation of
our fundamental educational principles." However, *Brown* resoundingly
focused on the legal process of desegregation, not integration. The 1954
case used forms of the word "segregation" forty-one times and only
incorporated two mentions of "integration." Similarly, the 1955 follow-up
case to *Brown*, which named the amorphous timeline for desegregating schools—"all deliberate speed"—highlighted "segregation" more
than "integration."[14] By framing *Brown* as representative of "educational
principles," the Board claimed that *Brown* reflected principles the Board
already held. However, although New York City public schools had not
been legally segregated for decades, other legal and social mechanisms,
including housing practices, cultivated school segregation.[15] Their argument distinguished New York City from southern states. While southern
states could not hide from the racism embedded in education because of
legal school segregation, New York City could. Rather than admit that
they had not implemented an abiding possibility, the Board emphasized
that the city had long prioritized the desegregation *Brown* put forth by
using a different term to describe the priority: integration. The difference mattered, and it allows us to witness how religion and race worked
together to sustain liberal values for white families.

The Commission's structure suggested that integration reflected an
investment in the whole community, from neighborhoods to schools.
The Commission included six subcommittees, which addressed systemic, lived inequality: zoning; guidance, educational stimulation, and
placement; educational standards and curriculum; teachers' assignments
and personnel; community relations and information; and physical plant
and maintenance. Each subcommittee's work was practical, oriented to-

ward desegregation. Zoning referred to "residential segregation," a term the Commission's final report used to avoid blame. Guidance, educational stimulation, and placement suggested a commitment to students' individual needs. Educational standards and curriculum addressed racist course materials. Teachers' assignments and personnel articulated a need for more Black and Puerto Rican teachers and administrators. Community relations and information sought to communicate with and learn from communities with predominantly Black and Puerto Rican students. Physical plant and maintenance recognized that many school buildings in Black and Puerto Rican neighborhoods were falling apart. Without the space to learn, learning could not happen. Taken together, the sub-commissions suggested that the Commission on Integration was committed to desegregating schools.

Moreover, committee members included Civil Rights Movement leaders who brought expertise to the table. Ella Baker, who became involved in the National Association for the Advancement of Colored People, the Southern Christian Leadership Conference, and the Student Nonviolent Coordinating Committee and later started Freedom Schools, served on the Zoning Sub-Commission. She edited the Zoning Sub-Commission's interim report to enforce greater accountability.[16] Baker and fellow sub-committee member Ethel Schwaber refused to approve the report unless it reflected her changes. Kenneth Clark— the psychiatrist whose doll study with his wife Mamie Clark became evidence for the Supreme Court in *Brown* to accept the argument that segregation harmed Black children—chaired the Educational Standards and Curriculum Sub-Commission. His sub-commission collected the previously mentioned report on offensive portrayals of "minorities" in textbooks.[17] The report included sections on "stereotypes," "distortions regarding slavery," "distortion of emancipation and reconstruction," "improper presentation of colonial peoples," and "questionable pictures and cartoons."[18] Clark offered a detailed analysis of a "compendium of so-called 'jokes,' anecdotes, etc.," "approved for use in libraries in the secondary schools of New York City."[19] Clark's sub-commission tried to emphasize African Americans' "dignity and worth[]" in curricula.[20] On the whole, Commission members came from across the ideological spectrum: Other Commission members, Board Members Vito Lanza and Andrew Clausen, had supported the moral and spiritual values curricula from the 1950s.[21] Yet, Baker's and Clark's significant roles indicate that the Commission's recommendations could have contributed to desegregation, had they been acted upon.

However, the Commission's final report exemplified that the Board's version of integration, the value, involved researching, meeting, and discussing, but not necessarily desegregating. Titled "Toward the Integration of Our Schools," the word integration announced that the document prioritized integration in principle, but the sub-commissions did not have the resources to turn their principles into action. "Toward the Integration of Our Schools" painted a less than rosy picture about whether the changes would actually be implemented, noting that, as "many of the changes recommended in the sub-commission reports entail budgetary increases which have not as yet been approved by the Board of Estimate, the implementation of these recommendations will be delayed to some extent."[22] The Commission's hard work could not stand alone; buy-in from the Board was necessary.

The Commission was mired in contradiction: The Board claimed it had long valued integration while the Commission admitted that segregation persisted. The Board formed the Commission to address what it called "residential segregation," a common American problem outside the Jim Crow South's *de jure* segregation. As the final report explained, "Although segregation has been illegal in the public schools of New York State since 1920, a substantial amount of *de facto* segregation has grown up in the New York City school system, as in other Northern cities, as a consequence of the prevailing *residential* segregation of white and Negro families." By relegating segregation to where people lived and neglecting to discuss redlining, the schools distanced themselves from segregation, even as they perpetuated stereotypes of redlined districts in juvenile delinquency prevention.

Although the report offered possible actions, because of lack of funding, it ultimately described a value, not an action, and a value that did not require action. The value mythologized the new tradition, Judeo-Christianity, and rendered change unnecessary. In moments of fleeting togetherness, the schools already enacted integration as a moral value. By supporting the *idea* of people from different backgrounds inhabiting the same spaces, the Board positioned itself against the Jim Crow South. At the same time, they cultivated New York's own religiously backed racism.

Brotherhood Week, a Temporary Expression of Family

Brotherhood Week ritualized integration by separating the value from everyday activities and suspending integration in time. From the 1930s to the 2000s, the NCCJ sponsored Brotherhood Week throughout the country during the last week of every February, encouraging students to celebrate co-existence.[23] As the era's most popular interfaith organization, the NCCJ began Brotherhood Week in the 1930s in response to the atrocities committed against Jews in Europe.[24] The NCCJ aimed to educate the masses about brotherhood through publications, radio spots, lesson plans for churches and synagogues, pamphlets for distribution, and more.[25] In the 1950s and 1960s, the NCCJ framed brotherhood as an antidote to a presumed enemy, especially the Soviet Union.[26] Against the backdrop of the Commission on Integration in the 1950s and the 1964 New York City school boycott for desegregation, the Board welcomed the NCCJ's celebration into public schools. The week's central teaching held that despite religious differences, everyone could join in "the brotherhood of man under the fatherhood of God."[27] The week represented integration as a temporary performance of an idealized white, Christian nuclear family. Moreover, with God as overseer, New Yorkers could step into the father theology, discussed earlier, as representatives from their ethnic backgrounds.

During Brotherhood Week, communities demonstrated integration by accepting the premise that they were all children of God, invited to family dinner. For example, in 1950, PS 168's Parents Association hosted a Brotherhood Week potluck. The NCCJ recommended that women from different backgrounds gather to "Eat Brotherhood" and "Illustrate brotherhood through food."[28] In doing so, they performed the roles of siblings who could take on roles of American leaders, as in the father theology. When the Brooklyn school's PA took the NCCJ's recommendation, the parents cultivated a ritual announcing inclusion in and respect for the human family. Women from different religious and racial backgrounds joined to taste food from each other's cultures at "an international buffet supper" with "family style" eating.[29] In Brotherhood Week's logic, people's cultures humanized them by making them members of a family: "brothers" under a Father God. Therefore, the logic went, religious and racial diversity reflected a Father God's creation.

Favorite dishes of all nations were sampled by parents and teachers of P.S. 168, Brooklyn, at an international buffet supper held in the school by the P. T. A. in celebration of Brotherhood Week. Italian spaghetti, Jewish gefulte fish, Southern fried chicken, Russian, German, Norwegian, Spanish and New England delicacies were served.

Figure 4.1. 1950 Parents Association Brotherhood Week Potluck at PS 168. "Brotherhood Nourished by PTA," Folder 93, Box 52, Subseries 8, Series 911, NYCBER.

During Brotherhood Week, schools directed students to learn about "the need for developing and for strengthening the bonds of friendship among all peoples."[30]

By eating the supper, parents performed commitment to integration, the seemingly universal, nonsectarian value. They assimilated from their particular culture to "brotherhood." Parents brought the most stereotyped and politically fraught edible representations of their cultures: Jewish families shared gefilte fish, African American families brought southern fried chicken. As Hillary Kaell has argued in a different context, eating food from other cultures paralleled Communion because diners tasted something spiritual but distant.[31] Here, the focus was easily consumable parts of their cultures. Food provided exposure without threatening conversion. The food became the small helping that each parent's culture offered to collective brotherhood. By eating each other's dishes, the parents did not suddenly become Jewish or African American if they were not already. Rather, parents ate to appreciate all cultures' humanity. The buffet table was plentiful; the women posing for the picture smiled.

At PS 168, women performed the emotional and culinary labor of family. Brotherhood named the week, but mothers led the charge. In the picture, the six women wear aprons and stand under a sign reading "Brotherhood." They smile, looking in different directions. Of the six women, only one is Black; the others, presumably, identified as some of the other ethnicities whose cuisines, the caption indicated, were served: Italian American, Jewish, Norwegian, Russian, German, and Spanish (a vague descriptor: did Spanish mean from Spain? From Puerto Rico?). One white woman puts her hand on the Black woman's arm, signaling affection, familiarity.

Together, the women sanctified the ritual through the notion that women were responsible for caring for their families and ensuring that their families practiced religion, but due to their auxiliary role in a Parents Association, their efforts were temporary. The press recognized the event as an example of the schools doing something. Their efforts highlight that the ritual practice of integration was often short-term. Schools devoted only one week of the year to the topic, suggesting that integration was separate from regular events, and therefore special, ritually set apart.

Each year, Brotherhood Week culminated February's honorific weeks as it immediately followed what was then called "Negro History Week." Negro History Week aimed to celebrate African American history by highlighting African Americans' contributions to many fields. During Negro History Week, students learned, among other things, that "the Negro participates in all phases of American life, e.g., in medicine, science, teaching, literature, art, music, factory work, agriculture, public service." Students also might have "Learn[ed] a poem by a Negro author (Teacher should select a poem free from dialect)."[32] Negro History Week acknowledged that schools often overlooked African Americans' contributions to American life and encouraged cultural sensitivity in learning about them. In contemporary terms, Brotherhood Week was the All Lives Matter to Negro History Week's Black Lives Matter. Schools concluded with universality above particularity.

General language in the weeks' programming—such as "services people have rendered to mankind" and "many lands"—highlighted that Brotherhood Week would universalize the history Negro History Week had particularized. In addition to reading books about brotherhood, possible activities included "reporting personal anecdotes in pupils' experiences in the home, school, or neighborhood which illustrate the ideal of brotherhood and of helpfulness," "preparing assembly program, e.g., dramatizing scene from a story or poem illustrating theme of brotherhood, preparing an original play based on services people have rendered to mankind," and "reciting appropriate selections in choral arrangements."[33] Brotherhood Week suggested that all cultures had idiosyncrasies, but the shared existence of idiosyncrasies was what students should celebrate. The theme emphasized togetherness without addressing histories of inequality, or why friendship among all peoples might be difficult.

For instance, the week turned a famous story of family strife, the biblical story of Cain and Abel, into an example of family care to highlight why integration mattered. In Genesis, Cain killed Abel. Then, with petulance, he asked God, "Am I my brother's keeper?"[34] However, President Dwight Eisenhower, the honorary chairman of Brotherhood Week in 1955, interpreted the story's message differently, to say that Cain failed his role as a brother. Eisenhower offered an alternative answer to "the first man who asked, 'Am I my brother's keeper?'": a lesson in tolerance.[35] Eisenhower continued, "Through thousands of years there have been many noble answers to this same question, answers which bravely affirm that all men—of all religions, of all colors, of all languages—are in fact brothers, that no man can live alone."[36] Caring for brothers saved lives, on Eisenhower's reading. Echoing Eisenhower, one newspaper editor argued that brotherhood meant responding affirmatively to Cain's question, "Am I my brother's keeper?," rather than adopting Cain's exasperated retort.[37] Given that in Genesis, God condemns Cain to a life of wandering because he killed his brother, these Brotherhood Week proponents interpreted God's punishment as a sign that humans failed when they did not keep each other.

Brotherhood Week presented integration as more than a school policy; it was taught as a national value. Each sitting US president served as the honorary chairman of Brotherhood Week. Presidents gave the occasion gravitas and moral authority. For instance, Eisenhower promoted Judeo-Christian values as a weapon to fight the Cold War. He connected the same biblical story of Cain and Abel to "our civilization," suggesting that national history participated in biblical history. His role meant that the parents sharing meals and the students singing songs were participating in a performance of the national family.

The NCCJ understood the nation as a family, though a family that was separate but equal—a principle at odds with the *Brown* decision.[38] As a metaphor, brotherhood represented the human family, where brothers were separate creatures equally worthy of dignity because brothers shared a creator. As brothers were related but physically separate, races and religions could share values but occupy independent bodies. The metaphor applied to diverse groups within the nation, where each group was a brother and the nation was the family. God could be a traditional Father God, or the deified American father-gods previously discussed, depending on who was talking.

The NCCJ's founder, Everett Clinchy, articulated religious uniqueness as key to brotherhood, which enacted the metaphor of family as separate but equal. Clinchy ardently opposed missions to Jews. When his colleague John R. Mott stated in 1931 that "'missionary work among Jews was a duty,'"[39] Clinchy responded by telegram to the *New York Times*, proclaiming, "Personally I do not want to see Jews proselyted to Christianity. . . . For Christians to talk about expressing good-will toward Jews and at the same time planning to annihilate Judaism shows a total ignorance of the anthropological laws of human behavior."[40] He called such ignorance "unbrotherly," signaling that to him, difference was a value itself. Making different religious groups the same erased an entire people, he expressed. His understanding of brotherhood relied on religious difference. Even decades later, the NCCJ pamphlet "Some Basic Beliefs" about brotherhood reflected Clinchy's vision: "NCCJ believes that brotherhood is giving to others the same dignity and rights one claims for himself . . . brotherhood can be achieved without seeking a union of religious bodies and without weakening the loyalties or modifying the distinctive beliefs of any creed."[41] To the NCCJ, each religion was distinct, and brotherhood maintained the separation. However, the NCCJ sought for all Americans to unite in commitment to difference, celebrating equality in separation together.

Despite the separate but equal framing, Brotherhood Week resonated with *Brown*. The central premise, that harmony between individuals of different backgrounds was easy, illustrates scholars' recent point that *Brown* grounded racism in individual psychology rather than systemic racism and socioeconomic disparity.[42] People turning on the radio between February 20 and 27, 1955 anywhere in the country could have heard the weather reporter announce: "There's a thaw in store for us today, according to the Weather Bureau, so go prepared for puddle-jumping. And, since this is BROTHERHOOD WEEK, go prepared to meet your fellow Americans with a nice thaw of understanding in your heart and spirit toward people of other races, religions, and nationalities. As Americans all, LET'S GET TOGETHER! . . . FOR BROTHERHOOD!"[43] In a splashy presentation of finding brotherhood even in playful puddle-jumping, the spot conveyed that brotherhood was about embodying the national family for a moment rather than implementing long-lasting change.

Pervasive Ritual Assimilation

Rituals both separate from and woven into everyday life made integration a moral value, a public good. While Brotherhood Week suspended integration in time through an annual festival, other rituals made integration habitual. Such rituals spread the value through pervasive acts of assimilation into white Christian norms.

For example, a 1950s program called the Puerto Rican Study assimilated Puerto Rican students to "American" culture. The PRS impressed a vision of citizenship upon Puerto Rican students based on white New York City school administrators' ideas about Judeo-Christian morality. The city and Ford Foundation provided financial support, and the NCCJ helped fund the program's summer workshops.[44] In New York City, Puerto Rican students' presence shaped integration as a value. Puerto Rico was part of the United States, but the PRS situated Puerto Ricans outside of US citizenship. The PRS articulated English as key to American citizenship, and citizenship as key to being worthy of integrating. The PRS helped the Board "develop policies, programs, and curriculum appropriate for the increasing number of students arriving from Puerto Rico."[45] In October 1958, estimates suggested that the Puerto Rican student population comprised about 15 percent of the school system. There were 137,000 Puerto Rican students enrolled in New York City public schools, 17 percent of whom the report estimated did not speak English.[46] The PRS was a stark example of the difference between the value of integration and the practice of desegregation: Because the study did not require students to change schools, Puerto Rican students remained in segregated schools.

Even though Puerto Rican students were US citizens, school personnel treated them as foreign. A sixteen-year-old student, "under the supervision of his teacher," wrote a class report for "his English 4 class at Morris High School" in the Bronx in May 1955. He described how he "especially came here attracted by an old Porto Rican rumor about the U.S. been an exajurated place" but "was so discouraged when I saw the real thing." "[A] gain I was discouraged," he wrote, because "The teachers in this school did not considered me, they were harsh and they made me feel like a complete stranger. They even told me to go back to where I came from. Although I couldn't speak English I understand every thing they ment. And all this I shall never forget it [sic]."[47] He summarized his research on Puerto Rico's economy and politics: "We are just as good 'American citizens' as you are."[48] The comments illuminated that school culture treated Puerto Rican students as "foreign" by framing them as in but not of the city.

Simultaneous US citizenship and perceived cultural foreignness made Puerto Rican students ideal candidates for assimilative integration. For example, in a speech at the National Education Association's 1954 Annual Meeting in New York City, Dr. Clare C. Baldwin, Assistant Superintendent of Schools, conveyed that Puerto Rican students' foreignness arose from living conditions:

> Those who left La Perla or El Fanguito have found their counterparts in the slums of New York. Many Puerto Rican families have been crowded together into cramped living quarters with inadequate ventilation and sanitary facilities, and a lack of ordinary housekeeping equipment. Frequently, the family unit does not consist of mother, father, brothers and sisters, but a mixed assortment of relatives, albeit there is a strong family bond which binds them together. The streets are the playground of the children. There exist hazards to health and morals in trying to bring up children under these conditions.[49]

Despite acknowledging that family was important to Puerto Ricans in New York, Baldwin ignored that migrant families often travel in waves and demeaned a sense of family beyond the biological. Education historian Madeleine E. López argues that the PRS challenged stereotypes of Puerto Ricans rooted in the "cultural poverty thesis" by including language learning classes. Yet, PRS leader Baldwin maintained views of Puerto Ricans as immoral, unclean, and unhealthy, due to where and how they lived.[50] To rectify problems the city contributed to, the PRS turned to assimilation. The study's subtitle, "A Report on the Education and Adjustment of Puerto Rican Pupils in the Public Schools of the City of New York," depicted Puerto Rican students as requiring "Education and Adjustment" into the city's public schools.[51] The schools were the constant; the students would need to change.

The PRS rarely mentioned students' religion explicitly. It focused instead on values and behaviors. However, a joint Council of Spanish-American Organizations and American Jewish Committee brochure suggests that religion informed the study's understanding of Puerto Rican children. The brochure estimated that 80 percent of Puerto Rico's population was Catholic and 20 percent was Protestant.[52] Furthermore, the brochure argued that religion imparted values to Puerto Ricans: "After hundreds of years of want and degradation, the Puerto Rican is an outstanding example of a person with strong family ties, generosity and warmth, pride of heritage, and a high standard of values."[53] It continued: "the Church can point with pride to its accomplishments in nurturing the people's finer qualities over centuries of heart-breaking adversities."[54] According to the brochure's logic, Puerto Ricans had already begun assimilation to church values in Puerto Rico and could translate those values to the New York City public schools.

PRS personnel demonstrated an enduring commitment to habituating assimilation as a national, public good. In PRS director Morrison's 1931 work, *Character Building in New York Public Schools*, he argued that "national morality" shaped public school norms. For example, he suggested that schools devote each month to specific virtues, including kindness, obedience, and cleanliness.[55] He cited George Washington's Farewell Address to demonstrate how religion could undergird public morality without being sectarian. In fact, he included the very lines sociologist Robert Bellah claims exemplified "civil religion": "And let us with caution indulge the supposition, that morality can be maintained without religion. Whatever may be conceded to the influence of refined education on minds of peculiar structure, reason and experience both forbid us to expect that National morality can prevail in exclusion of religious principle."[56] Bellah argues that "civil religion" is not Christian but "derive[s] from Christianity."[57] Similarly, Morrison's "national morality" claimed to be separate from religion, but inevitably influenced by religion.

The PRS acknowledged Puerto Rican culture as worthy of respect because schools also gave their personnel tools for interacting with Puerto Rican students. For instance, a publication titled "Interviewing Puerto Rican Parents and Children in Spanish" aimed "to help school personnel communicate with and achieve greater rapport with the Spanish-speaking child and parent."[58] The publication covered basic greetings and inquiries.

However, the PRS nevertheless prioritized school administrators' comfort by positioning them as necessary to assimilate students. The guide assured school administrators: "Don't be afraid or embarrassed to use the Spanish you know. After all, you are not a native, and you have not devoted years of study to conversational Spanish. For the most part you have been working along with Spanish and have done your best to pick up a few words or phrases to do your job more effectively."[59] Introducing school personnel to Spanish added some reciprocity to the relationship. However, including Spanish language lessons also supported personnel's role in assimilating Puerto Rican students to a national morality. Personnel only needed enough "to do your job"—i.e., assimilate the Puerto Rican students—more effectively.

While personnel faced minor adjustments, assimilation for the students was extensive. Assimilation shaped the moral goals of daily activities. For example, the PRS units aimed to introduce students to city neighborhoods, representing Puerto Rican students as otherwise lost in the big city. The lessons aimed to orient students to their surroundings, stating learning goals, such as:

- To acquaint pupils with various types of dwellings found in the neighborhood
- To point up the benefits of living in an apartment house, e.g., heat, hot water, access to washing machine

- To familiarize pupils with the types of rooms in homes and the functions of each
- To increase pupils' understanding of the responsibilities and rights of tenants
- To acquaint pupils with the unique features of their neighborhood[60]

To achieve these objectives, students identified dwellings and created a map of their school district with "construction paper, crayons, paints, [and] paste," "flat pictures of different types of houses and of various rooms in a house," "wedgies of members of family," and a "summary of regulations regarding sanitation and fire prevention in multiple dwellings."[61] The activities assumed that Puerto Rican students would have difficulties adjusting to a "foreign" environment.

The lesson plan also called for students to "dramatize" inhabiting the neighborhood, which taught etiquette through embodiment. To demonstrate "the correct way to cross the street," students pretended they were on the street corner. When one student vocalized that the light had turned to the walk sign, all the students turned their heads one way, then the other. One might have commented, "All clear." Then they would have walked across the front of the classroom. To dramatize a "dialogue between old resident and new resident in neighborhood," students engaged stereotypes about Puerto Rico. One resource unit described how parents needed to clothe their children, because, the unit said, children rarely wore clothing in Puerto Rico.[62] Finally, perpetuating a stereotype that Black and Puerto Rican neighborhoods were dirty because residents did not clean them, students would dramatize "The correct and incorrect way of disposing of garbage."[63] The PRS presumed that, left to their own devices, the students might arrive at school unclean and unclothed.

Another unit covered telephone use and police and fire departments to teach students to respect law enforcement. The implication was clear: The PRS researchers assumed Puerto Rican students lived in crime-ridden areas. Students rang emergency responders on fake telephones; played with toy police cars, normalizing police friendliness; wrote comic strips called "Our friend, the Fireman," and "Our friend, the Policeman"; and read "stories of heroism of firemen and policemen." All activities appeared in the same unit where students developed "directions for correct use of the telephone."[64] The unit conveyed that law enforcement was accessible to Puerto Rican students, and Puerto Rican students might not know how to or want to access law enforcement, given what PRS researchers assumed about the students' neighborhoods. The message that police officers were helpful contrasted with the scrutiny Puerto Rican students faced from police officers in their daily lives.

The PRS aimed to assimilate students to a place where they already lived by teaching a white, Judeo-Christian vision of America. The study thematized labor and citizenship to develop Puerto Rican students' self-actualization as American citizens. The lesson plan units encouraged students to get jobs, detailing how to acquire the necessary papers for an employer to hire someone younger than the age of eighteen. They described why Social Security cards helped secure employment. By connecting citizenship documents with employment, the units conveyed that holding the citizenship required for employment was both a student's right and an honor.

Each PRS resource unit concluded with lists of instructional films, films highlighting that the PRS wanted Puerto Rican students to adopt moral values from a white, Judeo-Christian culture. The collection included generic citizenship, morals and manners, and social studies films filled with white actors and produced by companies such as Encyclopedia Britannica and Coronet Films. Topics ranged from "Are Manners Important?" to "Cleanliness and Health" to a film on the "Airport." Schoolchildren generally were the target audience, not necessarily Puerto Rican students. However, the films' placement after each unit suggested that the PRS leaders thought Puerto Rican students needed to assimilate to the norms of white American middle-class life.[65] Many schools stocked the films in their libraries. Each borough also had repositories for the films. With Puerto Rican students as the audience, the films became tools for assimilating Puerto Rican students to "American" manners.

PRS activities also aimed to morally assimilate Puerto Rican parents, showing the significance of a nuclear family to Judeo-Christianity. They offered "technics [sic] with which the schools can promote a more rapid and more effective adjustment of Puerto Rican parents to the community and of the community to them."[66] Access to parents proved essential. Special occasions brought parents to school. At "Open School Week," parents observed what their children were learning. The PRS proposed that parents could better understand their children by seeing how *schools* taught children. Although Open School Week welcomed all family members, schools particularly reached out to mothers.[67] According to the PRS, scheduling a day where "Mother Comes To Visit" could "foster good home-school relationships by acquainting parents with the child's life in school and value of the school's objectives"; "show children the cooperation between home and school"; "help the children to learn social skills"; and "give children the opportunity to show and explain their school life to family."[68] The school was a multilayer assimilation mechanism, reaching Puerto Rican New Yorkers of all ages through the students. The nuclear family model allowed families to acculturate one another within and across households, while also echoing the brotherhood theology.

While public schools were supposedly removing religion, the Board claimed that Judeo-Christianity undergirded the schools' widely criticized assimilative plans for desegregation. In 1963, school administrators announced a new program: open enrollment. As noted, open enrollment represented "the blending of minority groups of all races and creeds into the American way of life," which was "a natural consequence of the morality of our American heritage and of our Judaeo-Christian tradition."[69] By claiming that open enrollment participated in an "American heritage" and "Judeo-Christian tradition," the administrators named integration a value in an established tradition. As noted, open enrollment placed the onus of assimilation onto Black and Puerto Rican students and their parents, presenting the tradition as one they were fortunate to join.

Open enrollment highlighted that the Board wanted to assimilate Black and Puerto Rican students into white, "American," "Judeo-Christian" culture while never allowing Black and Puerto Rican students to fully access white advantages. In open enrollment, parents could request to transfer children from schools with primarily Black or Puerto Rican students to schools with predominantly white students.[70] Despite Baker and Schwaber's work a decade earlier, schools remained segregated due to racially segregated zoning and housing discrimination. The Board called the predominantly Black and Puerto Rican schools "sending schools" and the predominantly white schools "receiving schools." Only students of color had to change.

As with the cultural pathology ascribed to criminalized children labeled "juvenile delinquents," the policy framed students seeking to transfer schools as potentially contaminating—medically, morally, and culturally—white "receiving" schools. According to the Board, open enrollment was a "right," not a "privilege."[71] If students from "sending" schools had behavioral or health conditions, they had to obtain special permission to transfer to a "receiving" school. The school system feasted on the consumable parts of cultures, while finding too much Black or Puerto Rican culture dangerous.

Panoramic Pedagogy

The school rituals that sustained *integration* failed to produce *desegregation*. However, in the mid- to late 1960s, Black and Puerto Rican New Yorkers challenged the assimilative and temporary rituals that had cultivated integration in the schools for more than a decade. Some still believed that integration could produce desegregation. Others looked in new directions to achieve what they took to be the aim of integration and desegregation alike: equal educational resources for Black and Puerto Rican students. They offered educational experiences drawing from an array of Black traditions, both within and beyond the public schools. Religion still sustained the experiences, but the religious resources differed from the Board's and NCCJ's. Black parents contested the schools' vision of pluralism through improvising on it. The improvisation cultivated aspirational visions of inclusive pedagogy that drew on Black traditions, including Pan-Africanism, the spirit and ancestors, racial uplift, and the practice of freedom.[72] Black New Yorkers extended the spaces where they taught and what students learned. In this way, the pedagogy was panoramic. It stretched beyond the public schools' limited view, offering something wider.

As noted earlier, a 1964 school boycott slogan read "Integration is an Education," tying the value of integration to the action of quality education. A flier for the boycott expanded: "OUR CHILDREN MUST BE GIVEN QUALITY EDUCATION IN A DE-SEGREGATED SCHOOL SYSTEM AND WE MUST KNOW WHEN THEY ARE TO BEGIN RECEIVING IT."[73] However, as the 1960s progressed, many Black and Puerto Rican parents continued to demand "quality education," but not all continued to require "a de-segregated school system," because the Board had shown little interest in structural changes. Education was still Black and Puerto Rican New Yorkers' priority, but the school board had proved that integration did not necessitate desegregation.

Figure 4.2. Students prepare signs for the 1964 boycott. Frank
Hurley/New York Daily News Archive via Getty Images.

Not all Black and Puerto Rican New Yorkers were Christian, let alone
followers of Black Liberation Theology (which did not emerge until the
end of the major desegregation movements), but liberation theologians
can help illuminate why Black and Puerto Rican New Yorkers sought alternatives to the Board's vision of integration. James Cone, a founding
figure in Black Liberation Theology, wrote in 1969, "If integration means
accepting the white man's style, his values, or his religion, then the black
man must refuse. There is nothing to integrate."[74] As open enrollment
and the PRS revealed, the Board's vision of integration matched this first
definition. However, Cone left room for a possible alternative definition of
integration: "if integration means that each man meets the other on equal
footing, with neither possessing the ability to assert the rightness of his
style over the other, then mutual meaningful dialogue is possible."[75] Cone
retained the possibility for an integration that looked like what he called
a future "Kingdom of God" while being direct about the present: "We are
not living what the New Testament called the consummated Kingdom,
and even its partial manifestation is not too obvious. Therefore, black
people cannot live according to what ought to be, but according to what
is." Cone articulated a Christian vision of integration that necessitated

Black self-determination. When Black parents in New York City refused the Board's vision of integration, they simultaneously refused to assimilate to whiteness and held out for a future where Black people controlled their own lives, even before Cone published his analysis.

For example, the children's librarian at Harlem's Countee Cullen Library and a parent of elementary school children at Harlem's PS 97, Amy Bush Olatunji, used Brotherhood Week to shift the temporality of integration. Blocks away from Cone at Union Theological Seminary, she changed the era when the temporary expression of togetherness occurred. Instead of the NCCJ's diverse imagined pasts to uphold the status quo, she imagined a future where the world celebrated people of color. In 1966, Bush Olatunji critiqued her school's Brotherhood Week for focusing on brotherhood without elevating people of color. A Black woman from Tuscaloosa, Alabama, Bush Olatunji engaged Brotherhood Week by encouraging students at the predominantly Black PS 97 to "'live with, learn with and grow up with their own.'"[76] *New York Amsterdam News* columnist Sara Slack praised Bush Olatunji's gumption: "What does a mother of tiny tots do when her school plans a Brotherhood Week celebration that doesn't please her? She sits down and writes a play that pleases her."[77] So she did, and the play "Panoramic View of Famous Negro Personalities, 1965–1966" was born.

The "Panoramic View" was unbroken; it saw things as they were, from the perspective of children of color. That year, the fifth and sixth grade classes at PS 97 in Harlem reimagined the school's annual Brotherhood Week by performing this play, set in 1990. Students at the predominantly Black school embodied "luminaries" such as then-Solicitor General Thurgood Marshall, then-Manhattan Borough President Constance Baker Motley, and then recently elected Prime Minister of India Indira Gandhi. A student narrator perched "atop a time capsule filling in supplementary descriptions" to create the panorama of the play's title. Written by Bush Olatunji with input from the children themselves, the play framed "brotherhood" as a mechanism for uplifting a broad portrait of people of color, including, but as the inclusion of Gandhi suggests, not limited to, Black people in the United States.[78]

Bush Olatunji's Brotherhood Week play critiqued brotherhood through a Pan-Africanist celebration of diversity amid a postcolonial Africa and the American Civil Rights Movement.[79] She joined ongoing critiques of the NCCJ by Black communities.[80] Like other Black Civil Rights activists, Bush Olatunji used the language of brotherhood in different theological registers than the NCCJ and apparently drew from different traditions.[81] Her theological register centered freedom and conjured ancestors, as African diaspora traditions often do. In 1951, the Countee Cullen Library where Bush Olatunji worked became the first public library in the city named after an African American.[82] Bush Olatunji's husband, the renowned Nigerian American drummer Michael Babatunde Olatunji, himself had been brought up through Baptist and Methodist church schools. In the United States, he promoted Black culture and Pan-Africanism, starting the Olatunji Center for African Culture.[83] Influenced by Bush Olatunji's context, where her husband promoted Harlem as a unifying space for the African diaspora, the school play was rooted in tradition and critique.

Bush Olatunji's play used Brotherhood Week's structure to critique Brotherhood Week. "Panoramic View of Famous Negro Personalities, 1965–1966" portrayed a panorama of what already existed, adapting the Judeo-Christian repertoire for her ends. Performing the play for Brotherhood Week rather than the earlier Negro History Week located the play in American consensus narratives of interfaith and interracial coexistence. The play presented an overarching vision, as the NCCJ did, synthesizing American peoplehood as popular American consensus narratives such as "faith in faith" or the later American civil religion did.[84] Yet, the panorama resisted common particulars of American consensus, such as presidential legacies and the white, tri-faith vision of American religion. The "panoramic view" capaciously represented people of color's lives from their perspectives.

Stylistically, the play was aspirational and improvisational, which highlighted its characteristically Black religiosity, in part "a practice of freedom" and "an open-ended orientation," to borrow Eddie Glaude's definition of African American religion.[85] It looked to the future and riffed on the explicit religious value of brotherhood while centering people of color in a multicultural view. The play's rhetoric and embodied performance transformed contemporary Black figures into ancestors, who played significant roles in African and African American religious traditions. African American religious studies scholar Josef Sorett claims that an Afro-Protestant spirit appeared in seemingly secular performances throughout the Black Arts Movement. While ancestors and spirits differ, the cultivation of future ancestors moved by an Afro-Protestant spirit shaped Olatunji's play as well.[86] The play used the practice of cultural representatives to imagine a future that celebrated people of color. Through its globally inclusive and unapologetically not-white perspective, it challenged the focus on retaining separate but equal American cultures. Moreover, students did not have to assimilate into the Board and NCCJ's view of brotherhood in the play, even as Bush Olatunji altered the Judeo-Christian repertoire. Rather than a vision of present togetherness to fight an imagined enemy, the play's uplift and multiculturalism turned the present into the past to imagine a freer future that students would create.

By setting the play in 1990, Bush Olatunji indicated that a multicultural celebration of people of color did not yet exist, but it could, through the young students' work. Bush Olatunji cultivated an inclusive pedagogy by encouraging students to use their own perspectives to produce knowledge, by, for instance, writing their own lines. Students, too, could become "luminaries," as Bush Olatunji's play also encouraged participation in the civic sphere. Moreover, she made Marshall, Gandhi, and Baker Motley luminaries by having students embody them, offering alternatives to the white moral exemplars of moral and spiritual values programming. Bush Olatunji encouraged student research and writing by connecting students to a particular racial history. The play resisted the assimilation of Black children into a norm of uncritical celebration of multicultural tolerance by encouraging students to share their thoughts. Students embodied well-known people of color in the process of making the figures and themselves crucial parts of history.

Bush Olatunji's inclusive approach participated in the student-centered pedagogy popular in Black churches and education movements, where freedom was the value and equitable education the action that emerged from it. Freedom was associated with integration; the school boycott leaders had named the boycott "Freedom Day." The alternative schools students attended that day were "Freedom Schools," insinuating that a desegregated school system generated freedom and previewing the efforts of Freedom Summer.[87] However, Freedom Schools also produced their own values, which participated in organizers' vision of integration. Freedom schools' goals were "to train and educate people to be active agents in bringing about social change," which required "provid[ing] an educational experience that is geared to the needs of the students, that challenges the myths of our society, that provides alternatives and directions for action."[88] The goals suggested that freedom as a value meant action, agency, and change. Change still invoked desegregation: "Integration is an Education" was Freedom Day's slogan, at a time when many Black and Puerto Rican New Yorkers still saw desegregation as key to equitable education.

Even as Freedom Schools took place on a day that was promoting desegregation, Freedom Schools' vision of integration did not require desegregation. Integration rather required Black students to reflect on their education. The Freedom School curriculum and pedagogy differed from the public schools', as Freedom Schools offered alternative programming and spaces to undo the public schools' myths. "Myths" here means narratives that shaped cultural practices *and* were false. To address the cultural myths, Freedom Schools' curriculum focused on asking students questions—a turn that empowered students with agency. For example, the curriculum asked students to compare their reality with other realities; to think about whether moving North was really a sign of Freedom, to consider the power structure, to compare the "poor Negro and the poor white," and to reflect on "Material Things versus Soul Things," or things that mattered on a deep level. The overarching questions were self-reflective and asked students to contemplate their education: "Why are we (teachers and students) in Freedom Schools? What is the Freedom Movement? What alternatives does the Freedom Movement offer?" Secondary questions produced racial and cultural integrity by showing how action and social change could emerge from Black students' agency: "What do 'white people' (the majority culture) have that we want? What do 'white people' have that we don't want? What do we have that we want to keep?"[89] These questions encouraged Black students to participate in their own education by reflecting on why Freedom Schools existed in the first place. By prompting a discussion of power structures and "the majority culture," the questions connected Black students' education to the country's racial power structure, and their ability to change it.

A self-cultivated missionary impulse shaped the vision of integration as the freedom to improve Black people's lives through education. For example, the East Harlem Protestant Parish offered alternative summer schooling opportunities for neighborhood kids in the mid-1960s. The

EHPP comprised four Protestant churches. It was originally a domestic city mission that received funding from the Home Mission Council of America. Its mission was to improve the conditions for people of low income and/or who were racial minorities in cities. Generally, the missionary impulse has idealized conversion to a "civilized," white child.[90] However, the EHPP's racial dynamics were not simply navigating relationships between white missionaries and Black converts. The EHPP's founders included white and Black leaders, many from Union Theological Seminary, in the years immediately preceding Black Liberation Theologian James Cone's presence there. The EHPP sought to introduce "a relevant religion" to Harlem kids.[91]

The EHPP was a mission *and* it focused on students teaching each other to cultivate agency. Though missions inherently have the power structure of converter and converted, an epigraph to an article in the EHPP newsletter discussing the summer reading program demonstrated an awareness of the tension. The epigraph quoted Sylvia Ashton-Warner, the New Zealand novelist, poet, and educator who worked with Maori children. Ashton-Warner saw education as collaboration between student and teacher: "What a dangerous activity reading is; teaching is. All this plastering on of foreign stuff. Why plaster on at all when there's so much inside already? So much locked in? If only I could get it out and use it as working material."[92] The EHPP's reading program started with the student, as it "has opted to perch itself on the very edge of the volcano."[93] By starting with the child, the EHPP demonstrated awareness that public school lessons could be alienating.

Acknowledging this alienation, the EHPP connected reading to students' lives to show them why reading mattered. In this case, quality education promoted students' agency by emphasizing Christianity's personal relevance. Through the reading program, older teenagers selected and taught books. Instead of assimilating students into prejudicial norms, the program allowed teacher and learner to each shape the educational experience. Students read Claude Brown's *Manchild in the Promised Land*, *The Autobiography of Malcolm X as Told to Alex Haley*, James Baldwin's *Go Tell It on the Mountain*, and Sammy Davis Jr.'s *Yes, I Can*, among other texts. According to the parish's newsletter, the teenagers' "method of teaching, though not 'professional', smacked of the stuff of life for their young pupils." For example:

One teenager used Claud [*sic*] Brown's *Manchild in the Promised Land* as his "primer." The reading was difficult for the boys, but the eagerness with which they worked indicated an interest which no other book had evoked before. They were overcome that a Negro had written a book about their lives—a book that was moreover a best-seller. Their interest in the book made it easy for the tutor to work on vocabulary, phonics, writing, debating, drama. They chose new vocabulary words, *they* wanted to learn. They wrote letters to Claud Brown and their own autobiographies. One youngster said, "If Claud Brown, a boy like us, did it, so can I." They enacted being picked up by the police. They brought in a former addict to talk to them about drugs and addiction. The word was made flesh in a very real way to them. Reading had something to do with life![94]

"The word was made flesh" referred to John 1 in the New Testament, in which the word was Jesus. Reading program students, then, could follow Jesus's path, as the parish interpreted Brown and others had done, by reforming themselves. The light gave them agency, as the parish presented it. Even as the schools drew on Christianity, the reading program's alternate approach suggested that schools were implying that Black students could not participate in Jesus's light.

The EHPP space welcomed students to read as part of the project of making religion relevant. Even though the program was an alternative to public schooling, some of its features mirrored ones students encountered in public schools. As the above extract shows, students learned the meanings of vocabulary words and dramatized life lessons. However, the approach to students differed from the public schools' approach because it engaged them in active dialogue with the text. They wrote letters to the author, adopted the genre of the assigned reading in a writing activity, and brought in a guest as a real-life example of issues the reading raised. In turn, the students reportedly became more engaged with the material because the curriculum connected to their own experiences. It did not evaluate students' familiarity with public school habits, as the PRS and open enrollment did. The parish's approach, the newsletter reported, excited students about the lessons because they had the opportunity to lead and exchange ideas. It was the parish's hope that when students took ownership of lessons, they would learn to articulate their place in the world and gain the skills to change it.

The EHPP's reading program highlights how some people, trying to realize integration, went beyond public schools to create space to imagine the future. Talking about juvenile delinquency prevention, EHPP co-founder J. Archie Hargraves, who was Black, described the need for each local church "to seek a new community orientation that implies it will cease existing for itself and will come to share its particular concerns, techniques and love with the whole neighborhood so that all may advance together."[95] In this instance, what the EHPP called "THE FAILURE OF PUBLIC EDUCATION" marked the churches' "particular concerns" and impetus for starting the reading program.[96] Of necessity, the church became the school, actualizing the education that integration promised.

* * *

The northern Civil Rights Movement included Freedom Day, Bush Olatunji's play, and the EHPP's reading programs. It also included attempts by the centralized school board to cultivate an appreciation for other cultures, without having to learn with people from them. The legal injunction to desegregate brought to center stage an educational value with religious origins—integration. For the schools, the value of integration set the framework of separate-but-equal religious traditions, transferred to racial communities. The framework prioritized equality, not equity. In their framing, integration neglected power dynamics, especially those connected to school opportunities. Simultaneously, it contributed to understandings of Black education as in constant need of saving, while Black communities did not seek salvation—they requested resources and to be treated with dignity.[97]

The competing visions of integration drew on disparate religious resources. While the Board sought for all races to come together under the fatherhood of God as conceptualized by mostly white Protestants, Catholics, and Jews, Black and Puerto Rican communities sought freedom from the Board's Father God figure and his heroic white American offspring. The competing visions reemerged in the community control movement, as Black and Puerto Rican parents sought separation from the centralized school board. More immediately, competing visions appeared in debates over government aid for Catholic schools, and the question of whether such schools promoted or prevented desegregation.

III

Purposes of Public Education

5

Government Aid and the Scope of Public Education

In 1965, a groundswell arose for a constitutional convention to revise the New York State Constitution. Support for the convention came from multiple factions, but the driving force was a vocal contingent of Catholic voters who sought to repeal a nineteenth-century constitutional prohibition against government aid to denominational schools because, they claimed, it discriminated against Catholicism. The timing was unusual. Since 1938, Article XIX, Section 2 of the New York State Constitution required the question "Shall there be a convention to revise the constitution and amend the same?" to appear on the general election ballot every twenty years, or as otherwise deemed appropriate.[1] However, the 1960s was an off decade, and New Yorkers had last significantly changed the constitution in 1894.[2] Therefore, Governor Nelson Rockefeller, responding to public pressure, went out of his way to place an off-cycle referendum on whether to hold a constitutional convention in 1967 on the 1965 general election ballot.

Also unexpected was the energy that was expended debating the little known and common constitutional prohibition against government aid to denominational schools: Article XI, Section 3.[3] Yet, this one small constitutional section captured New Yorkers' imaginations because it raised long-standing questions about the role of denominational schools in the American public. Attention fell to Catholic schools, the nineteenth-century prohibition's initial target. Thus, the 1965–1967 conversation about the prohibition provides a useful case study about which religions the state and its residents thought should educate the public. Some claimed that the public schools were the only truly public option; others saw more educational options, including Catholic schools, as capable of serving the public. While this debate centered on a marginalized religious group, discussion of inclusion and publicness inevitably led to more questions and debates about race and public life.

Despite the strangeness of the sudden swell, voters supported the off-year convention. In 1967, New York State held a nearly six-month-long constitutional convention to consider myriad issues, including welfare, redistricting, financial regulations, the environment, and the constitution's length. One hundred eighty-six delegates in Albany, close to ten thousand pages of transcript, and significant resources supported the convention. However, the most "controversial" and "the most emotional issue" according to the press and participants was whether New York should repeal the prohibition on government aid to denominational schools.[4] The prohibition magnified competing religious and racial identities and understandings of the public.

Although the prohibition mentioned only denominational schools, it implicated public schools as well as denominational ones in racial integration politics. Concerns proliferated that aid to parochial schools would fund racial segregation by supporting wealthy white Catholic schools rather than under-resourced Black and Puerto Rican public schools. The possible repeal of the prohibition elicited divergent arguments: Aid to denominational schools, usually Catholic schools, *promoted* religious freedom, according to some, and *prevented* religious freedom, according to others. Moreover, some argued that Catholic schools and aid to them *prevented* racial desegregation. Others argued the opposite: Catholic schools and aid to them *promoted* racial desegregation. The competing arguments raised key questions: Who counted in the public of public education? Could only public schools educate the public?

Disagreement abounded, and in September 1967, the delegates approved a Franken-constitution, meant to appease delegates' particularities. The revised state constitution cut the prohibition and included a version of the federal First Amendment instead. However, on voting day in November, New Yorkers rejected the constitution. As a "weathered political veteran" commented, the convention president seemed to forget "'the likelihood of the thing having something in it to offend everybody.'"[5] The efforts to revise the constitution had failed. New Yorkers ended with the same constitution that they started with, including the prohibition on aid to parochial schools.

Perhaps because the convention's efforts ultimately failed to produce a new constitution, and because scholars have identified more apparently consequential case studies, the 1967 convention has received little attention. Yet, even in the 1960s, critics did not understand the convention's meaning. Multiple news outlets published a cartoon that pictured a donkey and an elephant, symbolizing the Democratic and Republican parties, leaving the cinema where "67: An Off-Year Off-Beat Election Drama" was playing. The animals give each other befuddled looks, and the caption reads: "I'm sure it has a lot of significance, if I only knew what."[6]

This chapter offers one answer. The mess of the 1967 constitutional convention reveals how religion and race intersected to form conflicting definitions of public education because it brought to the surface New Yorkers' many underlying, and distinct, positions. The prohibition added kindling to already burning struggles over race, religion, and the American public.

The pairing of religious freedom and racial segregation created what one reporter called "strange bedfellows."[7] A wide range of people participated in the heated conversation, from predominantly white church-state separation advocacy groups to New York's Cardinal Francis Spellman to the Protestant Rev. Milton Galamison to Black Catholic organizations. Such diversity complicates typical portraits of debates over aid to parochial schools, which usually depict a duel between the federal establishment and free exercise clauses, or an example of nineteenth-century anti-Catholic nativism.[8] Yet, scholars studying segregation have shown that religion has signified racism, for example, with white Baptists forming private schools, supposedly in response to *Engel* and *Schempp*, but "really" to maintain segregation.[9] In 1967 New York, the positions and players were less straightforward. Nearly everyone claimed to support desegregation and religious freedom, unlike in the South. Nevertheless, Black Protestants argued with Black Catholics; Black and white Protestants disagreed; and though Jews generally opposed repeal, a Jewish delegate's proposal to repeal the prohibition won at the convention. Black New Yorkers worried about white flight to Catholic schools within the city, rather than white flight to the suburbs and evangelical "segregation academies."[10]

Why, then, did the convention fail, and what did it nevertheless produce? Figures with varied racial and religious arguments clarified that religion was essential to how New Yorkers talked about public education, but there was little space to clearly name religion's role. Ironically, religion became further institutionalized in imaginings of public schools' purpose as many tried to keep religion out of public schools.[11] Participants used the language of a Judeo-Christian morality they deemed appropriate for public space to argue for their visions of equitably educating the public. The language circumscribed the public role of religion and the possibility to draw on other religious reasoning to redistribute state funds toward desegregation, a theoretically shared goal.[12] This debate presaged advocacy for community control of schools, as some Black New Yorkers grew tired of relying on other people's control.

Prohibition or Repeal as Modern: Modernity as Religious and Racial Openness

The 1967 constitutional convention happened because enough New Yorkers across religious and political spectrums claimed the present constitution was too old. It was not modern enough, they argued, and it was prejudiced. The object of its prejudice depended on whom you asked.

With questions of religious and racial prejudice among the nation's most topical issues, the debate about the potential repeal became a perfect storm of clashing public concerns. Following the US Supreme Court's *Everson v. Board of Education* decision in 1947, the religion clauses of the US Constitution applied to the states, meaning that states, in addition to federal representatives and laws, now had to respect free exercise and non-establishment of religion.[13] Given this recent change, many argued that a constitutional prohibition against government funding of denominational schools too directly targeted religious schools when the law was supposed to remain "neutral" toward religion. The federal establishment and free exercise clauses of the First Amendment of the US Constitution, "Congress shall make no law respecting an establishment of religion, or prohibiting the free exercise thereof," sufficed.[14] Moreover, the Elementary and Secondary Education Act of Lyndon Johnson's "War on Poverty," among the most expansive pieces of federal education legislation in US history, funded materials for individual "needy" students, regardless of the school they attended.[15]

Locally, New York City faced the height of school segregation frustration. Although it was the largest school boycott of the Civil Rights Movement, the 1964 New York City boycott had not significantly changed school demographics. New Yorkers had different senses of desegregation's urgency.[16] The New York City Board of Education continued its commitment to integration as a value that did not require the practice of desegregation, while many Black and Puerto Rican parents viewed integration as a value that did require desegregation. The constitutional repeal thus became a new arena for ongoing discussions about how best to achieve the value of racial integration.

The prohibition itself, Article XI, Section 3 of the New York State Constitution, defined "public education" against "denominational" schools, especially Catholic schools. The prohibition's nickname, "the Blaine Amendment," was a misnomer. The prohibition mirrored a failed federal constitutional amendment proposed by Senator James Blaine in 1876, but Blaine was never directly involved with New York's prohibition nor, as a section of an article, was the prohibition a constitutional amendment. Instead, many states adopted similar prohibitions, even after Blaine's federal amendment narrowly failed.[17] Nevertheless, "denominational" in the New York prohibition was a dog whistle for "parochial" (Catholic), even as the prohibition technically applied more broadly. An 1871 Thomas Nast *Harper's Weekly* cartoon depicting crocodiles with miters heading toward frightened land-bound schoolchildren represented the widespread fear about federal aid to parochial schools. Blaine's proposed amendment specifically aimed to protect public schools from Catholic influence: "No money raised by taxation in any State for the support of public schools, or derived from any public fund therefor, nor any public lands devoted thereto shall ever be under the control of any religious sect; nor shall any money so raised or lands so devoted be divided between religious sects or denominations."[18] The cultural concern over parochial schools shaped the implications of New York's prohibition, which omitted reference to public schools:

Neither the state nor any subdivision thereof shall use its property or credit or any public money, or authorize or permit either to be used, directly or indirectly, in aid or maintenance, other than for examination or inspection, of any school or institution of learning wholly or in part under the control or direction of any religious denomination, or in which any denominational tenet or doctrine is taught, but the legislature may provide for the transportation of children to and from any school or institution of learning.[19]

While the language evoked fights between Catholic and Protestant schools, it also distinguished between "any religious denomination" and state-supported public schools.[20] New York's prohibition explicitly forbade state funding of denominational teaching and institutional control, while permitting the state to fund transportation to denominational schools. The allowance sent the message that members of the public had limited educational choice, and religious schools offered inferior public lessons.

Catholics formed a steady base of support for changing the constitution by referring to the anti-Catholic origins of public schools. For example, Charles J. Tobin Jr., secretary of the State Catholic Welfare Committee, told a gathering for the Temporary State Commission on the Revision and Simplification of the Constitution in Albany that the prohibition reflected "a time in our national history (1894) in which the proponents of universal education were fearful that major governmental support of religious elementary and secondary schools would prevent the development of a broad, well-financed system of public education." In the late nineteenth century, Protestants articulated that Catholic schools threatened a purportedly "universal education." Catholics felt excluded from public schools, and, as historians have shown, the schools promoted Protestantism.[21] Tobin continued, this time framing the prohibition itself as old-fashioned, turning the tables on nineteenth-century government figures' idea that Catholicism had become old-fashioned: "Such a fear has long since disappeared, but the amendment lingers on."[22]

In framing the constitution as old and outdated, Catholics repurposed historically anti-Catholic arguments for separation of church and state. At another hearing before the commission, "a spokesman for the Catholic Charities of Buffalo" called the prohibition an "unfortunate relic of a less enlightened past."[23] Using a classic anti-Catholic term—relic—and suggesting that anti-Catholicism, not Catholicism, was unenlightened, the speaker reignited nineteenth-century debates with a critical twist. Implying "we are the real modern ones!," New York Catholics positioned the embrace of Catholics as modern. They used traditionally anti-Catholic language, which claimed that Catholicism was anti-modern, against the constitution's prohibition to support Catholicism as a modern religion.

Since all debaters generally agreed that religious and racial openness were civic goods, each side signaled religious and racial progressiveness by calling their own views modern.[24] Non-Catholic advocates for repealing the prohibition also called the constitution old. In June 1965, a *New York Times* editorial argued, "The present Constitution is essentially an 1894 document," and described it as "a maze of statutory detail" that "ought to be simplified and clarified."[25] The *Times* urged Governor Nelson Rockefeller to sign the bill that would place a question on the November ballot asking New York State voters whether the state should hold a constitutional convention in 1967. He did, and New Yorkers, by a very thin margin, voted in favor of holding a convention.

The narrow victory foreshadowed conflict to come. In the days following the vote, the "nonpartisan" Citizens Committee for an Effective Constitutional Convention emphasized that a "modern and vital constitution" could not come fast enough.[26] In these early days, constituents framed modernity as a good constitutional quality because it rendered the constitution relevant, alive, and easier to read.

Similarly, Cardinal Francis Spellman, the Catholic Archbishop of New York, implied that supporting government aid to parochial schools was modern precisely because it represented open-mindedness in a Judeo-Christian tradition. Spellman responded to President John F. Kennedy Jr. after Kennedy opposed federal aid to nonpublic schools, a stance he, as the country's first Catholic president, may have taken to prove his loyalty to the United States over the Vatican. In a 1961 critique of Kennedy, Spellman issued a statement in support of government aid to nonpublic schools using language familiar in the integration debates: "As an American citizen interested in the welfare of the nation, I feel that the failure to do justice and to avoid discrimination in the field of elementary and secondary schools is contrary to the best interests of our country."[27] Spellman's references to discrimination, prejudice, and unity echoed the value of integration as presented in the Board's Judeo-Christian repertoire. He also framed his argument by America's best interests and indicated that all elementary and secondary schools, including Catholic schools, participated in the American public.

Before the convention, the prohibition took the election's center stage due to lobbying and polling by Catholic and parent groups. In a year of contentious races, especially for governor, all candidates announced positions on government aid to denominational schools.[28] Pollsters measured delegate candidates' temperatures on the prohibition as well. Citizens for Educational Freedom, a predominantly Catholic group, played an instrumental role in making the prohibition a key issue to delegates' campaigns. A statewide CEF survey captured the media's attention because of its size and CEF's clear position.[29] CEF claimed that the prohibition "had been conceived out of bigotry and hatred."[30] The CEF survey "showed that 79 per cent of the Democratic candidates and 75 per cent of the Republicans who responded favor repeal."[31] Concerns arose that delegate candidates may have been trying to appease CEF after the United Parents Associations, an organization that opposed repeal, completed a more limited, borough-based poll that showcased some contradictory statements by the same candidates.[32] Regardless of the exact survey results, the polls suggested that New Yorkers planned to elect delegates based on their position on the prohibition.

The stakes were high. New Yorkers asked: Was any segregation—religious or racial—inherently discriminatory? New York City and State had set the terms: Integration was a value because racial togetherness was good, yet integration did not necessarily require desegregation. Prohibition supporters refuted accusations that they were anti-Catholic by claiming that the separation of church and state preserved the possibility for desegregation. At the commission's gathering, Rev. Arthur W. Mielke, pastor of the First Presbyterian Church of Buffalo, framed the Catholic Church's position as a "'threat[]'" to "the principle of separation of church and state."[33] By repealing the prohibition, he proffered, "'We would be in the ironic position of giving support with one hand to religious segregation at the very time we are trying to overcome segregation by race with the other.'"[34] Mielke's appeal to desegregation efforts connoted that Catholic schools supported a religious segregation on par with racial segregation. However, he ignored the desires of Catholics, the segregated group. Many Catholics sought separation, while Black New Yorkers still generally sought inclusion. Mielke's elision of racial and religious segregation implied that Catholic education, and especially government aid to it, discriminated against non-Catholic students and the modern value of integration.

The "strange bedfellows" began to emerge. Mielke, the Protestant minister from Buffalo, the American Jewish Congress, and the national separationist (and at this point anti-Catholic) organization Protestants and Others Americans United for Separation of Church and State agreed that the prohibition was the inclusive, and therefore modern, option.[35] The American Jewish Congress brought representatives to the meeting who also rejected claims about anti-Catholicism, calling it a misunderstanding of history: "This provision of the state Constitution is not a monument to bigotry. It arose out of the need to protect religious freedom and it continues to have that effect today." By offering their own interpretation of the prohibition as symbolizing ever-expanding inclusion, the representatives also rejected the idea that the constitution's age was a problem. They focused on public funding, which showed what the public valued: "Parents undoubtedly have the right to send their children to the schools of their choice, but they have no right to demand use of the public purse to finance that choice."[36] The executive director of POAU, Dr. Glenn Archer, a Free Methodist, also critiqued Catholics' focus on money by calling it "a sad day when churches become so absorbed in political-welfare programs that they have little time for their primary mission—spiritual welfare."[37] By claiming that funding ("political-welfare") substantially differed from "spiritual welfare," Archer overlooked Catholic advocacy for Catholicism's higher moral and economic valuation in the American public. Archer incriminated those he perceived to be greedy Catholics taking away from the possibility for public schools to maintain racial integration and usher in their own modern, inclusive "spiritual welfare." In the months to come, the convention participants questioned who owned this "spiritual welfare."

The Convention: American Judeo-Christian Reasons for Supporting Repeal

A Catholic, a Jew, and a Protestant walked into a convention chamber, and they agreed. In his 1955 *Protestant-Catholic-Jew*, Sociologist Will Herberg famously argued that "faith in faith," rather than a particular religion, united Americans.[38] At the constitutional convention, commitment to the American Constitution as a modern, inclusive document brought people together across religious affiliations. "Modern" therefore had less to do with actual age (after all, the US Constitution was older than the most updated New York State one) than with perceptions of religious inclusiveness. Catholic Cardinal Spellman and two delegates to the convention, Jewish Blossom Graubard Saxe and Protestant Herman Badillo, formed a Herbergian troika of Catholic, Jew, and Protestant. They also reached across racial and ethnic lines: Spellman was the grandson of Irish immigrants, Saxe was the daughter of Romanian and Austrian immigrants, and Badillo was Puerto Rican. All supported repeal of the prohibition. Fault lines evaded neat religious identities or alliances (except Catholics, interested parties who generally wanted more funding). Instead, their reasoning for supporting the repeal institutionalized the American Judeo-Christian repertoire.

On April 4, 1967, the New York State Constitutional Convention began in Albany on a theological, pro-repeal note. Cardinal Spellman stood as the sole religious leader on the convention's first day. Delivering the invocation, Spellman urged that aid to parochial schools would embody an American democracy that God sanctioned. He set the stage for a convention that ultimately supported repeal of the prohibition on aid.[39] Speaking prior to welcoming addresses by New York's political leaders, Spellman called upon God to allow the democratic process to prevail at the convention: "With grateful remembrance we acknowledge the industry and sacrifice of our forebears, who labored at so great a price to give us as our birthright the democratic process of government to which this meeting renders witness. We beg You that this process may ever flourish in our land."[40] With the language of "forebears," Spellman tapped into the American theology that cast ancestral white men as deities. Spellman sought for democracy to prevail at the convention, and, given his long-time support of aid to parochial schools, it is reasonable to assume that he saw repeal as democratic.[41] Although Spellman avoided naming the prohibition, he had previously stated that denying aid to denominational schools infringed upon parents' religious freedom and educational choice. Spellman would later acknowledge that when he prayed for God to help delegates "forge with equity and fairness an instrument of justice for all our citizens," he prayed for repeal, because the prohibition instrumentalized injustice.[42]

From April to September, the prohibition loomed over the "Gothic Assembly chamber at Albany," where the 186 delegates met daily.[43] While the prohibition received more attention in the press than any other part of the constitution, days went by without discussing it in the chambers. Delegates had an entire constitution to review! They formed fifteen committees for different areas of the constitution.[44] Representatives from those committees proposed specific changes relevant to their areas. When a delegate wished to propose a change, Anthony Travia, Democratic Speaker of the New York State Assembly and President of the Constitutional Convention, asked the delegate to speak, and then called on other delegates to respond. After speakers had expressed their views on a proposal, the delegates voted. The final proposed constitution consolidated these votes. Upon the convention's closing in September, voters had six weeks to mull over the revised constitution before voting to approve or reject it.

The prohibition also hovered in the chamber air because the most promising proposed revision came from delegate Blossom Graubard Saxe, who fell ill before it was her turn to present the proposal. Saxe had prepared to propose the language of the First Amendment religion clauses in place of the prohibition on government aid to denominational schools. Instead of prohibiting a specific form of government spending, the federal religion clauses referred to more general categories: no government establishment of religion and no prohibition on the free exercise of religion. Her proposal had gained momentum, building on Manhattan Democrats' long-held interest in using First Amendment language.[45] When Saxe was hospitalized shortly before her presentation slot, delegates waited. Day after day, a delegate requested delaying presentation of the proposition on her behalf, each time saying something to the effect of:

> Mr. President, Mrs. Saxe, who everybody knows has been ill for these last two or three weeks is hospitalized and is now on the road to recovery. She telephoned this morning and said that she would like to lead the debate for her proposition. She expects that the doctors will allow her to appear here to at least read a statement on Monday. Accordingly, on her behalf, I ask this be laid aside until Monday.[46]

The repeated postponements revealed that many delegates wanted Saxe to deliver the proposal. For weeks, Travia repeated that Saxe's proposal was "Ready and laid aside" until she returned.[47] If Saxe's proposal had not been the most highly anticipated proposal of the convention before she became ill, it certainly was now.

The Manhattan Democrats strategically used Saxe as their leader, playing into tropes of integration and neighborliness. A daughter of working-class Jewish immigrants, Saxe modeled American diversity and assimilation into Judeo-Christian norms. Her father was born in Romania and her mother in Austria, which would later be ravaged by the Holocaust; their native language was Yiddish. From her own modest childhood, Saxe had risen through the ranks. She had practiced as a well-known government and community advocacy New York City attorney for thirty years.[48] At the convention, Saxe represented the 24th Senate District (New York County) as a Democrat, sat on the convention's Committee on Bill of Rights and Suffrage, and served as the secretary for the Legislature Committee.[49] Her story had all the elements of Judeo-Christian integration: She brought her individual background of struggle and difference (from white, American, male, Christianity) to pursue American freedom. Her proposal promised success because it played into her American dream narrative by focusing on the federal constitution's guarantee of religious freedom.

Applause and speeches welcomed Saxe's return. Taking the floor, Saxe wasted no time framing her recent experience in relation to love of neighbor, the same value she imagined her proposal would foster. Saxe thanked the delegates for "the warm welcome which you gave me today which touched me deeply," and "all of my colleagues who were so kind as to send me innumerable flowers, notes and cards, and to inquire about my health." In particular, she thanked delegates for "Your concern," which supplied "a great help to me during my hospital stay." Saxe suggested that her fellow delegates' care for her in illness exemplified human connection.[50] By beginning her speech with an expression of gratitude for the community, "I thank you all from the bottom of my heart," Saxe submitted that the delegates practiced her ideal community: people of different religious and racial backgrounds coming together to support someone in need.

The moment had finally come for Saxe to present her proposal, in which she contended that New York's constitution should reflect the country's. Saxe first introduced diversity as a fact in the district she represented: "We have all the religions—Catholic, Protestant and Jewish. We also have Coptics, Ukrainian and Greek Orthodox. Longshoremen, Fifth Avenue society folk and hippies live there. You name it and we have it." She emphasized that she both "represent[ed]" and "campaigned" in the district to imply that people of diverse religious and ethnic backgrounds had elected her precisely because they wanted to repeal the prohibition: "And in that area I pledged my voice on this issue."[51] With this opening, Saxe appealed to integration as a shared value. She also insinuated that the prohibition opposed integration, given that her diverse constituents, who modeled the "good neighbor" ideal, sought repeal. Building on this insinuation, she pointed to the prohibition's origins, saying that it "was included in our State Constitution by a convention rife with fear and filled with bigotry and prejudice against the minorities migrating to this country."[52] Situating her argument in relation to nineteenth-century immigration, Saxe asserted that the prohibition's "bigotry and prejudice" targeted religious and racial outsiders.

Saxe framed diversity as an educational value, much as the Board had done with integration. She described integration's value in capitalist terms: "In a competitive world, always requiring more knowledge, the existence of different types of schools will, through competition, diversity and freedom of choice, tend to raise the quality of all education."[53] Although Saxe drew on Catholic arguments for quality education and diversity of educational institutions in the public square, her primary claim commodified knowledge in the American spirit of accumulation: "Quantity and quality education combined may be."[54] Thus, when she argued that "in the fields of education, common to all schools, we should also insist that no child should be deprived of aid and opportunity because of his creed," her points resonated with Catholic religious freedom arguments while implying that schools must make children competitive in the American marketplace.[55] Addressing multiple reasonings at once, she concluded that: "Reason and hard economic practicalities, faith in the wisdom of our Legislature and Courts, and love for all of God's children demand the passage of this proposition."[56] Reason, economic practicality, faith in wisdom, and love led to her vision of religious and racial integration.

Saxe's supporters variously amplified the integration ideal. Unlike other Saxe supporters, Herman Badillo's reasoning had little to do with supporting aid to Catholic schools or even a diverse American educational system. Badillo (Democrat-Liberal, Bronx), a lawyer and accountant serving as Bronx borough president, opposed the prohibition and supported Saxe's proposition because he empathized with those experiencing prejudice. He explained that as a Puerto Rican Protestant, he was "a minority within a minority," an unlikely candidate for supporting repeal, given his family history with Catholics: "There are many legends about the Badillo family in Puerto Rico. One of them is that the Badillos smuggled the first Protestant Bible into Puerto Rico. Another one is that the Badillos were mostly ministers and lawyers; the ministers would practice the Protestant religion and the lawyers would get them out of jail."[57] He continued: "You may wonder how from that heritage you get to a point of supporting a proposition that would repeal the Blaine Amendment," as Catholics often supported repeal while Protestants opposed it.

Like Saxe and Spellman, who approached the prohibition from different religious and racial standpoints than Badillo, Badillo nevertheless framed the prohibition as prejudiced. Badillo's experience with prejudice as a Puerto Rican Protestant caused him to empathize with New York Catholics: "You get to a point where you have a special sensitivity to anything that smacks of prejudice towards a particular group and you seek perhaps a little deeper to root it out."[58] He appealed to Judeo-Christian inclusion by naming his double minority status, which uniquely positioned him to identify non-inclusive rules: "In my judgment, the present Blaine Amendment, the present Section 3 of Article XI, is a brutal provision."[59] Taken together, Badillo's, Saxe's, and Spellman's stances show that the American Judeo-Christian repertoire formed how repeal supporters discussed the prohibition. They reached to that American theology where America-talk replaced God-talk by gesturing to its categories of prejudice and democracy, rather than specific theologies within their religious traditions, such as grace or atonement. However, the American Judeo-Christian repertoire could only go so far.

Different Ways to Talk About Religion

Black New Yorkers concerned with Black students' education quickly reached the limits of the American Judeo-Christian repertoire's acceptable language. For example, school boycott organizer and Black Protestant Rev. Milton Galamison, who opposed repeal, and convention delegate Hulan E. Jack, the former Manhattan borough president and 1967 Democratic Party leader, a Black Catholic who supported repeal, never publicly debated the prohibition on aid to denominational schools. Yet, each aimed to provide more equitable education to Black students. To achieve this goal, they each pushed the boundaries of acceptable public ways to talk about race and religion. It is unclear if they ever met, but Galamison and Jack each asked New Yorkers to think about religion beyond its circumscribed public role. They recognized that limitations on public religion contributed to the impasses over the prohibition and desegregation. They each asked, implicitly: Would a different set of constraints around religion break open the possibility of achieving a more equitable education for Black youth? Was theology necessary to understand school segregation?

Putting Jack and Galamison in conversation amplifies two prominent positions among Black New Yorkers. Galamison represented Black New Yorkers who saw public education as the way to achieve equitable, quality education for Black and Puerto Rican students. Jack represented those for whom equitable, quality education for Black and Puerto Rican students required a broad educational system that included Catholic schools. While Galamison and Jack did not speak for all Black New Yorkers, positions for a public education restricted to public schools and positions for a public education including Catholic schools were well documented among Black New Yorkers.

Galamison and Jack both indicated that the "reality" of school segregation meant taking theology seriously. For Galamison, being realistic about the prohibition meant naming how its potential repeal could further racial inequality in schools for religious interests. In October, the month between the convention's September end and voters rejecting the proposed constitution in November, Galamison published a scathing critique of the proposed repeal of the prohibition. His opinion appeared as an article in the *African-American Teachers Association Forum,* which attracted readers immediately concerned with Black education but perhaps not the prohibition, and in a letter to the editor in the *New York Times*, for readers more concerned with the prohibition than Black education.[60] He began with an appeal to practicality: "It is time for black people to be realistic about the issue of repealing the Blaine Amendment, and by realistic, I mean analyzing it in terms of how it affects black parents and black children." For such analysis, "We cannot look upon this simply as a controversy within the white community or as a conflict between competing religious forces," because, "Whichever way it is resolved, the main effect will be on the next generation of blacks and Puerto Ricans, who are an ever-increasing majority in this city's public school system." Black and Puerto Rican education supporters would therefore need to consider both the religious and racial forces at play.

Galamison offered seemingly contradictory definitions of "religion." In the article, he stated that the prohibition was "not a religious issue," but, at the same time, argued that "The real religion of America—the one with the most serious and devout following—is racism." He continued his understanding of religion as commitment, "No matter how serious the political, religious or economic differences among whites, the one thing on which whites generally seem to agree is how to deal with blacks." Striking as it is, the claim that racism is "the real religion of America" could be read as a throwaway flourish: Perhaps Galamison used it for dramatic effect to solidify racism's extremity. However, the line was theologically meaningful. Galamison was concerned that the violent American theology within the schools' Judeo-Christianity would only further permeate school thinking and structure if the prohibition was repealed.

Simultaneously, Galamison postulated that the prohibition was "not a religious issue," because he separated racism from his ideal of religion. Inverting the anti-Catholic trope that Catholicism was antiquated, he named claims of anti-Catholic persecution as outdated thinking by writing, "Except for people who are still hung up on antiquated anti-Catholicism, this is not a religious issue." Galamison elucidated that "religious differences" and "a religious issue" related to a particular denomination. He also dismissed Catholic concerns about anti-Catholicism, expressing that race was more pressing: "But every day that passes makes it more and more a racial issue." It might seem like Galamison intimated that a religious issue could not be a racial issue, and therefore his point about racism being a religion would be contradictory. However, he implicitly advanced the position that the prohibition was religious insofar as New Yorkers zealously—even religiously—practiced racism. Given the public focus on religion and obscuring of race, he exhorted that addressing the problem of inadequate Black education required thinking differently, "realistic[ally]." Naming the problems with American theology could begin a new approach.

Jack also invoked the "realistic," but he did so to paint a broad vision of American public education that included Catholic schools: "And if need be, let us join hands with the Catholic schools, let us join hands with the authorities of the parochial schools and develop the kind of educational system, realistic, if you please, which will give to all our children the God given opportunities of a great future on the basis of our American tradition and our American society."[61] Given Galamison's generally direct approach and failure to mention Jack, and that the transcript may not have been available yet, Galamison's and Jack's shared use of the term "realistic" likely signified a meaningful coincidence rather than a response. Jack drew on interfaith features of the Judeo-Christian repertoire to authoritatively assert that working with Catholic schools was "realistic." He referred to opportunities that arose from "our American tradition and our American society," which God had blessed, and painted an image of people from different religious traditions joining hands. Jack saw religion as full of possibilities to create equitable, quality education for Black and Puerto Rican students.

Jack prioritized Black and Puerto Rican students' educational experiences, as Galamison did, but he pushed at the limits of acceptable public discourse about religion by claiming that Catholic values promoted his vision of public education. In Catholic education, Jack saw the possibility for social change because of Catholic schools' commitment to excellent education for all students. In fact, Jack argued that Catholic schools promoted integration by offering high academic standards. Addressing concerns that repeal would promote white flight from city public schools to city Catholic schools, Jack described his research at "The Catholic secondary school known as Rice High School in the heart of Harlem," with 913 students. Jack laid out the demographics: "Of these three hundred twenty-four are Negro and Spanish-speaking boys. More than five hundred white boys from white neighborhoods come into Harlem each day to get an education in this secondary school." According to Jack, the Catholic school so excelled academically that white students traveled to Harlem, a predominantly Black and Puerto Rican neighborhood and a place white parents generally avoided. He continued: "It ill behooves us to state that the repeal of the Blaine Amendment will bring about the doom of the public schools," due to fear of white flight to Catholic schools, "because let me say to you there is great ferment in Harlem, there is great ferment in the Stuyvesant area, there is great ferment in the areas labeled ghetto." The example circuitously supported his point. White students *were* attending Catholic schools, but their parents were not avoiding Black and Puerto Rican students, according to Jack. Rather, he reasoned, white parents wanted their children to learn with Black and Puerto Rican students, students like his own daughter. Jack said he had chosen to send his daughter to Catholic school because of the educational quality. The "great ferment," in Jack's view, unified New Yorkers committed to academics, despite religious or racial background.

Jack and Galamison participated in wider conversations. On the flip side to Jack, Black New Yorkers like Galamison, who expressed concern about white flight to Catholic schools, criticized religious arguments as false even as they used religion to make their arguments. Like Galamison, James Springer from the Bronx claimed in a letter to the editor of the *New York Times*: "The religious question is a smokescreen to disguise the true purpose of the article." Yet, this disingenuous argument nevertheless tapped into an American narrative of inclusiveness that permitted what Springer saw as the real issue of exclusion. With Black children's education taking place in dilapidated buildings and too few teachers and resources to support it, he contended, "Whether you believe in the education of black children through integration or separation, the article can only result in an even more inferior education for these children, as difficult as that may be to imagine."[62] Springer's comment reflected brewing conversations about community-controlled schools ("separation"), and put Black children's educational experiences front and center. He "urge[d] all the black voters of New York State to reject the new constitution" because "The repeal of the 'Blaine Amendment' contained in this proposed constitution is nothing more nor less than an attempt to strengthen the existing lily white 'Private and Parochial' schools and to encourage the creation of new ones." Springer critiqued the Judeo-Christian repertoire that framed the prohibition as inclusive by saying the prohibition was not theological, and yet his criticisms of it responded to American theological racism.

Some Black New Yorkers focused just on race, understanding that the prohibition was not only or even primarily a religious matter. Marietta Tanner, writing for the *New York Amsterdam News*, emphasized that repealing the prohibition would hurt the quality of education for students of color. She insisted that the parochial schools devalued integration, writing, "This all should be of special interest to quality public school education fighters. These parochial schools practice de facto segregation, since there is definitely no bussing." One feature of equitable education would be attaining well-trained, committed teachers, but she worried that "In the ghetto, the teacher shortage will become more acute once teachers in the parochial schools are on par with public schools salary-wise."[63] Tanner also situated her opposition within New York's broader educational failures on race, declaring that many of the delegates who supported repeal "were, by and large, the same old stalwarts of the anti-bussing measures."[64] Tanner advised that the prohibition conversation was entangled in the city's racial issues. However, it is no accident that a conversation about race also centered on religious schooling, because both got to the issue of whom schools valued and aimed to cultivate into moral citizens.

While a strong contingent of Black New Yorkers refuted the idea that the prohibition repeal was about religion as they held space for a more emancipatory view of religion, they simultaneously showed that religion permeated how New Yorkers spoke about education. For instance, months before Galamison's article, Lincoln Lynch, Assistant National Director of the Congress of Racial Equality, called nonpublic schools "a sanctuary for those who don't want their children sitting with black children in the schools" and said that public aid would be "supporting segregated education."[65] Lynch framed parochial schools as sacred sites for worship to a racist religion.

Religious understandings of public education framed white New Yorkers' arguments, too. For instance, Public Education and Religious Liberty published pamphlets against repeal, which concluded, "If public funds are poured into these private schools, an even faster exodus of middle-class white children to private schools may be expected."[66] The biblical image of an exodus of white children whose parents could not afford more expensive private education evoked an afflicted religious community. Yet since PEARL opposed a white exodus, the pamphlet mocked Catholics' proclaimed wound in the face of urgent Black needs.

Black Catholics echoed Jack's perspective and revealed that for some, the definition of "public education" included Catholic values. Social workers James R. Dumpson and Aminda Wilkins founded the predominantly Black Catholic organization Citizens United for Repeal of Blaine shortly after the convention concluded. Working from CURB's headquarters, Wilkins's Jamaica, Queens home, CURB aimed to convince voters that Catholic schools could offer quality and safe education to students in poor neighborhoods. CURB promoted repeal among people who were primarily concerned with Black and poor children's education.[67] Dumpson supported aid to parochial schools because "Denominational schools will continue to be the choice of many of the poor in the ghetto, because these schools have served nobly in both secular areas and in perpetuating value systems."[68] That denominational schools "served" "the poor in the ghetto" in academics and "value systems," suggested that Dumpson saw denominational schools as contributing to the public good. Moreover, Dumpson added that: "No state law should be more restrictive than the Federal Constitution,"[69] especially if it limited educational opportunity. Like others, he claimed Catholic schools' place in American public life through appeal to the federal constitution.

Black Catholics prioritized students in their pro-repeal, pro-government aid arguments by defending that Catholic schools promoted children's welfare as a public responsibility. In doing so, Jack and the CURB members also advocated for a broad vision of American public education, one that included Catholic schools in the American tradition. They argued that Catholic schools contributed to the public good. Galamison, by contrast, had a different way to talk about religion—as racism. This line of analysis landed him in an argument where the prohibition would further deflate funding for under-resourced Black and Puerto Rican public schools.

Galamison's Critique

The New York State 1967 Constitutional Convention failed to produce a new constitution, but it successfully ingrained intersections of
religion and race in how New Yorkers defined public education. Supporters and opponents of repealing the prohibition on aid to parochial
school used the Judeo-Christian repertoire deemed appropriate to the
American public sphere to make their claims before and at the convention. Yet, their circumscribed religion could not capture the core
areas of their disagreement. Some Black New Yorkers recognized the
limits of the language and pushed against them with different theological language: in Galamison's case, a language of anti-racism and
in Jack's, a Catholic universalism. From this different theological language, new attitudes toward public education emerged.

Galamison used the occasion of the prohibition to announce why
community control of schools was becoming more appealing to some
Black New Yorkers. Community control was the educational experiment that allowed Black and, to some extent, Puerto Rican, communities to control their own school curriculum, personnel, and funding
decisions. Community control represented grassroots efforts for self-
determination, efforts that presented religious and racial visions for
public education that differed from the Board's Judeo-Christian one.[70]
The hubbub surrounding the prohibition contributed to the community control movement's urgency in New York City. Community control is often framed as "separation," or "self-segregation," in contrast
to "integration" or "desegregation," yet these distinctions presume
overly stable positions. As historians have noted, Galamison seemingly "switched sides" on the integration versus separation debate: He
went from the leader of the boycott for school desegregation to a re-
luctant community control supporter.[71] He did not change his mind
philosophically, but practically, on the value of integration because
it became clear that the Board was not going to accede.[72] To assume
that separation and integration could not rest on the same principle
of equitable education for Black students would be to misunderstand
stances like Galamison's. Galamison pursued positive educational
experiences and belonging for Black students over particular school
structures.

Galamison's article on government aid to parochial schools suggests that he came to accept community control because of the colonial dimensions of religion, race, and public education. In community control, something other than what Galamison saw as the ugly American theology of racism, the one that mirrored the Judeo-Christian American father theology, was possible. To Galamison, the possible repeal was the nail in the coffin for business-as-usual public schools. He expressed concern that repeal would "result in two separate tax-supported educational systems—one for the white and well-to-do controlled by whites; the other for the black and poor, also controlled by whites."[73] He continued, "If the voters decide" to repeal the prohibition, they would be affirming "that blacks and Puerto Ricans shall be contained." Then, "the public school system with all its terrors and unfulfilled promises will be replaced." Yet, what would replace it when the public school system had become a monument to "the real religion of America" in Galamison's view? He argued that Black New Yorkers must turn "White bigots[']" intention to "defeat" "black aspirations" into an "advantage," writing, "While whites are reaching for public funds to finance private schools for white children, we can and must take our share of public funds to finance black-owned, black-controlled schools that will give black children the standard of education they never received under the present colonialist-operated school system." Galamison's vision for community control contained a narrative in which people on the ground claiming their own power could overturn colonialist power. "If this be black power," Galamison exhorted Black parents, "make the most of it." The Judeo-Christian repertoire animated his and others' frustration with the Board and their turn away from it and toward their own communities. There, Black and Puerto Rican New Yorkers transformed education through varied configurations of religious and racial uplift.

6

Community Control as Religious and Racial World-Making

For some Black New Yorkers, community control of public schools was a matter of life and death. The pro–community control newspaper, *African-American Teachers Association Forum* (originally *Negro Teachers Forum*), printed across the top of each issue: "WE MUST EDUCATE OURSELVES OR PERISH."[1] To survive, culturally and literally, Black New Yorkers turned to community control for self-determination. The term "community control" was widely used to designate individual school districts' responsibility for funding, hiring, testing, and curriculum within New York City's school system, rather than the centralized board having purview over those areas. In 1968, after more than a decade of failed attempts to desegregate the public schools, the city experimented with community control. Many Black and Puerto Rican community members who had supported desegregation as the means to educational equity and full participation in the American public turned to community control. The experiment created community-led and -elected boards of parents, educators, and community members in three predominantly Black and Puerto Rican test districts: East Harlem, Lower East Side's Two Bridges, and the Ocean Hill and Brownsville Brooklyn neighborhoods. While many Black New Yorkers supported community control as a practice, they offered different theories of who the community was and what Black agency looked like. They often employed theological ideas and religious rituals to cultivate their theories. The subtle eschatology of the *Forum*'s slogan was a case in point. The slogan suggested that the current school system, with its overwhelmingly white centralized board's unmet promises of universal, welcoming Judeo-Christian values such as "brotherhood," and "loving thy neighbor," would lead to Black people's demise.

Community control presented an opportunity for Black religious and racial world-making through the public schools. Community control might not seem religious on the surface, but analyzing the many, often opposing, theories that supported it reveals that religious under-standings of race undergirded Black New Yorkers' visions. For instance, the *Forum*—where Rev. Milton Galamison published his 1967 article announcing his resigned shift from supporting desegregation to ac-cepting what many viewed as separation, i.e., Black-controlled schools—collected diverse views in support of community control among Black educators.[2] Its pages were filled with articles by Black educators who answered the following questions in varied ways: Under which politi-cal community will we have control of our children's education, of our lives? Within which framework are we imagining ourselves as a self-determined community? Black community control advocates answered these questions differently depending on how they situated themselves in relation to larger political groups and religious traditions. Some saw themselves as the true inheritors of the American state; some saw them-selves as cultivating a Black nation; some aimed to form interracial and interreligious coalitions; some saw Black experiences as crucial to un-derstanding all humanity; and still others critiqued white Jewish New Yorkers to emphasize power imbalances and perceived abandonment. By studying examples of community control supporters who were not necessarily the most well-known but who nevertheless influenced public conversation on community control, we can see the varieties of religious and racial world-making opportunities community control of public schools advanced.

Religious and Racial World-Making: Disruptions and Interventions

As we have seen, the centralized New York City Board of Education cul-tivated a repertoire of moral values and practices influenced by Cold War Judeo-Christian universalism and understandings of race. Even as schools supposedly sought to secularize and desegregate, religion and segregation remained crucial to the Board's functioning. In serv-ing the entire city of one million students, the Board created policies and supported curricula and programs that framed Black and Puerto Rican students as needing to be saved and white students as inherently more capable of reaching a moral standard. The Board viewed Black and Puerto Rican students as situated outside society's moral fabric.

For instance, the Board's moral and spiritual values program deified the white male Founding Fathers to teach American history. The schools claimed that Black and Puerto Rican students in particular needed to learn to "love thy neighbor as thyself" to prevent city-wide delinquency. Moreover, the schools taught integration as a value that did not require the act of desegregation, leaving the Board claiming to value integration while schools remained segregated. The Board's efforts produced a standardized rubric for ranking student morality, as it claimed that all shared its values. Yet, as has been discussed, Black and Puerto Rican New Yorkers of various religious backgrounds and Catholics and Jews of various racial identities disagreed with the Board and offered alternatives to the Board's moral framework. Actions from boycotts to school plays challenged the notion that the Board's vision was in fact universal.

Analyzing a range of previously understudied perspectives on community control as Black religious and racial world-making shows that community control was part of the same story as *Engel* and *Schempp*, the US Supreme Court cases declaring school prayer and Bible-reading unconstitutional. Although the Court excluded those particular practices from public schools, religious and moral education for racial control existed before and after the decisions. Black New Yorkers knew that the quasi-pluralistic universalism promoted by the Board was always white and Judeo-Christian. The community control movement emerged in response to a single bureaucratic entity aiming to standardize morality for an entire school system. Its advocates attempted to destandardize that standard morality.

Community control presents another example of a school movement that the public claimed failed, as many also said of the constitutional convention discussed earlier, though the especially narrow metric of failure and success obscures what the event achieved. In this instance, failure seems to be defined by community control ending, the resulting system not reflecting community control advocates' demands, and, for some, the fact that segregated, unequal schooling persisted. Yet, community control advocates' visions changed education in New York City and created frameworks for possible greater transformations.

Community control led to a law that decentralized the city's public schools. Though decentralization may sound like another word for community control, and a central board with as much control as the decentralization law afforded it may sound like centralization, decentralization was its own complex rearrangement of school power. And, religious and racial dynamics fueled that rearrangement. Community control had ignited tensions between Black and white Jewish New Yorkers. Specifically, the Ocean Hill-Brownsville community board transferred or fired thirteen white teachers and six white administrators, some of whom were Jewish, whom they claimed were not fulfilling their job responsibilities. In response, the United Federation of Teachers, also composed of many Jewish teachers and led by Albert Shanker, who was Jewish, led a series of city-wide teacher strikes for a total of thirty-six days. Schools in Ocean Hill-Brownsville remained open by bringing in replacement teachers (70% of whom were white, and half of that 70% who were also Jewish) who were willing to cross the picket line, though 90 percent of city schools closed.[3] Police occupied schools in Ocean Hill-Brownsville, as predominantly white teachers struck over the firings and the community board structure that had led to them. While community control advocates supported keeping the three experimental districts of Ocean Hill-Brownsville, East Harlem, and Two Bridges and handing control over to sixty-four community districts, the UFT "favored a decentralized system that would preserve centralized hiring and eliminate" the experimental districts.[4] Eventually, the legislature passed the decentralization law, which created thirty-two districts with their own boards; however, these districts were larger than those proposed by community control advocates and combined white communities with communities of color, rather than giving communities of color control.[5] The experimental districts were dissolved with new districting. Interested parties negotiated who would control what under the decentralization law; eventually, the central board retained control over high schools, hiring and firing, finances, and more, while these larger local boards could appoint principals and superintendents.[6]

Historians have also framed community control as having failed because, they argue, Black and Puerto Rican communities wanted too much. One early documenter of the movement, education historian Diane Ravitch, showed disdain for the Black and Puerto Rican community control advocates. She referred to community control advocates as "militant protest groups"[7] and "militant advocates of total community control,"[8] who, she implied, could not settle things "rationally." Jerald

Podair's 2009 history offers a more nuanced view of the incompatible values of Black and white interests. Nevertheless, he also claims that the experiment "severely damaged the idea of community action as an instrument of social change" and "exposed local control's false promise of self-empowerment."[9] These lines criticized community control advocates, who were predominantly Black and Brown, for seeking to create their own space. The scholars neglect the material and religious needs that Black and Brown New Yorkers sought to meet through community control in favor of preconceived ideas about civil discourse.

More recently, the narrative about community control has shifted from blaming Black people for setting educational equity back to exploring community control's impact. Historians of education, participants in the movement, and journalists now echo what Harlem resident and author James Baldwin reflected at the time: "The experiment [in community control] was discontinued after three years, not because it failed but because it did not fail."[10] Baldwin grew up in Harlem schools and visited them as an adult, observing "there was a new climate in the halls and classrooms of the experimental schools"—different from the one he grew up in, where "most of us" experienced an "accumulating sense of one's own worthlessness."[11] As Baldwin implied, community control advocates sought for Black and Brown children to feel that they belonged by determining their own future. White school authorities perceived self-determination as a threat, Baldwin suggested, but to him, perceived threat signaled success, not failure. Education historian Heather Lewis and political scientist Jane Anna Gordon have argued that community control advocates, especially women of color, *succeeded* at grassroots organizing for self-determination. Advocates led their own districts on decision-making community boards and created models for future grassroots school organizing.[12] Building on this recent scholarship with Baldwin in mind, it is useful to shift our view from the failure/success paradigm to consider community control's impact on the larger movement surrounding religion in public schools.

Religion was vital to advocates' practice of community and thus community control. Scholars have not always recognized this, referring to the Black "critique of pluralism" and the "racial and religious antagonisms which had simmered in the schools for years."[13] Scholars correcting the typical narrative hint at religious connections as a site for grassroots organizing and the complicated racialization of Jews, many of whom opposed community control.[14] Each reference offers a glimpse into religion in New York City public schools.

We can go further. Community control was not a failed story about race; it was a successful story about religion, *because* religious registers created space for community control advocates to critique moral norms that valued people from different racial backgrounds differently. When seen as the culmination of a story about the centralized Board's Judeo-Christian repertoire, community control may not have achieved Black and Puerto Rican communities' original goals for integration— educational equity across racial groups—but community control did disrupt rather than preserve the Judeo-Christian norm.

Instead of a single, standard morality rooted in a Judeo-Christian imaginary, or a monolith of the loudest male voices, Black community control advocates offered diverse approaches to understanding the sacrality and morality of Blackness through public education, often drawing on what historian of religion Laurie Maffly-Kipp calls "black collective narration."[15] While Christianity shaped some Black narratives, the Christian interpretations centered liberation, rather than universalism, and Christianity was not the only influence. Traditions including Pan-Africanism and humanism also shaped the collective narration. Black women were often at the forefront, and some articulated what social historian and critical theorist Ahmad Greene-Hayes calls "anti-commodified Black Studies," meaning "grassroots educational institution-building and pedagogical innovation that democratizes the spread and reach of new knowledges for all people."[16] Judaism shaped the narratives as well insofar as Jews always held an unstable place in the schools' Judeo-Christian repertoire. Focusing on Black people could be viewed as reifying the idea that community control was only about Blackness. However, among Black New Yorkers, perspectives were diverse—intellectually, ethnically, and religiously.

Far more perspectives than are detailed here circulated, and, although community control's focus was Black self-determination, major organizers included Puerto Rican, other Caribbean, white Jewish (though in the minority among Jews), and Asian and Asian American New Yorkers. For instance, the Ocean Hill-Brownsville Board appointed the city's first Puerto Rican principal, Luis Fuentes, and first Asian American principal, David Lee.[17] Such coalition-building unsettles the notion of singular Black control. The movement's diversity spotlights that community control gave people space to share their voices, voices that ultimately undid the purported universality of Judeo-Christianity.

Across divergent visions of a Black collective future that exemplified alternatives to the schools' dominant Judeo-Christian paradigm, engaging in public educational debates meant engaging religion. Advocates needed to respond to a religious form, Judeo-Christianity. Engagement also surpassed mere response. Black people offered their own varied religious-moral visions for worlds where Black children could thrive in futures that community control could make possible, separate from the white gaze. Community control advocates unsettled the schools' Judeo-Christian norms, as community control prevented the central board from operating as it had before the experiment. Even though community control stopped after the teacher strikes, the advocates' work nevertheless made the whiteness and Christianness of Judeo-Christian norms visible to more New Yorkers. Advocates' work also revealed the possibility for public schools to liberate Black people from their American inheritance.

The US Nation

Narratives of Black Americans as the true inheritors of the US nation were a form of religious and racial world-making that engaged national rituals and stories. Schoolteacher Edwina Chavers Johnson may not have seemed like a candidate for a community control supporter given her widespread efforts to work with the government entities. If community control were only about separatism, she would not be. However, Chavers Johnson tried every strategy she could, and by the late 1960s she had become especially invested in educating Black teachers to teach Black children. She advocated for community control because, as she outlined in her 1968 essay, "An Alternative to Miseducation for the Afro-American People," history taught her that the American educational system would rarely defend Black people's place in American history and Black students' place in public schools. So, she argued, Black people must create their own educational spaces. She wrote that "The Afro-American was and is educated to serve that society (the colonies, the fledgling democracy, the technological world power) as a subordinate without human benefit or dignity."[18] In the society, she explained, Thomas Jefferson had determined that African Americans were "easily humored and ha[d] less brain capacity than the European."[19] Community control was necessary, she claimed, because "The African descendants in America, having passed through three phases of education in America—de-Africanization, dehumanization, and, finally, an inferior caste status—through application of self-determination and the establishment of a voluntary self-separated school system, can educate themselves."[20] She traced historical moments where Black Americans created their own spaces for education. Because the city failed to desegregate schools or educate Black children equitably, Chavers Johnson found the late 1960s to be one such moment, and community control an apt avenue to achieve educational resources for Black students.

Chavers Johnson grounded her work in the idea that Black people shaped America and were Americans. Even when public institutions had treated Black people as if they were separate from the US nation, and even when the national Judeo-Christian myth and those drawing on its attendant repertoire excluded Black people, Black people's Americanness remained. The following scene would have thrilled Chavers Johnson: third- and fourth-grade students at their desks, having read poems by Phyllis Wheatley and Gwendolyn Brooks, writing to the authors (even if Wheatley was no longer alive) or composing their own poems inspired by Wheatley and Brooks. In her 1963 "Guide for Teachers on Contributions of Afro-Americans to the American Culture" covering grades K-6, Chavers Johnson drew on her experience as a teacher and her knowledge of Black history to propose activities including this one. The intimate relationship born of addressing an author directly or emulating the author's style allowed Black children to participate in the same story as these Black women authors.

Chavers Johnson herself also contributed to that story. Born in Chicago, she grew up around Black achievement and artistry. She attended Englewood High School, where Brooks and Lorraine Hansberry also studied.[21] Though it is unclear if she and Brooks met, they would have overlapped for one year. Everyday educators and students, like Chavers Johnson, created America alongside well-known Black figures. By centering Black participation in and creation of the United States, she challenged the Board's narrative of the Founding Fathers as benevolent, heroic deities. Instead, she honored Black success through collective practice while maintaining the repertoire's American focus.

Chavers Johnson's project drew on religious dimensions of Black collective narration without being explicitly religious. The activity of writing to Brooks or Wheatley positioned the authors as the students' ancestors, elders with whom they could communicate. These American ancestors could give students their own narrative in the United States. As Maffly-Kipp has shown, reconstructing history for a people wrongly called "historyless" was sacred work.[22] In her essay summarizing the history of Black education in the United States, Chavers Johnson addressed imposed historylessness by describing how "The African was forbidden to speak his own language, to practice his own religion, he was, in effect, de-Africanized during the early colonial period." In short, "Learning for the African, then, was to lose his identity as an African, give up his African institutions, even his name," and "His education was in the field, in the enslaved persons quarter, where he adjusted or died in the state of servitude to whites."[23] Chavers Johnson scrutinized the hypocrisy of how enslavers allowed Black enslaved people to read—"Learning to memorize some bible passages was permitted for the sake of 'saving his soul'"—only to strengthen whites' own salvation.

Simultaneously, she enacted her own salvation narrative, which recovered Black history without honoring white Christianity. By the nineteenth century's end, "for at least some African-American Protestants, conceptions of race, religion, and national identity were indistinguishable: the notion of the 'African race' had been sacralized and understandings of national identity and purpose integrated into a sacred saga of emancipation, redemption, and salvation."[24] For Chavers Johnson, uplifting Black American figures in public education extended the "sacred saga" by inviting students into a community sustained by rituals.

By focusing on public schools, Chavers Johnson identified a complementary space to religious institutions to champion Black history. Public schools were historically Protestant institutions that the Board had reimagined as "Judeo-Christian." Her efforts thus fit within a broader Black commitment to "Protestantism as a source of belief, practice, and institutional structure."[25] Whatever her own religious background, Chavers Johnson reportedly "ran all around New York City, servicing schools, organizations, churches," and "received a grant from the Jamaica Branch N.A.A.C.P. for initial publication" of her guide, "Contributions of Afro-Americans." She recalled: "By 1962 I had personally serviced 225 schools in the New York City system"[26] and promoted the guide throughout the country. She amplified public schools as vehicles for redeeming America by positioning Black people as inheritors of the American nation. In her view, public schools could emancipate Black people from the inaccurate, dominating American narratives that positioned Black people as lesser humans.

Moreover, Chavers Johnson joined the tradition of Black women's historical work, which often took on religious dimensions. The religiosity sometimes emerged from denominational affiliation, or redemption narratives. As in the example of engaging with authors like Brooks, the religiosity also arose from ancestry, a key feature of African diaspora religions.[27] Delineating "women's work" could sound demeaning, suggesting that women operate in a separate sphere from "real" historical work, men's work. However, as Maffly-Kipp and religious studies scholar Kathryn Lofton argue, "Although few women, white or black, participated in the academic study of history until the mid-twentieth century," primarily because of barriers to entry, nevertheless, "women functioned as primary translators and teachers, offering explanations, allegories, and scholastic narrations of the past."[28] Naming women's work as history defines history and historians more capaciously and accurately than the limited definition of academic history because "Whether in schoolrooms or kitchens, state houses or church pulpits, women have always been historians."[29] Chavers Johnson worked when more women entered academia, but barriers to professional recognition still existed. Just because more women could pursue PhDs did not mean that academia was the only, primary, or best place for historical work. As in Chavers Johnson's case, public school curricula introducing and uplifting ancestors represented historical work that could reach a wide audience of children to create a world where Black people were recognized as American.

For Chavers Johnson, the public school proved a significant space for conveying a sacred race history because of its didactic structure and built-in futurity. Her approach saw time as supple, with the future intimately connected to the past. Her guide included a calendar with birth dates of important figures in Black history, so that children could mark

Harriet Tubman's leadership in March or Countee Cullen's on his May 30 birthday. Through ritually memorializing ancestors, pupils guided by Chavers Johnson tapped into how sacred race histories were prominently transmitted: through "commemorations, ritualized feasts, fasts, and celebrations that captured stories of the collective past, present, and future."[30] Chavers Johnson planned lessons with overviews of Black figures' contributions and activities related to the figures. Honoring Black figures in American history brought the past to the present, making these figures come alive as leaders for public school children. Rituals also brought the figures into the future through educating children who could create a new America. Though Chavers Johnson's uses of time were not outwardly biblical, her work resonated with the claim that Black women "authors often seem to construct an alternative world, in which biblical chronology is more vivid and predictive than the American social context," one that public school children could cultivate.[31]

Rituals associated with the school calendar restructured time so that a Black, rather than a white, collective defined America. In a piece she wrote for the *Forum* called "Teacher, Put Some Black on That Calendar!," Chavers Johnson referred to her earlier guide by contrast to the Judeo-Christian patriotic calendar that put aside time to honor former US presidents, the flag, brotherhood, and Christmas. Re-emphasizing the importance of dates, she pointed out how just in September, teachers could use the many "examples of how dates can be commemorated, taking a birth date of an important Afro-American and weaving the lessons and activities around that person's life."[32] For instance, "September we can celebrate *Owijira*, the West African New Year. September we can dramatize *Jesse Owens'* Olympic feats. September we can present *Hiram Revels*, the first Afro-American Senator, and *James Forten* who was an inventor and an abolitionist. September we can discuss *Alain Locke* and the Harlem Renaissance."[33] By punctuating the broad possibilities for just one month, her plan conveyed to students that Black accomplishment permeated an array of fields—sports, government, industry, and arts—across space and time. Instead of relegating Black history to a particular month, she aimed to saturate the curriculum with religious and racial world-making rituals to correct the notion that only white students ought to see people who looked like them in tales of historical figures.[34] The world to be made was a new America, redeemed by Blackness.

Although she followed other Black women's historical work and uplifted Black women's voices, and even as her recommendations for classroom celebrations and lessons ran contrary to Black Power's anti-institutionalism, Chavers Johnson also participated in the masculinist language of Black Power. Many of her descriptions appeared value-neutral regarding gender; however, Chavers Johnson also used femininity to disparage Black people she saw as trying to please white people: "We will be swinging our own parades down the avenue, not effeminately attempting to be in somebody else's parade."[35] Her use of "parade" accentuated the importance of taking up space, "the avenue," to claim Black presence in the United States. At the same time, she implied that those Black people "attempting to be in somebody else's parade" were "effeminate[]," and in doing so, she associated femininity with helplessness. Her efforts to secure the guide in the schools contradicted the association, as she was anything but helpless. Nevertheless, despite challenging the gender status quo herself, she adopted patriarchal values to critique others.

Chavers Johnson was pro-America, but the America she sought to create fundamentally challenged white visions of the nation by rejecting assumptions about which racial groups populated the schools' Judeo-Christianity. In a letter she wrote to Martin Luther King Jr., she described "The appalling crisis in the country" as "due very largely to what is recorded as 'The American Heritage' and its continued debasement of African and Africa and African descendants, through all media of communication, particularly in public school textbooks which are paid for with our tax money."[36] She addressed the crisis by reframing who the deified figures were, "reimagining the relationships among national identity, religious affiliation, and racial lineage" to produce "a radical overturning of fundamental 'American' assumptions."[37] No longer abiding the Board's focus on the white male Founding Fathers, she spread the celebration around. If her activities deified the Black figures they honored, gods proliferated, and Black children could see themselves in school deities.

Chavers Johnson's religious and racial world threatened the centralized Board because its contents challenged the status quo. In her article for the *Forum*, she wrote, "the Board of Education of New York City," i.e., the centralized generator of curriculum, "called me in for some meetings,—my work had stamina,—could it be an official document?" However, "That was a consideration which was squelched by some very well-executed Uncle Tomming,"[38] i.e., by Black people whom she understood to be playing into white interests. The response further motivated her to work around educational bureaucracy: "I went into business" and "reached 32 of the 50 states in this country—from a small office which is in my home."[39] Because of her dedication to trying multiple strategies and her frustration with the Board, her support for community control emerged.

Chavers Johnson's experience with the Board also inspired her focus on educating and activating Black teachers to better teach about Black history and culture. Community control became an opportunity to challenge the white Judeo-Christian norm. Following the confrontation, she shifted from her focus on all teachers to Black teachers because "Waiting for the Boards of Education or for the Bureaus of Curriculum or Title Projects to initiate action is to wait for the line-up to crematorium. Forget it."[40] Instead, she sought to identify resources within Black communities through working with the "*talented, knowledgeable black educators WHO KNOW OUR HISTORY and who are not being recognized by us because they are not recognized by white people due to their unswerving, uncompromising attitudes*." She wanted to complete the work soon: "There is enough material called units or lesson plans written already by black people for us to put into our home libraries this forthcoming summer, pur [*sic*] over, and get going with a bang in September, 196[9]."[41] Chavers Johnson organized Black communities because white (and some Black) people had rejected her ideas, not because she unilaterally rejected white people.

Chavers Johnson sought unity among Black people because "Black educators are not teaching them anything to help bring about self-love, self-acceptance, and self-respect,"[42] which were "the total commitment of the late Malcolm X whose depth of knowledge and projection of black unity sprang from his having learned black history, that is, African and African-American history."[43] Black unity also enabled control over which values and history schools taught. For Chavers Johnson, solidifying Black people's belonging in America created a world where Black children would facilitate Black history's reproduction for future generations. Chavers Johnson articulated an American vision of Black life separate from whiteness but fully American.

Black Nations

As white teachers struck for more than thirty days in New York City, they carried signs that read "Stop Teaching Race Hatred to Children" and "End Racism in Schools."[44] In doing so, they implied that Black and Brown people were the racist ones. By contrast, Black community control advocates, including Ocean Hill-Brownsville administrator Rhody McCoy, countered with signs demanding "A Future for Our Children NOW," "United We Stand for Community Control," "Schools of the People for the People by the People," and "Let My People Go" with "Please please pretty please" around the sign's border.[45] "Our," "We," "the People," "My People" were unapologetic claims to Black dignity, to Black children's right to shape public schools and the various religious and racial worlds they enacted. Drawing on the African American spiritual sung during slavery, "Go Down Moses," the reference to Exodus 5:1, "Let My People Go," placed Black community control advocates in a long line of Black freedom fighters.[46] While some, such as Chavers Johnson, sought to transform the American nation through uplifting Black people's contributions to it, for other community control advocates, restoring or creating a Black Nation would free Black people from America's violence.

Community control took place at the height of Black Nationalism, a complicated term that meant different things to different people. References to Black nations offered some Black people religious and racial worlds all their own. The distinctly masculine and heteronormative dimensions of Black Nationalism are notable, even as its participants sometimes used the more inclusive language of Black peoplehood. One form Black Nationalism took was Pan-Africanism. The Pan-African movement aimed to build solidarity among all people of the African diaspora. It began in the late nineteenth century and saw many iterations during decolonization in Africa and the Civil Rights Movement.

Pan-Africanism took hold in New York City during and after community control. In 1970, under decentralization and without the full control that advocates had fought for, some of the former community control leaders formed a Pan-African school to realize their vision. They called the school "Uhuru Sasa Shule," meaning Freedom Now School in Swahili. The school operated alongside the Pan-African cultural center

Figure 6.1. "Dr. McCoy, holding sign at left, and the Rev. C. B. Marshall at a demonstration outside Dr. McCoy's office during the 1968 teachers' strike." Patrick A. Burns/The New York Times.

the leaders founded in 1969 called "The East" (opposed to the dominant "West"). Uhuru Sasa Shule began as an after-school program in February, but it became a full-fledged elementary school by spring.[47] Former students have said they were the first children, or among the first children, to learn the Seven Principles of Blackness, developed at the height of Black Power. That students learned the principles in school was no accident; the principles provided a critical alternative to the public schools' Judeo-Christian values.

The Seven Principles of Blackness faulted Christianity for creating white supremacy. To counter this history, at Uhuru Sasa, the school became a mechanism for creating a religious and racial world where first principles rest on Blackness. The Seven Principles of Blackness are: "UMOJA—Unity; Kujichagulia—self-determination; Ujima—collective work and responsibility; Ujamaa—cooperative economics; Nia—purpose; Kuumba—creativity; Imani—faith."[48] Black Nationalist and professor Maulana Karenga developed the seven principles alongside the Pan-African holiday Kwanzaa. First celebrated in 1966 as an antidote to Christmas, Kwanzaa lasts seven days and celebrates one principle each day. Amiri Baraka, the poet and activist, also wrote about the principles in what he called "The Black Value System."[49] Baraka played on the idea of a "value system." The principles took a similar form to moral and spiritual values lessons taught in New York City public schools, which promoted values such as "brotherhood" and "love thy neighbor." Yet the principles magnified different values for a different audience—Black people. Baraka explicitly connected the seven principles of Blackness to the Ten Commandments, writing in "The Black Value System": "The 7 principles are '10 commandments' yet more profound to us—US because they are pre and post 10 commandments at the same time. If there is Umoja, for instance, thou cannot kill, steal, bear false witness, commit adultery, or any of the things the western world thrives on. The commandments are fulfilled by the initial need of blackness for unity—oneness."[50] "The western world," according to Baraka, perpetuated the values it commanded against, so Black people needed a new world. Former community control advocates had learned that radical possibilities could emerge from educating a public. Education could oppress, but it could also liberate.

Interfaith and Interracial Coalitions

Chavers Johnson's work and Black Nationalisms also operated in a milieu of interfaith and interracial grassroots organizing. Such organizing fostered multi-racial, multi-religious coalitions to support a world where Black people could determine their educational rights and experiences. Thus, on-the-ground critiques of the Judeo-Christian norm came from many directions. In particular, community control's success depended on interracial coalitions, as historian Heather Lewis and Charles Isaacs, a white Jewish math teacher community control advocate turned journalist who wrote a deeply researched book on his experience, have shown.[51]

In addition to interracial coalitions, success also relied on the coalitions' interreligious nature. In Ocean Hill-Brownsville, the governing board included Father John Powis, a white priest; Herbert Oliver, a Black minister at Westminster Bethany United Presbyterian Church; parent Thelma Hamilton, who was African American; and parent Dolores Torres, who was Puerto Rican. Powis, Hamilton, and Torres were all involved in Christians and Jews United for Social Action, "a grassroots organization committed to organizing Brownsville's poorest residents."[52] Together, they promoted the district's goals for self-determination. The interreligious, interracial community board existed because Torres and others had laid the groundwork years before.

Community control was built on existing interfaith work that was rooted in direct action for justice, rather than promoting images of tolerance, as with the Board's implementation of Brotherhood Week. CUSA spurred direct action by mobilizing religiously and racially diverse New Yorkers to advocate for issues facing their communities to people in institutional power seats. Yet CUSA members reportedly felt stigmatized in their own districts. According to Torres's *Eyes on the Prize* documentary interview, CUSA "dealt with problems in the community: with housing, with welfare, with the schools, with drug addiction. Anything that pertained to the community, any problem that was there." Torres describes how, in 1967, following complaints from parents about PS 144, CUSA "went into the local school board that represented, supposed to represent, our district. We found not one person on that board lived in our district. Most of the people on that board were White, we were a district of mostly Hispanic and Black families. The ones that did have children in public schools went to public schools in good neighborhoods. We were a poor neighborhood." Before the community control experiment, she was already practicing direct action for Black and Brown children and running up against the barriers white control built.

Torres sought to break the local board's barriers with interfaith and interracial organizing that responded to community needs. Such organizing revealed inaction and insensitivity to Black and Brown peoples' needs, even as the Board professed unity across religious and racial difference. The alienation Torres reported at the previous local school board meeting carried over to a visit CUSA made "to 110 Livingston Street, to the Board of Education," to "present our case, and they kept telling us to go to the local school board, and these people, we felt, did not represent us. They had no children in the schools in our district, we felt they weren't paying any attention to us because we were the ignorant people, these were the educated people, these were the people with all kinds of degrees, and we felt that they didn't care about us or our children."[53] When responses to direct actions made CUSA members feel their children were uncared for, they looked elsewhere for support so that their voices were heard. For instance, Hamilton had sought to work within the city system as a major organizer of the 1964 boycott for integration—the moral value that *did* require desegregation. Torres and Hamilton directed their efforts to the community boards, drawing on their interracial and interreligious organizing experiences.

Black Humanism

Black Humanism was another form of religious and racial world-making that influenced public schools. Like visions centering nations or communities, Black Humanists also offered a religious and racial perspective, but the scope of the political community extended beyond nations and communities to all of humanity, albeit defined by hu*man*ity. Preston Wilcox, a professor in the Columbia University School of Social Work and member of the Harlem test community control district's ad hoc parent advisory committees, ensured that New Yorkers heard that Black people were human. Although Wilcox is recognized as a veritable force in the movement for community control, his written work on religion and race has been understudied. In his widely circulated article "Education for Black Humanism" from the volume *What Black Educators are Saying*, he asserted the first principle of Black Humanism: "All black children are human and educable."[54] Here, as in presentations at Black Power conferences and in guidelines for confronting white institutional racism, he named white school systems' wrong views about Black children as the biggest obstacle to educating Black children.[55] He dated their views back to colonialism and slavery. Indeed, white people have justified the view that Black children were inhuman and ineducable through Christian categories such as "heathen" and interpreting Black people as carrying the biblical curse of Ham.[56] In Wilcox's published and unpublished writings, Black Humanism meant belonging to humanity. Yet, Wilcox suggested, because the white world invalidated Black people's humanity, Black Humanism required separate spaces for Black people to affirm their dignity. Community control would allow such space for children, who were Black communities' future.

In two words, "human" and "educable," Wilcox invoked a history of denying Black children's humanity through inaccess to formal education.

If Christianity takes as foundational that God created all people and there-fore all people deserve dignity, an accusation that Christians did not see Black children as human struck at the heart of Christian doctrine. Further, it brought to light the legacies of colonialism and slavery in public educa-tion. The statement "All black children are human" implied that the cen-tralized Board and the teachers it hired were oblivious to Black children's humanity. Wilcox's assertion that Black children were "educable" sug-gested that, as humans, they could be taught. Moreover, education was a human right that schools still refused Black children. Under enslavement, formal education for Black children had been rare (although some white people, especially in New England, sought to educate African Americans for theological reasons).[57] Even when Horace Mann cultivated common schools purportedly for everyone, his ideology "did little to ensure that black people would be included—let alone included equally—in public schools."[58] By bringing educational history to the surface, Wilcox made visible intersecting religious and racial violences in public schools.

Wilcox's need to state Black children's humanity and educability in the late 1960s suggested that the centralized Board had failed Black students, even in attempts at inclusivity through school-specific Judeo-Christianity. Wilcox's Black Humanism took aim at the Board's assump-tion that the divine created humans. While the Board used God language less often than it had fifteen years earlier, the notion that a divine force created humans persisted in the deification of white Protestant men as creators of the nation and, thus, of Americans.[59]

By contrast, Wilcox sought Black agency without divinity. This quest drew Wilcox to Humanism. Twentieth-century organized Humanism generally rejected organized religion. Some humanists claim a spiritual religiosity; others support a theory of humans as agents that dates to the Enlightenment and ancient Greece.[60] Wilcox formulated his own ver-sion. He only referred to religion in "Education for Black Humanism" when he wrote that, to be free, each individual Black person needed to achieve "Resolution of his religious hangups, i.e., freeing himself from the need to be saved by first finding his own salvation within himself."[61] Wilcox rejected a brand of religion that promoted a white savior com-plex, where Black people lacked agency. Yet, he did not outright reject all religion. Instead, Wilcox directed Black people to save themselves because doing so gave them agency that traditional religion did not.

Attentive to the school-as-savior complex, Wilcox situated Black Humanism in conversations about the coloniality of public schools that were widespread among community control advocates. Charles Wilson, educational director of the experimental Harlem district, also described the schools as "shot through with colonialism."[62] During community control, "Black nationalists and left-wing groups associated the UFT and the Board of Education with a colonial structure whose mission was to maintain a system of racial exploitation."[63]

Evocations of America's exploitative history found specificity in Wilcox's identification of colonialism as scientific. Wilcox unraveled school colonialism by implying the intersecting coloniality of religion, race, and public education; he argued that public schools participated in "*scientific colonialism* by white America."[64] He named academic testing and crime statistics as cultivating a scientifically backed image of Black students as inferior to white students—morally, intellectually, behaviorally. Wilcox challenged assumptions that testing and crime rates were race-neutral by highlighting the ways systems that tracked students by race prioritized white students. Public school standards overvalued white students at the expense of Black students.

Wilcox more than responded to public schools' Judeo-Christian universalism. He created values for public schools to teach. To counter the overvaluation of white students, Wilcox proposed that Black Humanism required "A Reordering of Values" for Black people, especially Black men, so that they could liberate themselves from white control. The disruptive reordering was rooted in Black tradition. Instead of the Board-promoted narrative where white people starred and Black people reacted to center stage from the wings, Wilcox clarified that "Neither is it [authentic blackness] solely a reaction to white rejection" because it was proactive. For Wilcox, "authentic blackness" preceded whiteness. He defined "authentic blackness" as "a soul-searching, excruciatingly difficult attempt to undo four hundred years of de-Africanization, dehumanization, and colonization—to reach deeply into the instinct and belief systems of Black people to restore them to a self-defined level of *experienced* humanity, *figurative* Africanization, and *literal* collective liberation."[65] Liberation *from* asked Black people to imagine their purposes and possibilities without white control. "Authentic Blackness" restored collective and individual peoplehood that Europeans and white Americans had stolen through colonization and the Atlantic slave trade. It rejected the public schools' teachings: the deified white Founding Fathers, the requirement to "love your neighbor," and the inherent goodness of integration without restructuring public school resources to create more equity.

Wilcox's Black Humanism directed the reordering of values at Black people, which significantly reframed who could exemplify the "values." The schools assumed that the default good public school student was white. "Values" were an unmarked white category, though sometimes school practices directed values learning at Black or Puerto Rican students so that students would act more like white students, who were perceived as good, as in the case of "loving thy neighbor" and the cleanup parades.[66] By contrast, Wilcox argued that Black people could reorder their values by reframing their relationships to white people and society. For instance, he asserted, "1. Black people must forget their *isolation* from white people and deal with their *alienation* from black people" and "2. Black people must replace their *need to belong* with a sense of *functional marginality* as it relates to their membership in this society."[67] Wilcox proposed forgoing dependence on white people's approval and adopting a practical approach to living on society's margins to sever any reliance Black people had on white people for their self-understanding. A third reordered value further developed Wilcox's idea that Black people should recognize their own worth: "3. An effort must be made to distinguish *needs* from *wants*; the economic consequences are crucial."[68] Educational opportunities therefore marked essential human *needs*, in Wilcox's framing. For Black people to achieve such self-determination, "4. Peer and mutual relationships across age, class, and sex lines should come to be valued more than superordinate and/or subordinate relationships."[69] In his gesture to relational power dynamics, Wilcox aimed for a broadly equitable society, one that extended beyond white/Black dynamics. This reordering of values offered Black people a way of thinking outside the constraints of the schools' white, Judeo-Christian moral framework without having to situate themselves in reaction to it. They could determine the terms of their own humanity through reorganized structures such as community control.

Black reclamation, a much longer tradition than the schools' Judeo-Christian one, catalyzed Black Humanism. Listing what "black humanism asserts," Wilcox identified common ground across Black Americans,

writing: "Blacks hold in common African descendancy and victimiza-
tion by white institutional racism." He later elaborated that educators
needed to recover stolen education because: "Education for blacks is
essentially a retooling process: rehumanization, re-Africanization and
decolonialization." Wilcox further explained what "retooling" meant:
"i.e., authentic black men enjoy only one kind of freedom as a conceptual whole: a respect for native cultural differences, a resistance to all
kinds of oppression, and recognition of one's right to defend his right to
become who he wants to become as long as the expression of that right
does not demand the oppression of others."[70] Because Black people often
were denied the opportunity to inherit pre-slavery and pre-colonization
traditions, the "retooling" recognized the exploitation that Black people
had experienced and the need to reclaim a shared African descendancy.

Black Humanism also drew on more recent influences in the ongoing civil rights struggle, with its complicated relationship to gender. On
multiple occasions, Wilcox perpetuated the masculinist nature of Black
Power.[71] Citing how "white America" pigeonholed Martin Luther King
Jr., Malcolm X, Harold Cruse, and Eldridge Cleaver into labels that Wilcox claimed did not fit, Wilcox focused on Black men in "Education for
Black Humanism," largely ignoring Black women's voices: "The peculiar
ability of this nation to assign to black men equal status as it relates to
antisocial behavior and to deny them the accreditation of humanness has
compelled an increasing number of black men to begin to define themselves on their own terms—*to rid themselves of the need to be defined in
a positive sense by white America*."[72] Wilcox cited that Malcolm X was
not "antiwhite," as he claimed "white America" argued, but rather "Malcolm X's real message was that *one's right to be human is non-negotiable*."
While Malcolm X influenced Wilcox's argument about Black children as
humans in a generally ungendered manner, in other moments, Wilcox
defended misogynist behavior. For instance, he tacitly accepted Cleaver's
actions as "a convicted rapist," suggesting they were merely emblematic
of systemic racism and misogyny because Cleaver "knew too well that
the system produced rapists."[73] While Cleaver's case is complex, Wilcox's
silence on women and misogyny while uplifting Cleaver suggests that
women could not access Black Humanism as men did.[74]

Wilcox's standard Black human was male. Throughout "Educating for
Black Humanism," he used he/him/his pronouns to describe the Black

human. Lest this be seen as just a default (which would reveal its own assumptions anyway), he clarified that he was talking about men when he described male/female relationships, writing that liberation required "Resolution of his relationships with the opposite sex, i.e., male strength and feminine assets should become liberating instruments rather than weapons."[75] He recognized power inequities in male-female relationships, later writing, "Collective survival within the black world can never be achieved as long as institutionalized conflict and colonialism exist within male-female relationships." However, Wilcox still differentiated "male strength" from "feminine assets," implying that women should contribute to liberation delicately, from the sidelines. Wilcox framed education as experience, indicating that even without a supportive public school system, Black children learned because "The black community was *their* black university," and "The content of the curriculum was real life."[76] If we take Wilcox at his word, then in learning from "real life," any Black person who did not conform to male standards would have also learned about male dominance in Black Humanism and beyond.

Wilcox critiqued the schools' values as those of the "WASP," meaning the "White Anglo-Saxon Protestant." In a collection on School Control, Wilcox declared that community control advocates made "an effort to redefine and control public educational institutions serving Black People and to eliminate the WASP quality which requires Black to become culturally white inside; to not disturb the chains on their minds; and to participate in their own miseducation."[77] WASP signaled assimilation and foreshadowed Wilcox's critique of multiculturalism: "If it failed to materialize, it was precisely because it required the hyphenated American groups to play the game of 'Follow the WASP.' Most hyphenated American groups have over-subscribed to 'Wasp behavior' as appropriate public behavior; they have clung to cultural imperatives as private and ethnic group behavior."[78] With "WASP" as the default, according to Wilcox, anyone who was not a white Protestant themselves privatized parts of their identities because the "WASP" was by default public in America. Moreover, language such as "ethic" and "myth" described how "WASP" views permeated public schools: "The deliberate crushing of views that are culturally radical to the WASP ethic by the public school system appears to be part of an effort by white America to make equality a myth and white supremacy a reality."[79] He used "myth" to mean "lie." However, equality was also a myth because it was a story that gave public schools meaning, purpose, and moral guidance. "WASP" and "Judeo-Christian" have different origins, the first a name applied from without and the second from within. Nevertheless, both point to public institutions' Protestant power. Even as Jews and Catholics perpetuated and reimagined status quo power dynamics through their involvement in the Judeo-Christian repertoire, Wilcox's critique of "WASP" power in public education poked holes in Judeo-Christianity's origin stories.

Wilcox also turned to Malcolm X to criticize the intersection of whiteness and Christianity in public institutions' Judeo-Christianity. In 1963, Malcolm X sat down for an interview with Kenneth Clark, the psychologist from the *Brown* case and co-founder of Harlem's Northside Children's Center with fellow psychologist Mamie Clark, his wife. Malcolm told Clark, "I firmly believe that it was the Christian society, as you call it, the Judaic-Christian society, that created all of the factors that send so many so-called Negroes to prison."[80] Malcolm blamed on Christianity the religious desire to punish Black people rather than "reform" or "rehabilitate" them. His sentence notably started with "Christian" before moving to "Judeo-Christian." He put "Judeo-Christian" in someone else's voice, suggesting his ambivalence with Jews' roles in the Judeo-Christian.

Jews' unstable role in the idea of "Judeo-Christian" came to a head in accusations of anti-Semitism during the community control experiment. The questions came front and center: Did Jews foster Black self-determination in the public schools and the broader spheres the schools represented—nations, coalitions, humanity? Or, did Jews perpetuate Black alienation?

Anti-Semitism, Calling Out Jews, and the Unstable Role of Jews in the "Judeo-Christian"

Ocean Hill-Brownsville is often framed as a standoff between Black parents and Jewish teachers. However, this picture is incomplete. Advocacy coalitions were more religiously and racially intersectional than single identity groups. The conflict between Black and Jewish New Yorkers, such as it was, has been blown out of proportion. And, Jews' role in the conflict was more complex than simple antagonists because they did not quite belong in the "Judeo-Christian" either.

The "Black parents versus Jewish teachers" framing arose in part because New York City public school teachers were overwhelmingly Jewish, so when Black people criticized teachers, some understood them to be criticizing Jews. However, when Black and Brown people resisted the centralized board, they usually challenged its Judeo-Christian universalism, not Jews. Even those who interrupted the Judeo-Christian fantasy of tolerance proclamations by critiquing Jews did so through a nuanced discussion of Jews and whiteness. For instance, Baldwin called Jews out for adopting whiteness, given Jewish history. He argued that whiteness was inseparable from the Christianity that had oppressed Jews. Instead of succumbing to the power and incognizance of whiteness, he proposed, Jews might demonstrate solidarity with Black and Brown community control advocates.[81]

Jews have consistently been among the most politically liberal ethnic and religious groups, supporting the Civil Rights Movement and the New Deal. Conflicts among Jewish liberals have arisen when Jews must decide between assimilation into American culture and progressive values. Jewish Studies historian Marc Dollinger argues that at such inflection points, around issues like affirmative action, Jews historically have often chosen assimilation over social liberalism.[82] Arguments like Baldwin's primarily critiqued Jews for not choosing social liberalism.

Whatever intrinsic issues were at play in anti-Semitic statements, or even critiques of Jews, some Black New Yorkers tested the idea that Jews comfortably fit in the Judeo-Christian worldview by directing their ire at Jews. In turn, the Board's image of interfaith and interracial tolerance, which had so harmed Black people, collapsed. White Jews joined Judeo-Christianity by virtue of their acceptance into whiteness.[83] Yet their whiteness had limits. Signs of difference, whether dress, practice, or physical appearance, and supersessionist theology persisted.

Some community control advocates made undeniably anti-Semitic remarks. When Brownsville teacher Leslie Campbell read a poem by a fifteen-year-old student on the radio, pandemonium erupted. Called "Anti-Semitism (Dedicated to Albert Shanker)," the President of the United Federation of Teachers, the poem began, "Hey, Jew boy, with that/ Yarmulka on your head, You, pale-faced Jew boy, / I wish you were dead."[84] The poem used derogations of Jewish dress and appearance to justify a death wish on Shanker, whom the student denigrated with repeated use of the term "boy," when in fact he was a powerful man. The rhyme made the poem more memorable, the image of wishing death on a Jew for wearing Jewish garb easier to retain. Isaacs, the math teacher-turned-journalist, interprets the poem as expressing frustration with Jewish participation in whiteness, specifically Shanker's participation in white oppression of Black students, because of the reference to the boy's "pale-face[]." The student later explained that she had learned that the original Semites were Black, so she was reflecting on how Jewish teachers treated Black students.[85] Two things were true at once: The poem contained anti-Semitic language *and* a critique of Jews' participation in anti-Black oppression. In this climate, the anti-Semitic death threat, which Campbell amplified when he took the poem from the classroom to the airwaves, stirred up attention. The radio station received much hate mail and the person who interviewed Campbell learned of a plot to kidnap him. The Jewish Defense League (a group Isaacs calls "paramilitary") got involved.[86] The event was nothing short of painful and inciting.

Anti-Semitism among some Black community control advocates nastily caricatured Jews. For example, an anonymous author wrote an article titled "The Unholy Sons of Shylock" for the *Forum* that used volatile language to argue that "the political objective of black people is power," and that "These objectives," such as running schools, the police, dealing with delinquency, etc., "run counter to Jewish interests."[87] The author trafficked in stereotype, writing: "Our communities are sucked dry and exploited by a Jewish Mafia, which has its tentacles in our groceries, our dwellings, in our schools, indeed in every area of our lives. These shylocks are the principal instruments of suffering and privation in our black communities."[88] Pointing out that Black and Jewish interests may have conflicted if both groups sought power was not inherently anti-Semitic. However, invocation of Shylock, the stereotypically greedy and cheating character in William Shakespeare's *The Merchant of Venice*, certainly was, as was the description of Jews as monsters with tentacles, which conjured images of sneakiness and wicked subhumanity. Tentacles also imply overwhelming power, suffocating prey from all directions.

At the same time, the author echoed other conversations about Jews and whiteness, using violent imagery to argue that Black control was necessary given the failure of perceived Jewish control to help Black children. Similarly, when parents called the UFT President "Adolf Shanker," instead of Albert Shanker, to comment on the UFT's authoritarian nature, the anti-Semitic insult conveyed that Shanker, himself Jewish, was now oppressing people as Hitler had done.

Community control advocates used the widespread phrase "educational genocide" to describe what the Board and UFT promoted. For instance, the *Forum* published an article titled "Needed: A Responsible Jewish Voice" that asked: "How long shall we tolerate the unholy conspiracy of the teachers, the principals, the Board of Education, the superintendent of schools, the custodians and Mayor Lindsay to crush the splendid effort of the community of Ocean Hill-Brownsville to reverse the established patterns of Black educational genocide?"[89] "Conspiracy" echoed the sneaky, powerful Jewish monster, who now inflicted genocide on another group after suffering one themselves. The characterization of the "conspiracy" as "unholy," as the other article also called the "sons of Shylock," pointedly claimed that Jews, as a religious people, ought to do better, and, given the anti-Semitic stereotypes in the articles, even suggested that Judaism itself was unholy.

The phrase "Black educational genocide," in addition to its invocations of the Holocaust, spoke to the high stakes of community control. Rallying cries around "educational genocide" could thus sometimes participate in anti-Semitism and sometimes describe the need for Black survival, often in the same breath. Even those who did not employ anti-Semitic rhetoric used "educational genocide." For example, Wilcox offered "An Alternative to Black Educational Genocide," where he elaborated his views on Black Humanism. Early documenter Ravitch has characterized "educational genocide" as depicting white monstrousness (not explicitly tied to Jews in her reading), which "contributed to an atmosphere in which flamboyant hyperbole replaced rational discourse."[90] Yet, naming "educational genocide" was also a safeguard against obliteration; it spoke to the broader theme of belonging and survival in educational institutions.

One critic took on both Black and Jewish figures. John Hatchett, a Black teacher at PS 68 in Harlem's community control test district, penned a *Forum* article on "The Phenomenon of the Anti-Black Jews and the Black Anglo-Saxon: A Study in Educational Perfidy." As Jews had also been oppressed, Hatchett explained, some Black people wanted Jews to join Black people, instead of dominating them: "I hate the misery, degradation, racism, and cultural genocide daily practiced against my people by a group of people whose entire history should have told them no, this is morally and spiritually wrong."[91] He noted that New York City schools presented an unusual situation where a group typically in the minority, Jews, had seen a "systematic coming of age." The result, to Hatchett, was that Jews "dominate and control the educational bureaucracy of the New York Public School system," given the sheer numbers—Hatchett estimated that 80–85 percent of the teaching staff was Jewish. Hatchett was also concerned with what he called "their power-starved imitators, the Black Anglo-Saxons," Black people whom Hatchett identified as assimilating to white culture instead of looking out for Black children.[92] Calling the relationship between "the Anti-Black Jews and the Black Anglo-Saxon" "coalition or collusion," he blamed the relationship for why "our Black children are being educationally castrated, individually and social devastated to the extent that they are incapable of participating in, and carrying through to a reasonable conclusion, any meaningful educational experience."[93] Hatchett remained unclear regarding whether Blackness or Jewishness rendered his article's subjects untrustworthy, but he saw support for the continued "educational genocide" of Black children as a perversion of Jewishness and Blackness alike.

His argument got to the heart of the purported universalism of the schools' Judeo-Christian morality. Setting "morality and spirituality" apart from "racism," he wrote, "Morality and spirituality are games some people love to play. The prime motivation behind the educational charade being played with Black children is racism—raw naked contempt for Black folk as a people without the Book and therefore without culture or a history and therefore not really human and therefore all that is done is right—because things are made to be manipulated and in the eyes of white America we Black folk are objects to be used, not human beings fully entitled to justice and freedom and knowledge."[94] In other words, claims to morality within the schools perpetuated centuries-old ideas of Black people having no religion, of a deprivation theory of

Black culture, because they erased Black people's humanity.[95] Dollinger's scholarly point that Jews sometimes chose assimilation over otherwise liberal values echoed Hatchett. Like others, Hatchett explained why he thought Jewish assimilation was especially harmful to Black students. In doing so, he sometimes played fast and loose with anti-Semitism.

The most attention-grabbing incident regarding anti-Semitism during community control involved two leaflets in Ocean Hill-Brownsville that the UFT reproduced and distributed, the provenance of which is widely debated. The first pamphlet did not refer to Jews explicitly but Isaacs writes, "it could be argued" that its tone was "strongly pro-black" and "anti-white." The second included "rantings" of "a decidedly anti-Zionist and possibly anti-Semitic nature."[96] It "called Jews 'Middle East Murderers of Colored People' 'Bloodsucking Exploiters' who should not teach African-American history because they would only 'brainwash' black children. The leaflet closed with a warning that an enraged black community was preparing to oust all 'outsiders' and 'missionaries.'"[97] The leaflet's origin was never determined. Isaacs argues that the leaflet was likely fraudulent, "fabricated" by "someone at the UFT."[98] Shanker himself printed half a million copies of the leaflet in UFT headquarters and circulated copies throughout the city "with a message from the teachers union 'Is this what you want for your children? The U.F.T. says no!'"[99] Historian Clarence Taylor reads the leaflet printing as Shanker's "attempt to prove to New Yorkers and the nation that the real threat to education came from black nationalists."[100] Surely, the leaflets aimed to divide Black and Jewish New Yorkers. Leaflets left in Isaacs's mailbox included a cover sheet reading "Please circulate to your Jewish colleagues."[101] Community control participants have since posited that Shanker sought to rile up New Yorkers and pin isolated incidents of anti-Semitism on the whole movement.[102]

Many strike and community control participants later recalled that anti-Semitism was rare in the movement. When asked if anti-Semitism played any role in how parents involved in community control felt toward teachers, organizer Dolores Torres reflected years later in the *Eyes on the Prize* documentary: "I don't think there was any kind of racial, ah, ah, hard feelings there. I mean, every teacher that we had wasn't Jewish. All of the nineteen that we reassigned, they weren't all Jewish. I don't think there was any kind of anti-Semitism." She did not comment on Jewish teachers' allegations that there was anti-Semitism.[103] Isaacs, the white Jewish math teacher community control advocate, however, did agree with Torres when he said he did not experience anti-Semitism or see signs of it. Perhaps most tellingly, twenty years later, Shanker attested that anti-Semitism had nothing to do with the strike but was rather how the public saw it. Given that at the time, Shanker was one of the loudest voices saying anti-Semitism was a core issue, his retraction is remarkable.[104]

The debate about anti-Semitism curiously excluded the impact of anti-Semitism on Jews. Christians began the "tri-faith" alliance of Protestants, Catholics, and Jews with a proclamation to fight against anti-Semitism. Thus, when the UFT blamed the whole community control movement for anti-Semitism, the UFT accused the movement of flouting the schools' central morality. The strategy worked because in the Judeo-Christian worldview, making anti-Semitic statements was among the least Christian things one could do.[105] Jews, however, were not concerned with being un-Christian. In the Judeo-Christian worldview, making anti-Black statements, or creating and perpetuating educational institutions where Black children felt they did not belong, was par for the course.

* * *

Community control advocates disrupted the school-specific Judeo-Christian repertoire. By staking claims to Blackness in public education, community control advocates offered their own visions of what public education looked like when Black children felt they could create their own futures. These visions drew on diverse religious perspectives, including Black Humanism, Black Protestantism, and Pan-Africanism. They also revealed the whiteness of the Judeo-Christian repertoire and its underlying false claim to universality. That the school system's structure changed after the community control experiment is no accident. Community control advocates had shown that the Judeo-Christian center could not hold.

Community control was a form of racial and religious world-making that sought to mold a different world than the one that existed, the one from which *Schempp* and *Engel* had emerged. The advocates' question was not "should there be religion in public schools?" That question assumed a shared understanding of religion as something that could be inserted into or removed from public schools. It assumed that religion was unrelated to the schools' privileging of white students' needs, or assumptions that white students were inherently more moral than Black and Brown students. Rather, their question was: "given that religion made public schools in concert with efforts for racial control, how can we imagine religion differently? What would public education for children of color look like then?"

This book's story ends here, with a moment of change and disruption. Rather than a defeat, the time of community control was when people asked different questions about old institutions to produce new futures. Community control advocates did so in America's quintessential disciplining institution; hope is not lost. As James Baldwin told public school teachers back in 1963, "The paradox of education is precisely this—that as one begins to become conscious one begins to examine the society in which he is being educated."[106] Education disciplines. Education disrupts. All of us who work and learn in educational institutions live in this paradox.

Conclusion

Religion, Race, and the Structure of Public Education

This book has demonstrated that religion and race are continuous dynamics in American public education. It does not make sense to think of them separately.

Let us return to the bifurcation of secularization and desegregation on the September 9, 1963, *Public Schools of New York Staff Bulletin*'s front page. With one column dedicated to *Engel* and *Schempp* and the other dedicated to New York City's integration plan, the bulletin's above-the-fold articles literally framed religion and race as distinct issues occurring in the same place, the public schools. Yet, both articles referred to a shared morality. The article, "Rulings Obeyed, Bible Reading in Assembly Ends," stated, "The Superintendent of Schools and the staff recognize and will fulfill their continuing obligation to inculcate in our young people the fundamental moral values underlying our Nation's cultural heritage."[1] The article immediately to its left, "Integration Plan Sets 4 Main Areas," described the first goal of the school system's racial integration plan: "On the *moral* front the professional staff of the school system commits itself to pursue vigorously the unequivocal integration policy established by the Board of Education."[2] Each article suggested that its topic, religion or race, undergirded the moral formation of New York City students and educators.

Religion continued to shape public schools after the 1960s, Court decisions on prayer and Bible-reading because on-the-ground understandings of religion were embedded in how public schools addressed race and their educational aims. Secularization failed because schools followed the courts in aiming to "de-religionize," or remove religion, through identifying particular religious practices. Desegregation failed, in part, because the Board tried to "de-race" the schools by teaching the value of integration as a color-blind sense of human equality without actively changing who attended which schools.[3] Nevertheless, when articulating the purposes of public education post-*Engel* and *Schempp*, New Yorkers leaned on varied religious resources and visions of American race relations.

Public schools were one site where religion and race morally formed Americans, but public education expands beyond a single setting. Prisons, politics, and families educate the public. Religion and race were active, changing processes that influenced each other. Courts could not lift religion out of morning exercises when administrators used religion's tools to explain their positions on desegregation and juvenile delinquency, or when Black parents recognized the existential and eschatological stakes of public education. From white Jewish Board of Education members to Black Catholic parents, people understood religion and race differently, but each dynamic significantly affected how New Yorkers approached public schools because they were entangled.

New York City public schools became sites for Cold War and Civil Rights religiosity to intersect. Racialized ideas about morality formed New York City public schools' definitions of religion. The Regents' prayer—the prayer at issue in *Engel*—was part of widespread Cold War–era pedagogical practices that institutionalized whiteness by naming moral and spiritual values as a national inheritance. With the educational context surrounding the landmark case in mind, the Regents' prayer more than supported religion or rejected Godless communism. The prayer, and the moral and spiritual values program from which it emerged, instantiated a historical narrative of whiteness into students' curricula. When moral and spiritual values programming came to New York City, Catholic, Jewish, Protestant, teacher, and parent organizations contended over the terms' specific meaning, all weighing in on draft moral and spiritual values programming. The Founding Fathers replaced God in the revision. What seemed like secularization was a theological change, one that implemented Jewish and Catholic theological forms to uphold white Protestant men.

Religion also undergirded school practices relating to the Civil Rights Movements' calls for racial justice, juvenile delinquency prevention, and desegregation, even as public schools were supposedly secularizing. In anti-vandalism cleanup parades through redlined neighborhoods, films, jingles, and more, public schools used "love thy neighbor" to signal racist social scientific ideas about neighborhoods. The embodied enactment of a religious idiom taught that good neighborhoods were white and bad neighborhoods were Black. Ideas about integration as a moral value also contributed to segregation. Integration was a moral value with multiple religious influences. For Black and Puerto Rican communities, the moral value required the act of desegregation; for the Board, it did not, but rather contributed to what the Board identified as an existing Judeo-Christian tradition. Desegregation failed because white New Yorkers could not reconcile, or in some cases, even recognize, different moral definitions of integration.

New Yorkers' understandings of religion and race underlay their views of public education's purpose. The language of Judeo-Christian morality the participants used in the constitutional convention debate circumscribed the public role of religion, and in doing so, narrowed the imaginative possibilities for desegregation funding. Through debates about whether government aid to Catholic schools supported or prohibited desegregation, New Yorkers clarified that they found that one purpose of public or publicly funded education was to teach that respecting religious and racial difference was moral. Yet, this lesson did not produce material change for Black and Puerto Rican New Yorkers, and their concerns birthed community control as an experiment in equitable education. A change in who controlled resources, curriculum, and hiring, community control allowed for Black religious and racial world-making through the public schools among Black New Yorkers who offered distinct, often conflicting, theories to support the same practice. Black New Yorkers had had enough of false promises and laid bare the non-universality of the schools' Judeo-Christianity. Yet, Black New Yorkers did not abandon schools as sites of religious meaning making and moral formation but sought to tailor public schools consistently with visions of liberation and collectivism. Thus, New Yorkers' improvisations with religious and racial national projects contributed to the 1969 decentralization of the city's school system.

To articulate the intersections of religion and race in public education, I have looked for each in archival sources beyond those strictly relating to one or another. Archival institutions are organized much like our siloed understanding of education, religion, and race—the Board of Education Archives, the Archives of the Archdiocese of the City of New York, the Schomburg Center for Research in Black Culture. I visited widely—physically and through online databases. In my analysis, I did not assume sources in education archives would only tell me about schools, sources in religious institutions' archives would only tell me about religion, or that sources in Black history archives would only tell me about race. Rather, building on scholarship across fields that identifies modern religion, race, and education as products of colonialism, I looked for all three across all sources and archives. I applied my method to New York City in the 1950s and 1960s, but any host of regions, time periods, or institutions could be equally fruitful to show that religion and race do not merely signal each other, they sustain each other through educating the public.

Moreover, I have taken seriously Winnifred Fallers Sullivan's proposition to think otherwise about "church-in-law," i.e., the notion that in American law religion is "church-shaped."[4] Hegemonic stories appear alongside counter-hegemonic stories and historical figures whose visions imagined power beyond the simple binary structures of hegemony and counter-hegemony, such as Harlem children's librarian Amy Bush Olatunji, who wrote the Brotherhood Week play, "Panoramic View of Famous Negro Personalities, 1965–1966." Religion and race in public schools persisted even as New Yorkers improvised upon them, rendering any one form impermanent.[5] Such flexibility amidst recognizable power has likely existed in times, places, and institutions to-be-studied, too.

Religion and race in public schools have continued to influence the United States since the 1960s. Studying their intersections offers one historical narrative for how the Cold War and Civil Rights Movement led to the Culture Wars. The parental-theological language of "moral and spiritual values" and the disciplinary practices surrounding youth crime and movement under the ritualized banner of love and brotherhood produced controversies over who and what public schools were (good) for. These controversies developed concepts such as family values, religious freedom, and racial self-determination that have become key to the Culture Wars.[6]

Their intersections can also illuminate the countless news stories on religion and race in public schools with which we are inundated. In the summer of 2022, the Supreme Court of the United States decided two religion cases that many liberals interpreted as "pro-religion": *Kennedy v. Bremerton School District* and *Carson v. Makin*. *Kennedy* found a Washington football coach's post-game prayer at center field a protected expression of the free exercise of religion and of free speech. *Carson* found Maine's requirement that tax dollars only fund "nonsectarian" schools to violate the free exercise clause, thus permitting tax dollars to fund vouchers for sectarian schools. With Charles McCrary, I have argued that beyond concerns about church-state separation, these cases evince that the Court is destroying the common good that public schools promise by further privatizing religion.[7] Privatization enables book banning, censorship, and the discourse about so-called critical race theory in public schools because it is a logic wherein individual parents and students can choose to learn only what makes them feel comfortable, rather than what actually happened in the past. The deification of the Founding Fathers is now law. *Carson* may also be a response to the panic about teaching white children about race in schools, as it adopts school choice as a good.

Kennedy, *Carson*, and the recent siege against teaching about race in schools also demonstrate, again, that religion never disappeared from public schools, even after *Engel* and *Schempp*. Public education is a process of moral formation that instills national values about religion and race in children. Some may abhor and some may celebrate the form that religion takes in *Kennedy* and *Carson*, but the cases are one part of a larger story that is not so much chronological as repertory. The larger story may have predictable features, but it is not already written. Just because religion stayed in public schools does not mean it must look the way it looks now, that it looks the same everywhere, or that such a conservative Court would inevitably be adjudicating these cases. Religion and race in public schools will always share histories and conceptual shapes, but understanding who gains access to the public of public education and how can help us see what people are doing when they talk about religion and race in public schools.

We can see that at their worst, educational institutions inhibit and destroy community; at their best, they formalize and foster it. As participants in such institutions, we play a role in forming the communities we inhabit.

ACKNOWLEDGMENTS

This book is for the teachers and students I have learned from over the years, as well as the ones who might read it.

Thank you to everyone who has made this project possible. I have learned so much from you.

First, thank you to my editor at New York University Press, Jennifer Hammer, who significantly improved this book with her time and keen intellect. I am also grateful to the editors of the North American Religions series, Tracy Fessenden, Laura Levitt, and David Watt, for their support of and enthusiasm for the book. Comments from the two anonymous reviewers helped me better frame my contributions. Many others helped in important ways throughout the production process.

I was able to keep writing with a heavy teaching load thanks to my thoughtful friends with whom I have regularly exchanged drafts for years. Genevieve Creedon, Charles McCrary, Andrew Walker-Cornetta, and Shannon Winston: This book exists, and is better, because of you. Charlie in particular has read versions of this book many times and offered invaluable feedback at each turn. Thanks as well to Nimisha Barton for her sharp insights. Cara Rock-Singer has been a boon intellectual companion and collaborator.

Transylvania University has supported my research through the Bingham Start-Up Funds, David and Betty Jones Faculty Development Fund Grant, and the Dean's Professional Development Fund. I am grateful to Transylvania colleagues who have offered encouragement, especially Priya Ananth, Carole Barnsley, Matthew Bauman, Sharon Brown, Daniel Clausen, Ellen Cox, Jamie Day, Deidra Dennie, Simona Fojtova, Melissa Fortner, Qian Gao, Emily Elizabeth Goodman, Kerri Hauman, Iva Katzarska-Miller, Wei Lin, Melissa McEuen, Martha Ojeda, Bethany Packard, Jeremy Paden, Ken Slepyan, Tiffany Wheeler, Scott Whiddon, and Dean Rebecca Thomas. Thank you to Charlene Harris and Kim Naujokas for coordinating grant logistics, and undergraduate research assistants Sydney Tye and Elia Zonio. Elia deserves special recognition—my ideal reader, she has read every word of this book and offered her insights.

The Young Scholars in American Religion 2020–2023 cohort inspire me and made me believe that I had something to stay. With a bond forged in the pandemic, you all have become lifelong friends whose ideas I always want to hear: Tazeen Ali, Philipp Gollner, Darrius Hills, Courtney Irby, Emily Johnson, Alyssa Maldonado-Estrada, Max Perry Mueller, Samuel Perry, and Ansley Quiros, along with mentors Penny Edgell and Jonathan Walton. Thank you. A special thanks to Tazeen Ali for reading the first two chapters of the book and offering helpful feedback.

I was fortunate to attend graduate school in the Religion Department at Princeton University, where I learned how to be a part of a supportive academic community. Judith Weisenfeld is the best advisor anyone could ever ask for because of the time, energy, resources, and wisdom that she offers her students. Wallace Best cared for and supported my project from start to finish. Thanks as well to faculty Jessica Delgado, Kathryn Gin Lum, Eddie Glaude Jr., Seth Perry, Jeffrey Stout, and Robert Wuthnow for their incredible guidance over the years. In addition to these remarkable formal mentors, the brilliant scholars with whom I attended graduate school are dear friends who changed the way I think about the world: April C. Armstrong, Alda Balthrop-Lewis, Vaughn Booker, Eden Consenstein, Madeline Gambino, Ahmad Greene-Hayes, Rachel Gross, Ryan Harper, Rachel McBride Lindsey, Caleb Maskell, Alyssa Maldonado-Estrada, KB Dennis Meade, Kelsey Moss, Anthony Petro, Beth Stroud, Stephanie Mota Thurston, Andrew Walker-Cornetta, and Kristine Wright.

At Princeton, I regularly shared work with the Religion in the Americas and Religion in Public Life Workshops. In addition to the people mentioned above, Gillian Frank, Kellen Funk, Samantha Jaroszewski, Jenny Wiley Legath, Dan Vaca, Alexander Wamboldt, and Jenny Wiley Legath each responded to my work and offered helpful comments. The Princeton Writing Program also taught me important lessons about motive and managing writing time that allowed me to complete this book. Thanks especially to Christopher Kurpiewski, Judy Swan, and Amanda Irwin Wilkins, as well as others named above. Administrators at Princeton make so much research and learning possible, including this book: thank you, Mary Kay Bodnar, Patricia Bogdziewicz, Melinda DeNero, Margie Duncan, Lorraine Fuhrmann, Jeff Guest, Kerry Smith, Keith Thomas, and Dionne Worthy.

Thank you to the archivists who helped me find sources for this project: at the New York City Municipal Archives, Board of Education archivist David Ment and Dwight Johnson, Linnea Anderson at the Social Welfare History Archives who helped coordinate the Clarke Chambers Travel Grant at the University of Minnesota Libraries, Kate Feighery and Elizabeth Alleva, Archdiocese Archives of New York at St. Joseph's Seminary, Alexsandra Mitchell and Tiana Taliep at the Schomburg Center for Research and Black Culture, Vakil Smallen at the National Education Association Archives at George Washington University, and the helpful archivists at the main branch of the New York Public Library, the Tamiment Library and Robert F. Wagner Labor Archives at New York University, the Columbia University Manuscripts Division, the Brooklyn Public Library, the Library of Congress, the New York State Archives, and the National Archives. Librarians at Princeton University and Transylvania University also aided with research: Princeton librarians Wayne Bivens-Tatum, David Hollander, and Audrey Welber; and Transylvania Librarians Susan Brown, Helen Bischoff, Beth Carpenter, Jason Cooper, Kevin Johnson, Ann Long, and Phillip Walker.

I appreciate all the people who have created opportunities for me to share this work at conferences and on blogs, including Mike Graziano and Zitsi Mirakhur. Thanks also to Adam Becker and Wei Wu for clarity about Rabbi Hillel and Confucius, as well as Shana Sippy for information about juvenile delinquency and the Ten Commandments.

Thanks to those with whom I was able to exchange ideas about this project at many conferences over the years, and especially to those who responded formally: Candy Gunther Brown, Sarah Barringer Gordon, Stefan Lallinger, John Lardas Modern, Winnifred Fallers Sullivan, and Jonathan Zimmerman.

Undergraduate mentors and teachers from Barnard College motivated me to become an academic, especially Randall Balmer, Courtney Bender, Patricia Denison, Evan Haefeli, Wayne Proudfoot, and James Runsdorf. The generous Beinecke Scholarship also made graduate school possible.

Thank you to dear friends for support over the years: Natalie O'Neal Clausen, Nicholas Cummins, Rebecca Feinberg, Jacob Finch, Hyun Young Kim, Kirsten Lindquist, Laura Maranto, Sam Massie, Bryant Rolfe, Rebecca Taylor, Rebecca Tropp, Nicolas Alvear Velastegui, Wenchi Wei, and especially Laura Marostica.

I am grateful to my family for their curiosity and encouragement: the Albas, Hershes, Keefes, Lincolns, Mandarinos, Pozgays, Rawlinsons, and Riboviches especially Elaine Alba, Lisa Alba, Ann Arata, Nick Keefe, Nancy Lincoln, Katherine Lincoln Pozgay, Rome Pozgay, Max Ribovich, Natalya Ribovich, and the late Betty and Harry Lincoln. My parents Deborah Hersh and John Ribovich inspired my love of learning and made it possible for me to learn. I am sad that I never got to know my parents' parents, Genevieve (Joseph) Foster, Morris Hersh, Joseph Ribovich, and Pauline (Woldenberg) Hersh Shulman. Pauline attended James Monroe High School, Bronx, NY, class of 1949. I would have loved to talk to her about this project.

August Lincoln Pozgay, my husband, has been my best conversation partner and biggest champion since before this project began. I am grateful that he has always imagined his dreams as part of our dreams. He has moved to New Jersey and Kentucky for my work, read countless drafts, and watched our child so I could work. August, I could not have done this project without you.

I am grateful for my child, Amelia Beth Pozgay; I submitted the full version of the manuscript two weeks before giving birth to her and the final version in her first year of life. Amelia, I wonder what you think of all this and am so excited to find out.

NOTES

INTRODUCTION

1 Gaston, "Interpreting Judeo-Christianity in America," 301–302, points out that while Judeo-Christianity may seem a classic "invented tradition," the term obscures that all traditions are invented. However, it can also illuminate the same. I see the school-specific Judeo-Christianity as a tradition that, like all traditions, was invented, and invented by twentieth-century New Yorkers.

2 On collective memory as a mode of interpreting the past, see Elizabeth Castelli, *Martyrdom and Memory: Early Christian Culture Making* (New York: Columbia University Press, 2004), 10–32.

3 For example: Biondi, *To Stand and Fight*; Sugrue, *Sweet Land of Liberty*.

4 *Everson v. Board of Education*, 330 U.S. 1 (1947); *McCollum v. Board of Education*, 333 U.S. 203 (1948).

5 Eliza Shapiro, "Segregation Has Been the Story of New York City's Schools for 50 Years," *New York Times*, March 26, 2019, www.nytimes.com.

6 Lorrin Thomas, *Puerto Rican Citizen: History and Political Identity in Twentieth-Century New York City* (Chicago: University of Chicago Press, 2010); Isabel Wilkerson, *The Warmth of Other Suns: The Epic Story of America's Great Migration* (New York: Random House, 2010).

7 Cone, *Black Theology and Black Power*; Hucks, *Yoruba Traditions and African American Religious Nationalism*; Sorett, *Spirit in the Dark*; Weisenfeld, *New World A-Coming*. I use "religio-racial movements" here in Weisenfeld's meaning on 5–8.

8 For instance, see: Delmont, *Why Busing Failed*; Isaacs, *Inside Ocean Hill-Brownsville*; Lewis, *New York City Public Schools from Brownsville to Bloomberg*; Brian Purnell, *Fighting Jim Crow in the County of Kings: The Congress of Racial Equality in Brooklyn* (Lexington: University Press of Kentucky, 2013); Taylor, *Knocking at Our Own Door*.

9 "Episode 4: Agitate! Educate! Organize!," *School Colors Podcast*.

10 "Episode 3: Third Strike," *School Colors Podcast*; Podair, *The Strike that Changed New York*; Ravitch, *The Great School Wars*.

11 Lewis, *New York City Public Schools from Brownsville to Bloomberg*, 10 and 15.

12 James W. Fraser, *Between Church and State: Religion and Public Education in a Multicultural America* (New York: St. Martin's Press, 1999); Gordon, *The Spirit of the Law*; Green, *The Third Disestablishment*; David Komline, *The Common School Awakening: Religion and the Transatlantic Roots of American Public Educa-*

tion (New York: Oxford University Press, 2020); Kruse, *One Nation Under God*; Schultz, *Tri-Faith America*.

13 For instance, Jonathan Zimmerman studies religion and race together. He suggests that the "myth" of American history prevailed in history curriculum throughout the twentieth century, and that in the "history wars," "the combatants rarely subjected America itself to analysis: even as different groups struggled to insert their own heroes into the national story, they rarely challenged that narrative's broader contours and themes." Zimmerman challenges the mythological narrative by arguing that "the infusion of 'diversity' into American textbooks—however laudable in its own right—actually delayed rather than promoted the critical dialogue that a healthy democracy demands." *Whose America?*, 8. By looking at how the "history wars" and "religion wars" were not so separate in New York City, I show that people on the ground also challenged the American myth and the Judeo-Christian values that school officials claimed went with it. Tracy Fessenden and Kathleen Holscher offer important exceptions to the general undertheorizing of religion in *Culture and Redemption* and *Religious Lessons*, respectively.

14 Kristy Slominski, *Teaching Moral Sex: A History of Religion and Sex Education in the United States* (New York: Oxford University Press, 2021), 4–5.

15 Charles Long, *Significations: Signs, Symbols, and Images in the Interpretation of Religion* (Aurora, CO: Fortress Press, 1986); J. Z. Smith, "Religion, Religions, Religious," in *Critical Terms for Religious Studies*, edited by Mark C. Taylor (Chicago: University of Chicago Press, 1998), 269–282.

16 Carter, *Race*; Conroy-Krutz, *Christian Imperialism*; Masuzawa, *The Invention of World Religions*; Moss, "On Earth as It Is in Heaven."

17 Imhoff, "Belief," in Dubler and Weiner, *Religion, Law, USA*, 26–39.

18 Charles Taylor, *A Secular Age* (Cambridge, MA: Harvard University Press, 2007), 22, 530–531, among others.

19 Cooper, *Family Values*; Hartman, *A War for the Soul of America*; James Davison Hunter, *Culture Wars: The Struggle to Define America: Making Sense of the Battles over the Family, Art, Education, Law, and Politics* (New York: Basic Books, 1991); Kruse, *White Flight*; Lassiter, *The Silent Majority*; Petrzela, *Classroom Wars*; Zimmerman, *Whose America?*.

20 Finbarr Curtis, *The Production of American Religious Freedom* (New York: New York University Press, 2016); Dubler and Weiner, eds., *Religion, Law, USA*; Gordon, *The Spirit of the Law*; McCrary, *Sincerely Held*; Winnifred Fallers Sullivan, *The Impossibility of Religious Freedom* (Princeton, NJ: Princeton University Press, 2007) and *Prison Religion: Faith-Based Reform and the Constitution* (Princeton, NJ: Princeton University Press, 2009); Tisa Wenger, *We Have a Religion: The 1920s Pueblo Indian Dance Controversy and American Religious Freedom* (Chapel Hill: University of North Carolina Press, 2009).

21 Gaston, "Interpreting Judeo-Christianity in America," 297; Gaston, *Imagining Judeo-Christian America*; Schultz, *Tri-Faith America*; Mark Silk, "Notes on the Judeo-Christian Tradition in America," *American Quarterly* 36:1 (1984): 65–85, 67.

22 Examples of this include Balmer, *Bad Faith*; Kruse, *White Flight*; Lassiter, *The Silent Majority*.

23 Ribovich and Rock-Singer, "Educating for the New Jerusalem."

24 Education scholars have long considered public schools' purpose and have sometimes engaged religion in doing so. For example: Robert N. Gross, *Public v. Private: The Early History of School Choice* (New York: Oxford University Press, 2018); David Labaree, "Public Good, Private Goods: The American Struggle Over Educational Goals," *American Educational Research* 34:1 (1997): 39–81; David Tyack and Larry Cuban, *Tinkering Toward Utopia: A Century of Public School Reform* (Cambridge, MA: Harvard University Press, 1995).

25 Courtney Bender, "How and Why to Study Up: Frank Lloyd Wright's Broadacre City and the Study of Lived Religion," *Nordic Journal of Religion and Society* 29:2 (2016): 100–116. Bender's full quotation on p. 112 is "part of 'the secular' imagination has also been less punitive and restrictive." While I argue that it is less restrictive, the public school mode of governance can punish.

26 Talal Asad, *Formations of the Secular: Christianity, Islam, Modernity* (Stanford, CA: Stanford University Press, 2003), 1; McCrary, *Sincerely Held*, 7–12.

27 Influenced by Courtney Bender and Ann Taves, eds., *What Matters?: Ethnographies of Value in a Not So Secular Age* (New York: Columbia University Press, 2012), 1–33. Also see Elayne Oliphant, *The Privilege of Being Banal: Art, Secularism, and Catholicism in Paris* (Chicago: University of Chicago Press, 2021), 4, on how people "had to overlook how Catholic objects, images, and spaces—from crucifixes to paintings of Christian narratives to neogothic churches—inundate public life in Paris alike" to claim "that Catholicism can no longer be seen in the nation today." In mid-century New York City, New Yorkers would have to overlook religious configurations beyond Protestantism to argue that religion no longer influenced the nation, *and* many did not share that perspective. Though Lois Lee's interlocutors separated religion from nonreligion more than the historical actors I study, she describes secularity, religion, and nonreligion as ongoing processes, which helps frame my approach to thinking beyond Protestant hegemony's epistemic categories. Lois Lee, *Recognizing the Non-religious: Reimagining the Secular* (New York: Oxford University Press, 2015), 13–16.

28 Gin Lum, "The Historyless Heathen and the Stagnating Pagan."

29 Dubler and Lloyd, "Mass Incarceration is Religious (and So Is Abolition)," makes a similar point about prisons.

CHAPTER 1. THE RACIALIZED MORAL AND SPIRITUAL VALUES OF NEW YORK STATE

1 For names of the Regents in 1951, see "Regents of the State of New York," in "Moral and Spiritual Values in Education," Folder 16, Box 41, Series B0459, Deputy Commissioner James E. Allen's Subject Files, New York State Archives (hereafter cited as Allen Files). I have determined race and gender demographics through Ancestry database searches, locating draft registration cards and census

records. I have also consulted Albert B. Corey, Hugh M. Flick, and Frederick A. Morse, eds., *The Regents of the State University of New York, 1784–1959* (Albany: University of the State of New York, 1959), https://babel.hathitrust.org. Finally, multiple sources refer to psychologist Kenneth Clark as the first African American Regent, such as "Kenneth Bancroft Clark," Robert Penn Warren's Who Speaks for the American Negro?: An Archival Collection, Jean and Alexander Heard Library, Vanderbilt University, https://whospeaks.library.vanderbilt.edu. At the least, Roger Williams Straus was Jewish, and John F. Brosnan was Catholic. Wenger, *Religious Freedom*, 143–146, 160; "Roger Williams Straus and Gladys Guggenheim Straus," Straus Historical Society, Inc., Newsletter, 12:2 (February 2011), www.straushistoricalsociety.org; Wolfgang Saxon, "John Brosnan and, Former Head of State U. and Regents Unit," *New York Times*, April 15, 1982, www.nytimes.com. Schultz comments that the 1951 Regents "included members from the three major faiths" in *Tri-Faith America*, 123. On working with religious leaders, see Gordon, *The Spirit of the Law*, 86.

2 "The Regents' Statement on Moral and Spiritual Training in the Schools," Meeting Minutes, February 7, 1952, Folder 484, Box 29, Series 281, New York City Board of Education Records, New York City Municipal Archives (hereafter cited as NYCBER).

3 Gordon, *The Spirit of the Law*, 86. For more on the uproar, see Benjamin Sasse, "The Anti-Madalyn Majority: Secular Left, Religious Right, and the Rise of Reagan's America," PhD diss. (Yale University, 2004), https://blurblawg.typepad.com.

4 Gordon, *The Spirit of the Law*, 86–89.

5 "The Regents' Statement on Moral and Spiritual Training in the Schools," 1951, Meeting Minutes, February 7, 1952, Folder 484, Box 29, Series 281, NYCBER; Folder 34, Box 43, Series W0104-77, Allen Files; and *Jesuit Education Quarterly*.

6 1954 for the Pledge; 1956 for currency. Jeffrey Owen Jones and Peter Myer, *The Pledge: A History of the Pledge of Allegiance* (New York: Thomas Dunne Books St. Martin's Press, 2010); Richard J. Ellis, *To the Flag: The Unlikely History of the Pledge of Allegiance* (Lawrence: University Press of Kansas, 2005).

7 Anne Blankenship also suggests that the roots of this religious boom are in Franklin Delano Roosevelt's administration's incarceration of Japanese Americans. Anne Blankenship, *Christianity, Social Justice, and the Japanese American Incarceration* (Chapel Hill: University of North Carolina Press, 2016), 5.

8 Robert Wuthnow, *The Restructuring of American Religion: Society and Faith Since World War II* (Princeton, NJ: Princeton University Press, 1989), 11.

9 Kruse, *One Nation Under God*.

10 For one example of a morality tale, see: *Boy with a Knife*, Film, directed by Laslo Benedek. Also: *The Ten Commandments*, Film, directed by Cecil B. DeMille (1956; Los Angeles: Paramount Pictures); Weissman Joselit, *Set in Stone*.

11 Taylor, *Reds at the Blackboard*, 3, 178.

12 "The Regents' Statement on Moral and Spiritual Training in the Schools."

13 *Engel v. Vitale*, 370 U.S. 421 (1962).

14 Some scholars have highlighted this program. Bruce Dierenfield notes that the Regents' statement sought to curtail juvenile delinquency in *The Battle Over School Prayer: How* Engel v. Vitale *Changed America* (Lawrence: University Press of Kansas, 2007), 70–71; Kruse discusses how the debate over the Regents' prayer and moral and spiritual values "foment[ed] religious tension" in *One Nation Under God*, 170–178; Jonathan Zimmerman mentions moral and spiritual values programs as one way that American public schools sought to identify "a 'common core' of values and practices that could bind the different faiths together" in *Whose America?*, 153–155.

15 "The Regents' Recommendations for School Programs on America's Moral and Spiritual Heritage," the University of the State of New York, The State Education Department, Unanimously Adopted by the Regents on March 25, 1955, Folder 1, Box 44, Series W0104-77, Allen Files.

16 The New York State Education Department, "For Immediate Release," June 29, 1962, Folder 34, Box 43, Allen Files.

17 This mode of control parallels that examined in Hulsether, "The Grammar of Racism."

18 Arthur Levitt to the Members of the Board of Education and the Superintendent of Schools, October 20, 1952, Folder 42, Box 48, Subseries 8, Series 911, NYCBER.

19 Commissioner James E. Allen Jr. to City, Village and District Superintendents of Schools, Re: Moral and Spiritual Values in the Schools, Sept. 9, 1957, Folder 35, Box 43, Series W0104-77, Allen Files.

20 "Religion In Schools Is Still a Controversy," The Religion News Service, Folder 135, Box 55, Subseries 8, Series 911, NYCBER. The "American Way of Life" rhetoric invokes Herberg, *Protestant-Catholic-Jew*. For critical analysis of the cultural fractures in "American Way" language, see Ronit Stahl, "A Jewish America and a Protestant Civil Religion: Will Herberg, Robert Bellah, and Mid-Twentieth Century American Religion," *Religions* 6:2 (2015): 434–450; and Wendy L. Wall, *Inventing the "American Way": The Politics of Consensus from the New Deal to the Civil Rights Movement* (New York: Oxford University Press, 2008) for a discussion of how Americans were not united in belief but in the politically useful concept of the "American Way."

21 Benjamin Fine, "Education in Review: Regional Discussions Are Preparing the Way for the National White House Conference," *New York Times*, June 26, 1955; Alfred E. Parker, "Consensus on Religion in the Schools," *The Phi Delta Kappan* 38:4 (Jan. 1957): 145–147, 147.

22 "Religion In Schools Is Still a Controversy"; Zimmerman, *Whose America?*, 155.

23 "Moral and Spiritual Values in the Public Schools," Folder 3, Box 1050, Educational Policies Commission Series, National Education Association Records, Special Collections Research Center, George Washington University (hereafter cited as NEAR). Also quoted in Judah Goldin, "Public Education and Spiritual Values," *Religious Education*, January 1, 1953 (48): 81–84, 83; and Rt. Rev. John J. Voight, "Moral and Spiritual Values in Public Education," 93.

24 "Moral and Spiritual Values in the Public Schools."
25 Voight, "Moral and Spiritual Values in Public Education," 93. The following identifies that his appointment was for the Archdiocese of New York: "Program Twenty-Second Annual Convention the American Catholic Sociological Society," *American Catholic Sociological Review*, 167.
26 Voight, "Moral and Spiritual Values in Public Education," 93.
27 The State University of New York, The State Department of Education, "Moral and Spiritual Values," Tentative and Confidential, undated, Folder 15, Box 41, Series B0459, Allen Files, cites William James as inspiration for "spiritual," drawing in interesting ways on pragmatism and New Thought to expand beyond Christianity. "Progress Report on Teaching Moral and Spiritual Values in the Public School," November 1953, Folder 5, Box 20, Series W0103–78, Education Department Commissioner Lewis A. Wilson Subject Files, New York State Archives (hereafter cited as Wilson Files), includes more details that echo the quoted document.
28 "The Regents' Recommendations for School Programs on America's Moral and Spiritual Heritage."
29 "The Regents' Recommendations for School Programs on America's Moral and Spiritual Heritage."
30 "New Crises for Education," *Newsweek* Platform Issue, January 1952, Folder 33, Box 40, Series B0459, Allen Files.
31 "Fireworks on the Academic Front," *Newsweek* Platform Issue, January 1952, Folder 33, Box 40, Series B0459, Allen Files.
32 "Fireworks on the Academic Front."
33 "Fireworks on the Academic Front."
34 "Fireworks on the Academic Front."
35 "Report of Special Committee of the Board of Regents in the Inquiry Relative to Subversive Organizations," September 24, 1953, Folder 1, Box 18, Series W0103–78, Wilson Files.
36 "Report of Special Committee of the Board of Regents in the Inquiry Relative to Subversive Organizations."
37 Murray Illson, "State's Teachers Declare Loyalty," *New York Times*, November 26, 1952, Folder 33, Box 40, Series B0459, Allen Files.
38 "A Message from Your Public School: Moral and Spiritual Values for Your Children," National Education Association, Folder 13, Box 8, Series W0103–78, Wilson Files.
39 "Fireworks on the Academic Front."
40 See chapter 3 of this book; Ribovich, "Saving Black Boys."
41 Wenger, *Religious Freedom*, 160; "Roger Williams Straus and Gladys Guggenheim Straus."
42 Gaston, *Imagining Judeo-Christian America*, 32–39.
43 "Address by Roger Williams Straus," New York Academy of Public Education, May 19, 1953, Folder 15, Box 41, Series B0459, Allen Files.
44 "Address by Roger Williams Straus."

45 "Address by Roger Williams Straus."
46 Herberg, *Protestant-Catholic-Jew*; Schultz, *Tri-Faith America*.
47 Gaston, *Imagining Judeo-Christian America*, 21–46.
48 Performance here does not mean untrue, but the enactment of rituals, habits, and behaviors that cultivate ways of being in the world.
49 Robert Tracy McKenzie, "The Founding Fathers and Warren G. Harding," *Faith and History*, June 22, 2015, https://faithandamericanhistory.wordpress.com.
50 For more on conversations about the revisions, see "Regent Brosnan's First Revision of Doctor Getman's Report" and "Suggestions for Revision—made by Doctor Getman September 1954" in Folder 18, Box 41, Series B0459, Allen Files.
51 "Suggestions for Teaching Moral and Spiritual Values in Public Schools," June 1953, Folders 17 and 18, Box 41, Series B0459, Allen Files.
52 "The Role of Jews in American History," in "Suggestions for Teaching Moral and Spiritual Values in Public Schools," June 1953, Folder 18, Box 41, Series B0459, Allen Files.
53 On Jews in early American history, see: Michael Hoberman, Laura Arnold Liebman, and Hilit Surowitz-Israel, eds., *Jews in the Americas, 1776–1826* (New York: Routledge, 2018); Jonathan Sarna, *American Judaism: A New History* (New Haven, CT: Yale University Press, 2004).
54 "Suggestions for Teaching Moral and Spiritual Values in Public Schools," June 1953, Folder 18, Box 41, Series B0459, Allen Files.
55 L. A. Wilson to Clarence Linton, February 13, 1952, Folder 15, Box 8, Series W0103–78, Wilson Files.
56 L. A. Wilson to Clarence Linton; Frederick Moffitt to L. A. Wilson, February 20, 1953, Folder 6, Box 20, Series W0103–78, Wilson Files; and Special to the New York Times, "Dr. Arthur Getman, State Educator, 81, *New York Times*, September 15, 1968, www.nytimes.com.
57 Paul Meacham to James Allen, Jr., October 5, 1959, Folder 50, Box 12, Series B0444–78, New York State Education Department Commissioner's Interim Subject Files, New York State Archives.
58 "Progress Report on Teaching Moral and Spiritual Values in the Public School," November 1953, Folder 15, Box 41, Series B0459, Allen Files.
59 "Progress Report on Teaching Moral and Spiritual Values in the Public School."
60 Mrs. Irving (Bella) Crown to Board of Regents, February 27, 1952 and L. A. Wilson to Mrs. Irving Crown, March 4, 1952, Folder 15, Box 8, Series W0103–78, Wilson Files.
61 See, e.g., Herzog, *The Spiritual-Industrial Complex*; Kruse, *One Nation Under God*; Schultz, *Tri-Faith America*.
62 Wilson to Crown.
63 "The Regents' Recommendations for School Programs on America's Moral and Spiritual Heritage."
64 "The Regents' Recommendations for School Programs on America's Moral and Spiritual Heritage."

65 Thomas Jefferson to Benjamin Rush, September 23, 1800, Founders Online, National Archive, https://founders.archives.gov.

66 Brett Bertucio, "The Political Theology of Hugo Black," *Journal of Law and Religion* 35:1 (2020): 79–101, doi: 10.1017/jlr.2020.10, describes Black's "syncretic civil moralism," Black's participation in the Klan, and his anti-Catholicism, 86–87; *Engel v. Vitale*, fn 21 of majority opinion. Also see Hamburger, *Separation of Church and State*, 422–434.

67 Taylor, *Reds at the Blackboard*, 3.

68 "Report of Special Committee of the Board of Regents in the Inquiry Relative to Subversive Organizations."

69 "Report of Special Committee of the Board of Regents in the Inquiry Relative to Subversive Organizations," 319; Clarence Taylor, "Dreamers and Fighters: The NYC Teacher Purges," http://dreamersandfighters.com. Andrew Hartman discusses the Teachers Union as explicitly anti-racist and the Board, especially Jansen, as racist in *Education and the Cold War*, 81–84. See chapter 2 for more.

70 "Report of Special Committee of the Board of Regents in the Inquiry Relative to Subversive Organizations."

71 "More bias-fighting teachers fired in N.Y.," *National Guardian*, Folder 6, Box 1, Series 591, NYCBER. Undated, best guess 1952, given its adherence to a letter from March 1952.

72 Committee for the Reinstatement of the 8 Suspended Teachers, "An Appeal to the Jewish People of New York From Eight Teachers Suspended from the Schools by Superintendent Jansen," undated, Folder 6, Box 1, Series 591, NYCBER.

73 Hartman, *Education and the Cold War*, 84; Weiner, *Power, Protest, and the Public Schools*, 115–116.

74 Jewish Teachers Association, A Press Release, June 1, 1950, Folder 6, Box 1, Series 591, NYCBER.

75 Committee for the Reinstatement of the 8 Suspended Teachers, "An Appeal to the Jewish People of New York From Eight Teachers Suspended from the Schools by Superintendent Jansen."

76 "An Appeal to the Jewish People of New York From Eight Teachers Suspended from the Schools by Superintendent Jansen."

77 "Brief Amicus Curiae of the New York City Council of the American Jewish Congress," Folder 6, Box 1, Series 591, NYCBER.

78 "Statement adopted by the New York Board of Rabbis on Wednesday, December 26, 1951," Folder 144, Box 55, Series 911, NYCBER.

79 "Resolution Sent by the New York Board of Rabbis to New York Board of Education," April 21, 1955, Folder 6, Box 1, Series 591, NYCBER. Thanks to Cara Rock-Singer for helping me parse this reasoning.

80 "The Jewish Law Pertaining to the 'Mosor' or Informant," Folder 6, Box 1, Series 591, NYCBER.

81 "Brief Amicus Curiae of the New York City Council of the American Jewish Congress."

82 "Brief Amicus Curiae of the New York City Council of the American Jewish Congress."

83 This example presents a different case than Tisa Wenger's claim that Jews "became white" by adopting their religiosity as a form of difference in tri-faith work. Here, Jews partook in pro-America, pro-religion work while also underlining their own alterity, religiously, racially, and politically. Wenger, *Religious Freedom*, 143–187.

84 McCrary, *Sincerely Held*, 7–12.

85 Resolution, City School District of New Rochelle, February 5, 1952, Folder 145, Box 55, Subseries 8, Series 911, NYCBER; Donald K. Phillips to All Members of the Professional Staff, February 7, 1952, Folder 145, Box 55, Subseries 8, Series 911, NYCBER; and *Rochellean Yearbook*, New Rochelle High School, New Rochelle, NY: 1958, E-Yearbook.com, www.e-yearbook.com, 12.

86 "Statement adopted by the New York Board of Rabbis on Wednesday, December 26, 1951," Folder 144, Box 55, Series 911, NYCBER.

87 "Statement adopted by the New York Board of Rabbis on Wednesday, December 26, 1951."

88 "For Immediate Release, March 6, 1952," Folder 144, Box 55, Subseries 8, Series 911, NYCBER; "For Immediate Release, February 7, 1952," Folder 144, Box 55, Subseries 8, Series 911, NYCBER.

89 Schultz briefly summarizes the "America" alternative in *Tri-Faith America*, 123–124.

90 "Col. Arthur Levitt Explains Strength of Religion," *Jewish Teachers Association Bulletin*, May 1, 1953, Folder 6, Box 1, Series 591, NYCBER, 1 and 4.

91 Levitt to the Members of the Board of Education and the Superintendent of Schools.

92 Interesting parallels to Rock-Singer, "A Prophetic Guide for a Perplexed World."

93 Levitt to the Members of the Board of Education and the Superintendent of Schools. For more on "America," see Robert James Branham and Stephen J. Hartnett, *Sweet Freedom's Song: "My Country 'Tis of Thee" and Democracy in America* (New York: Oxford University Press, 2002), 56–65.

94 Levitt to the Members of the Board of Education and the Superintendent of Schools.

95 Levitt to the Members of the Board of Education and the Superintendent of Schools.

96 "The Development of Moral and Spiritual Ideals in the Public Schools."

97 "4th Stanza of 'America' Subterfuge for Introducing Prayer in Schools," *New York Teachers News*, January 10, 1953, Folder 145, Box 55, Subseries 8, Series 911, NYCBER.

98 Lillian Ashe to Clauson, January 21, 1953, Folder 145, Box 55, Subseries 8, Series 911, NYCBER; Meeting Minutes, January 15, 1953, Folder 484, Box 29, Series 281, NYCBER.

99 Clauson to L. Ashe, January 23, 1953, Folder 145, Box 55, Subseries 8, Series 911, NYCBER.

CHAPTER 2. NEW YORK CITY AND THE DEIFICATION OF THE FOUNDING FATHERS

1 Arthur Levitt to the Members of the Board of Education and the Superintendent of Schools, October 20, 1952, Folder 42, Box 48, Subseries 8, Series 911, NYCBER; "The Regents' Statement on Moral and Spiritual Training in the Schools," Meeting Minutes, February 7, 1952, Folder 484, Box 29, Series 281, NYCBER.

2 Lillian Ashe to Clauson, January 21, 1953, Folder 145, Box 55, Subseries 8, Series 911, NYCBER; Meeting Minutes, January 15, 1953, Folder 484, Box 29, Series 281, NYCBER.

3 "The Development of Moral and Spiritual Ideals in the Public Schools," adopted by the NYC Board of Education on October 4, 1956, Folder 120, Box 14, Series 668, NYCBER.

4 Hartman, *Education and the Cold War*, 84; Weiner, *Power, Protest, and the Public Schools*, 115–116.

5 "Jansen Discounts Religion 'Balance,'" *New York Times*, December 12, 1952, 31.

6 "Moral and Spiritual Values and the Schools," Office of the Superintendent of Schools, Board of Education of the City of New York, June 14, 1955, Folder 135, Box 55, Subseries 8, Series 911, NYCBER.

7 "The Development of Moral and Spiritual Ideals in the Public Schools," adopted by the NYC Board of Education on October 4, 1956, Folder 120, Box 14, Series 668, NYCBER, 10.

8 On theology, see Sullivan, *Church State Corporation*.

9 Green, *The Third Disestablishment*; Greenawalt, *Does God Belong in Public Schools?*; and Holscher, *Religious Lessons*; Adam Laats, "Our Schools, Our Country: American Evangelicals, Public Schools, and the Supreme Court Decisions of 1962 and 1963," *Journal of Religious History* (Australia) 36: 3 (September 2012): 1–16, for example.

10 Todd, "The Temple of Religion and the Politics of Religious Pluralism," in Bender and Klassen, eds., *After Pluralism*, 203; and Wenger, *Religious Freedom*, 143–187.

11 Schultz, *Tri-Faith America*, 59.

12 "Moral and Spiritual Values and the Schools."

13 Gaston, *Imagining Judeo-Christian America*, 21–45.

14 McCrary, *Sincerely Held*, 138–139, 145.

15 "Moral and Spiritual Values and the Schools."

16 Joshua Dubler, "Review: Religion and the Practices of Popular Constitutionalism: Sarah Gordon's 'The Spirit of the Law,'" *Law and Social Inquiry* 36:4 (2011): 1062–1088, 1079, doi: 10.1111/j.1747-4469.2011.01261.x; and Gordon, *The Spirit of the Law*, 2, 214. Gordon indicates that "The tension between popular and technical constitutionalism reflected the difference between the spirit and the letter of the law."

17 UPA to The Board of Education of the City of New York, Re: "A Guiding Statement for Supervisors and Teachers" on "Moral and Spiritual Values and the

Schools" adopted by the Board of Superintendents on June 14, 1955, November 21, 1955, Folder 134, Box 55, Subseries 8, Series 911, NYCBER. Underline in original.

18 Thomas Jefferson, "Virginia Statute on Religious Freedom," 1786.

19 *Everson v. Board of Education*, 330 U.S. 1 (1947); Thomas Jefferson to Danbury Baptists, January 1, 1802, Library of Congress, www.loc.gov, accessed August 21, 2020; and *Reynolds v. United States*, 98 U.S. 145 (1879).

20 Stanley Rowland Jr., "School Spiritual Guide Approved by 2 Faiths, Opposed by Rabbis," *New York Times*, November 25, 1955, 1.

21 William G. Blair, "Andrew Clauson Jr. Is Dead," *New York Times*, August 1983, D15.

22 Andrew Clauson to Interested Organizations, November 10, 1955, Folder 134, Box 55, Subseries 8, Series 911, NYCBER.

23 *Everson v. Board of Education*, 330 U.S. 1 (1947).

24 UPA to The Board of Education of the City of New York.

25 UPA to The Board of Education of the City of New York.

26 Abraham Lefkowitz, "The Guild Protests the Report on 'Moral and Spiritual Values and the Schools,'" Folder 1, Box 61, WAG 022, United Federation of Teachers Records, Tamiment Library/Robert F. Wagner Labor Archives, New York University (hereafter cited as UFTR).

27 "Statement adopted by the New York Board of Rabbis on Wednesday, December 26, 1951," Folder 144, Box 55, Series 911, NYCBER; "The Development of Moral and Spiritual Ideals in the Schools." Spelling in above is "fibre" and here is "fiber."

28 On Lefkowitz leading the break with the Communist "Rank and File" of the Teachers Union in 1935 and helping create the Teachers Guild, see Taylor, *Reds at the Blackboard*, 1, 2, 5, 16–33.

29 *Abington v. Schempp*, 374 U.S. 203 (1963); and Sarah Imhoff, "The Creation Story, or How We Learned to Stop Worrying and Love *Schempp*," *Journal of the American Academy of Religion* 84:2 (2016): 466–497, doi: 10.1093/jaarel/lfv060.

30 Specific quotations from "Moral and Spiritual Values and the Schools," critiques in: "Teachers Fight Spiritual Code: Their Guild Favors Teaching Moral Values but Objects to Proposed Method," *New York Times*, September 14, 1956, 14; Lefkowitz, "The Guild Protests the Report on 'Moral and Spiritual Values and the Schools,'" Folder 1, Box 6a, UFTR.

31 Samuel Moyn, *Not Enough: Human Rights in an Unequal World* (Cambridge, MA: Harvard University Press, 2019).

32 Rowland, "School Spiritual Guide."

33 For more on Catholic theology around human rights in this time, see Sarah Shortall, *Soldiers of God in a Secular World: Catholic Theology and Twentieth-Century French Politics* (Cambridge, MA: Harvard University Press, 2021).

34 Rowland, "School Spiritual Guide."

35 "Schools Alter Their Code on Moral Values," *New York Times*, July 29, 1956, Folder 134, Box 55, Subseries 8, Series 911, NYCBER.

36 Leonard Buder, "Hearing Put Off on School Code," *New York Times*, August 23, 1956; "Summary of Contacts with Organizations Re The Development of

Moral and Spiritual Ideals in the Public Schools," August 20, 1956, Folder 134, Box 55, Subseries 8, Series 911, NYCBER; Siegel to Hon. Charles Silver, Telegram, July 27, 1956, Folder 135, Box 55, Subseries 8, Series 911, NYCBER; For Release, Re: Board of Education's Statement on Moral and Spiritual Ideals in the Public Schools, July 30, 1956 Folder 134, Box 55, Subseries 8, Series 911, NYCBER, among others.

37 "Moral and Spiritual Values—Current Developments," Folder 134, Box 55, Subseries 8, Series 911, NYCBER.

38 Isadore Fried to Executive Council Members, August 13, 1956, Folder 134, Box 55, Subseries 8, Series 911, NYCBER.

39 Gladys Harburger to "President," August 24, 1956, Folder 135, Box 55, Subseries 8, Series 911, NYCBER.

40 Meeting Minutes, October 4, 1956, Folder 120, Box 14, Series 668, NYCBER.

41 Gene Currivan, "School Board Member Resigns; Brooklyn Minister Cites Health," *New York Times*, February 5, 1958, 17.

42 Rodney G. S. Carter, "Of Things Said and Unsaid: Power, Archival Silences, and Power in Silence," *Archivaria* 61 (2006): 215–233; Michel-Rolph Trouillot, *Silencing the Past: Power and the Production of History* (Boston: Beacon Press, 1995).

43 Jansen and Allen, *Distant Lands: Part Two*, 151.

44 Weiner, *Power, Protest, and the Public Schools*, 114–116.

45 Weiner, *Power, Protest, and the Public Schools*, 116. Also see chapter 1 of this book.

46 Weisenfeld, *New World A-Coming*, 201, quoting the *Norfolk Journal*.

47 Meyer, "Medium."

48 "The Development of Moral and Spiritual Ideals in the Public Schools."

49 "The Development of Moral and Spiritual Ideals in the Public Schools," and "Moral and Spiritual Values and the Schools."

50 "Moral and Spiritual Values and the Schools."

51 "Moral and Spiritual Values and the Schools," and "The Development of Moral and Spiritual Ideals in the Public Schools."

52 "Moral and Spiritual Values and the Schools."

53 "The Development of Moral and Spiritual Ideals in the Public Schools."

54 "Hebrew Culture Contest," WNYC, June 4, 1952, www.wnyc.org , accessed August 21, 2020.

55 "Hebrew Culture Contest."

56 Levitt's language resembled Will Herberg in 1955's *Protestant, Catholic, Jew*. The draft contained a Herberg-sounding section heading, "MORAL AND SPIRITUAL VALUES IN OUR AMERICAN WAY OF LIFE." The Regents' 1951 Statement also discussed an "abiding belief in the free way of life." The timing alone suggests that although school leaders may have been reading Herberg, his language circulated before his book. The "feeding" discussion echoes bell hooks, "Eating the Other: Desire and Resistance," in *Black Looks: Race and Representation* (Boston: South End Press, 1992), 21–39.

57 "The Development of Moral and Spiritual Ideals in the Public Schools."

58 Eden Consenstein, "Religion at Time Inc.: From the Beginning of Time to the End of Life" (PhD diss., Princeton University, 2022).

59 Eden Consenstein and Leslie Ribovich, "Teaching Religion, 1955," *Sources*, October 2020, www.american-religion.org; Masuzawa, *The Invention of World Religions*.

60 Boyarin, *Intertextuality and the Reading of Midrash*, 22.

61 Boyarin, *Intertextuality and the Reading of Midrash*, 23.

62 "Jansen Discounts Religion 'Balance.'"

63 Anglican common law follows precedent. Further research could examine common law's intertextuality.

64 "Moral and Spiritual Values and the Schools."

65 "The Development of Moral and Spiritual Ideals in the Public Schools."

66 David Morgan, "A Generative Entanglement: Word and Image in Roman Catholic Devotional Practice," *Entangled Religions* 11:3 (2020), doi: 10.13154/er.11.2020.8443.

67 Meyer, "Medium," 60.

68 James Baldwin, "A Talk to Teachers"; Frederick Douglass, "Appendix," in *Life of an American Slave* (Boston: Anti-Slavery Office, 1845). See Ribovich and Rock-Singer, "Educating for the New Jerusalem" for further discussion of Baldwin.

69 Baldwin, "A Talk to Teachers."

70 Meeting Minutes, October 4, 1956.

71 See chapter 1 of this book.

72 For more on these controversies, see Strub, *Perversion for Profit*, 2–14.

73 Meeting Minutes, October 4, 1956.

74 Meeting Minutes, October 4, 1956.

75 "The Development of Moral and Spiritual Ideals in the Public Schools."

76 Zimmerman, *Whose America?*, 7.

77 Alicia Cox, "Settler Colonialism," *Oxford Bibliographies*, 2017, doi: 10.1093/OBO/9780190221911-0029; Patrick Wolfe, "Settler Colonialism and the Elimination of the Native," *Journal of Genocide Research* 8:4 (2006): 387–409, doi: 10.1080/14623520601056240, 387-388.

78 Cox, "Settler Colonialism."

79 Moss, *Schooling Citizens*, 10; and Stephen Tomlinson, "Phrenology, Education and the Politics of Human Nature: The Thought and Influence of George Combe," *Journal of the History of Education Society* 26:1 (1997): 1–22, doi: 10.1080/0046760970260101.

80 Stephen Tomlinson, *Head Masters: Phrenology, Secular Education, and Nineteenth-Century Social Thought* (Tuscaloosa: University of Alabama Press, 2013).

81 Weiner, *Power, Protest, and the Public Schools*, 114.

82 Jansen and Allen, *Distant Lands*, 151.

83 "Churchmen Back New School Code: Protestant Council of City Endorses Report on Which Hearing Is Slated Today," *New York Times*, September 17, 1956, 28.

84 Paulo Freire, *Pedagogy of the Oppressed*, trans. by Myra Bergman Ramos (New York: Continuum International Publishing Group, 1970, rep. ed., 2005), 72.

85 Freire, *Pedagogy of the Oppressed*, 72.

86 M. Jacqui Alexander, *Pedagogies of Crossing: Meditations on Feminism, Sexual Politics, Memory, and the Sacred* (Durham, NC: Duke University Press, 2005), 92.

87 Meeting Minutes, October 4, 1956.

CHAPTER 3. JUVENILE DELINQUENCY AND THE LOVE OF NEIGHBOR

1 *Rebel Without a Cause*, Film, directed by Nicholas Ray (1955; Los Angeles: Warner Brothers).

2 *Boy with a Knife*, Film, directed by Laslo Benedek; and Strub, *Perversion for Profit*.

3 Stephanie Coontz, *The Way We Never Were: American Families and the Nostalgia Trap* (New York: Basic Books, 1992).

4 Muhammad, *The Condemnation of Blackness*, 8–9.

5 Agyepong, *The Criminalization of Black Children*; Juvenile Delinquency Evaluation Project of the City of New York: Final Report No. I: The Planning of Delinquency Prevention and Control, February 1961, https://babel.hathitrust.org.

6 James Gilbert, *A Cycle of Outrage: America's Reaction to the Juvenile Delinquent in the 1950s* (New York: Oxford University Press, 1988); Sherrie Inness, ed., *Delinquents and Debutantes: Twentieth-Century American Girls' Cultures* (New York: New York University Press, 1998); among others.

7 "Full Text of Board's Delinquency Program," *New York World-Telegram*, February 5, 1958, Folder 108, Box 53, Subseries 8, Series 911, New York City Board of Education Records, Municipal Archives (NYCBER). Emphasis added.

8 Rachel Ellen Lissy, "From Rehabilitation to Punishment: The Institutionalization of Suspension Policies in Post–World War II New York City Schools" (PhD diss., University of California Berkeley, 2015), 14–15. Lissy uses John Kingdon and James Thurber's phrase "focusing event," meaning an event that "puts a problem on the policy agenda," to describe the lye incident.

9 Robert Alden, "Hennings Scores Leibowitz Plan to Cut Migration," *New York Times*, September 26, 1959, 1; "Courts v. Schools," *New York Times*, February 2, 1958, E2; "Jail Young Thugs, Leibowitz Urges," *New York Times*, August 13, 1954, 17; "Leibowitz Hits Slums," *New York Times*, October 9, 1959, 9; "Leibowitz Orders School Crime Study," *New York Times*, November 7, 1957, 37.

10 "Leibowitz Orders School Crime Study"; "Lye-Attack Sentence," *New York Times*, September 28, 1960, 37.

11 "Three Statements about Violence in City's Schools," *New York Times*, January 31, 1958, 14.

12 Lawrence Fellows, "Jansen Opposes Police in Schools," *New York Times*, November 27, 1957, 1.

13 Gene Currivan, "Proposal for a Policeman in Every School Is Strongly Resisted by the Board," *New York Times*, December 15, 1957, Folder 107, Box 53, Subseries 8, Series 911, NYCBER.

14 Judith Crist, "Mayor Calls Top School Officials," *New York Herald Tribune*, February 1, 1958; "How New York School System Handles Delinquents," *New York*

Times, February 16, 1958, Folder 108, Box 53, Subseries 8, Series 911, NYCBER; Lou Schwartz, "School Board in City Attacks Jury's Probe," *Newsday*, January 31, 1958, 3.

15 "Courts v. Schools"; Judith Crist, "Board Offers a Plan Against School Crime," *New York Herald Tribune*, February 8, 1958, 1; "Leibowitz Hits Slums"; Harrison E. Salisbury, "Well-Run Schools Solving Problems in City 'Jungles,'" *New York Times*, March 29, 1958, 1; and Gertrude Samuels, "The Schools, the Children, the Dilemma," *New York Times*, February 16, 1958, SM14.

16 Emma Harrison, "Boy Hurls Lye in Classroom," *New York Times*, September 20, 1957, 1; "Boy in Lye Attack Continues to Gain," *New York Times*, September 22, 1957, 50.

17 Bellah, "Civil Religion in America"; Gaston, "Interpreting Judeo-Christianity in America"; Herzog, *The Spiritual-Industrial Complex*; and Schultz, *Tri-Faith America*.

18 Brotherhood Week 1955, Box 5, Series 4, National Conference of Christians and Jews Records, Social Welfare History Archives, University of Minnesota Libraries (hereafter cited as NCCJR).

19 Brooke Granowski, "Ten Commandments Monument of Faribault," Religions in Minnesota, https://religionsmn.carleton.edu; Weissman Joselit, *Set in Stone*, 30–32. The judge helped ignite the movement for Ten Commandments monuments to appear on government buildings nationwide. Thanks to Shana Sippy for pointing me to the Granowski source.

20 "The Development of Moral and Spiritual Ideals in the Public Schools."

21 Gil Anidjar, *The Jew, The Arab: A History of the Enemy* (Stanford, CA: Stanford University Press, 2003), 19.

22 Robert Elliott Allinson, "Hillel and Confucius: The Prescriptive Formulation of the Golden Rule in the Jewish and Chinese Confucian Ethical Traditions," *Dao* 3:1 (2003): 29–41, doi: 10.1007/bf02910339; Jacob Neusner, "The Golden Rule in Classical Judaism," *Review of Rabbinic Judaism* 19:2 (2016): 173–193, doi: https://doi.org/10.1163/157007008786777677. Thanks to Adam Becker for pointing me to Hillel's Golden Rule, a reviewer for pointing to the ambiguity in Confucius, and Wei Wu for information regarding Confucius. See *Analects*, 12:2, Chinese Text Project, https://ctext.org: "Zhong Gong asked about perfect virtue. The Master said, 'It is, when you go abroad, to behave to every one as if you were receiving a great guest; to employ the people as if you were assisting at a great sacrifice; not to do to others as you would not wish done to yourself; to have no murmuring against you in the country, and none in the family.' Zhong Gong said, 'Though I am deficient in intelligence and vigor, I will make it my business to practice this lesson.'" Also, *Analects*, 15:24, Chinese Text Project, https://ctext.org: "Zi Gong asked, saying, 'Is there one word which may serve as a rule of practice for all one's life?' The Master said, 'Is not RECIPROCITY such a word? What you do not want done to yourself, do not do to others.'"

23 Muhammad, *The Condemnation of Blackness*; Murakawa distinguishes the terms by arguing conservatives aim to preserve the status quo and liberals seek individual uplift in *The First Civil Right*, 3, 10, 16, and elsewhere.

24 Muhammad, *The Condemnation of Blackness*, 8.

25 Muhammad, *The Condemnation of Blackness*, 9.

26 Wiley B. Sanders, Review of *Unraveling Juvenile Delinquency*, *Social Forces* 29:4 (1951): 459–460, https://academic.oup.com/; Sheldon Glueck, "Crime Causation Study: Unraveling Juvenile Delinquency, 1940–1963," Murray Research Archive Dataverse, Harvard Dataverse, https://dataverse.harvard.edu.

27 The Gluecks' predictive tables were widely criticized. For example, a two-part critique of the Gluecks' work was published in the September 1951 issue of the *American Journal of Sociology*, 57:2, the first part by Sol Rubin and the second by Albert J. Reiss Jr. Sheldon Glueck responded in "Ten Years of 'Unraveling Juvenile Delinquency': An Examination of Criticisms," *Journal of Criminal Law, Criminology, and Police Science* 51:3 (1960): 283–308, doi: 10.2307/1140483.

28 Glueck and Glueck, *Unraveling Juvenile Delinquency*, 5.

29 Eleanor T. Glueck, "Body Build in the Prediction of Delinquency," *Journal of Criminal Law, Criminology and Police Science* 48:6 (1958): 577–579, doi: 10.2307/1140253, 577; Vertinsky, "Physique as Destiny."

30 Vertinsky, "Physique as Destiny," 300.

31 Glueck and Glueck, *Unraveling Juvenile Delinquency*, 38.

32 Glueck and Glueck, *Unraveling Juvenile Delinquency*, 40.

33 Sheldon Glueck, "Ten Years After 'Unraveling Juvenile Delinquency.'"

34 Ralph W. Whelan, "An Experiment in Predicting Delinquency," *Journal of Criminal Law, Criminology, and Policy Science* 45:4 (1954): 432–441, doi: 10.2307/1140014, 436.

35 Ralph W. Whelan, *God's Rascals* (Washington, DC: National Conference of Catholic Charities, 1943), www.lib.cua.edu.

36 Eleanor T. Glueck, "Status of Glueck Prediction Studies," *Journal of Criminal Law, Criminology, and Police Science* 47:1 (1956): 18–32, doi: 10.2307/1140191, 18.

37 Agyepong, *The Criminalization of Black Children*; Muhammad, *The Condemnation of Blackness*; Ribovich, "Saving Black Boys."

38 Robert MacIver, "The City of New York Juvenile Delinquency Evaluation Project: A Progress Report," January 1958, https://babel.hathitrust.org.

39 "Robert MacIver: 1882–1970," *American Sociologist*, February 1971, accessed October 14, 2018, www.asanet.org.

40 *Juvenile Delinquency Evaluation Project of the City of New York: Final Report No. II: Delinquency in the Great City*, Princeton University Library, Public Administration Collection, July 17, 1961, 11.

41 JDEP, *Final Report No. II*, 32.

42 "The 90-Year Old Financial Policy that Harms Our Health," NYC.gov, https://a816-dohbesp.nyc.gov. For more on redlining and schools throughout the north, see: Delmont, *Why Busing Failed*; Ronald P. Formisano, *Boston Against Busing: Race, Class, and Ethnicity in the 1960s and 1970s* (Chapel Hill: University of North Carolina Press, 2004 [1991]); Richard Rothstein, *The Color of Law: A Forgotten History of How Our Government Segregated America* (New York: Liveright Pub-

lishing, 2017); and Keeanga-Yamahtta Taylor, *Race for Profit: How Banks and the Real Estate Industry Undermined Black Homeownership* (Chapel Hill: University of North Carolina Press, 2019).

43 Muhammad, *The Condemnation of Blackness*, makes a similar argument outside of schools.

44 JDEP, *Final Report No. II.*

45 "An Invitation to Urban Ethnography," in *The Urban Ethnography Reader*, edited by Mitchell Duneier, Philip Kasinitz, and Alexandra Murphy (New York: Oxford University Press, 2014), 6.

46 Clifford R. Shaw, *Delinquency Areas: A Study of the Geographic Distribution of School Truants, Juvenile Delinquents, and Adult Offenders in Chicago* (Chicago: University of Chicago Press, 1929).

47 JDEP, *Final Report No. II*, 32.

48 Robert MacIver, "My Religion," *American Weekly*, March 6, 1947, 27, New York Public Library, David Spitz Papers, Box 10, Miscellaneous Essays by MacIver (2).

49 MacIver, "My Religion."

50 Clarence Taylor, *The Black Churches of Brooklyn* (New York: Columbia University Press, 1994); Weisenfeld, *New World A-Coming.*

51 Hartman, *Education and the Cold War*, 84. See chapter 2 in this book for more.

52 Robin Nagle, *Picking Up: In the Streets and Behind the Trucks with the Sanitation Workers of New York City* (New York: Farrar, Straus and Giroux, 2013), 102.

53 For a bibliographic essay on the history of cleanliness, see Kathleen M. Brown, *Foul Bodies: Cleanliness in Early America* (New Haven, CT: Yale University Press, 2009), 431–436.

54 "[] Fights, Vandalism," Folder 5, Box 3, Series 521, NYCBER.

55 "Program for Participating in Independent Anti-Vandalism and Care of Neighborhood Plan, P.S. 27, April 1953," Folder 5, Box 3, Series 521, NYCBER.

56 See responses in Folder 5, Box 3, Series 521, NYCBER.

57 George L. Kelling and James Q. Wilson, "Broken Windows: The Police and Neighborhood Safety," *The Atlantic Magazine*, March 1982, www.theatlantic.com.

58 Boxes 1 and 2, Series 521, NYCBER.

59 "Program for Participating in Independent Anti-Vandalism and Care of Neighborhood Plan, P.S. 27, April 1953."

60 Smith, "Using Films in Group Guidance with Emotionally Disturbed Socially Maladjusted Boys," 206.

61 "The '600' Day Schools," Juvenile Delinquency Evaluation Project, April 1957, Folder 18, Box 6, UFTR.

62 "The '600' Day Schools."

63 "The '600' Day Schools."

64 "The '600' Day Schools."

65 "The '600' Day Schools."

66 "The '600' Day Schools."

67 Smith, "Using Films," 206–209.

68 Smith, "Using Films," 206.

69 *Neighbours*, Film, directed by Norman McLaren; and Albert Ohayon, "*Neighbours*: The NFB's Second Oscar Winner," NFB/blog, February 27, 2011, http://blog.nfb.ca/blog/2011/02/27/neighbours-the-nfbs-second-oscar-winner/.

70 *Neighbours.*

71 Smith, "Using Films," 208.

72 Smith, "Using Films," 206.

73 Perry, *More Beautiful and More Terrible*, 46.

74 "Photo Book, J.H.S. 188, Man., Clean Street Parade, May 1953," Folder 4, Box 3, Series 521, NYCBER.

75 "Report: Vandalism and Clean-Up Campaign," Folder 5, Box 3, Series 521, NYCBER. Underline in original.

76 "Report on Vandalism, P.S. 23," Folder 5, Box 3, Series 521, NYCBER.

77 Joseph Schroff, Principal, "Clean-Up Campaign, P.S. 188, Manhattan," June 16, 1953, Folder 4, Box 3, Series 521, NYCBER.

78 Schroff, "Clean-Up Campaign, P.S. 188, Manhattan."

79 "Citizenship Project-Schools North of West 82nd Street," Folder 4, Box 3, Series 521, NYCBER.

80 PS 72, Manhattan Commitment Pledge, Folder 4, Box 3, Series 521, NYCBER.

81 "The Clean-Up Campaign'-P.S. 72, Manhattan," Folder 4, Box 3, Series 521, NYCBER, underline in original.

82 The Children of Public School 34 to Neighbors, Spring 1953, Folder 4, Box 3, Series 521, NYCBER.

83 "Neighborhood Cleanup Campaign P.S. 4B Statement," Folder 2, Box 3, Series 521, NYCBER.

84 Arthur L. Swift, Jr., "Gangs and the Churches," *Union Seminary Quarterly* 11:4 (May 1956): 43–50, 43.

85 Lee, "Delinquent Youth in a Normless Time," 1475.

86 Lee, "Delinquent Youth in a Normless Time," 1475.

87 Hargraves, "The Local Church and Juvenile Delinquency," 180.

88 Hargraves, "The Local Church and Juvenile Delinquency," 180.

89 Milton Matz, "How Religious Institutions Can Combat Juvenile Delinquency," *The Reconstructionist* 21:15 (December 2, 1955): 17–19, 17.

90 Wilkerson, *The Cross and the Switchblade*, 76–77.

91 Wilkerson, *The Cross and the Switchblade*, 7, 78.

92 "Nicky Cruz Outreach," https://nickycruz.org/.

93 *Everson v. Board of Education*, 3301 U.S. 1 (1947) discussed the concept of a "secular purpose," though *Abington School District v. Schempp* 374 U.S. 203 (1963) more fully established religious v. secular purpose.

94 Randolph White, "Harlemites Help Puerto Ricans Battle Slums," *New York Amsterdam News*, June 10, 1950, 1.

CHAPTER 4. CONFLICTING RELIGIOUS VISIONS OF INTEGRATION

1 Jennifer Ayscue and Erica Frankenberg, "Desegregation and Integration," *Oxford Bibliographies*, February 25, 2016, doi: 10.1093/OBO/9780199756810-0139; Chana Joffe-Walt, "Nice White Parents," podcast, July 2020, www.nytimes.com.

2 "Joint Statement by Mr. Charles H. Silver, President of the Board of Education, and Dr. John J. Theobald, Superintendent of Schools (2 P.M. Wednesday, August 31, at press conference in office of Superintendents of Schools, Room 1016, Board of Education Headquarters, 110 Livingston Street, Brooklyn, New York)," Folder 88, Box 71, Subseries 10, Series 911, NYCBER.

3 "East Harlem Protestant Parish Newsletter," Folder 49, Box 69, Subseries 10, Series 911, NYCBER.

4 Diana Eck, *A New Religious America: How a "Christian Country" Has Become the World's Most Religiously Diverse Nation* (San Francisco: HarperCollins, 2001), 6. Amanda Lewis and John Diamond, *Despite the Best Intentions: How Racial Inequality Thrives in Good Schools* (New York: Oxford University Press, 2015), 83–118, 122, distinguishes between "integrated" and "diverse" schools.

5 For more on tri-faith, see Gaston, *Imagining Judeo-Christian America* and Schultz, *Tri-Faith America*.

6 Bender and Klassen, eds., *After Pluralism*; Wendy Brown, *Regulating Aversion: Tolerance in the Age of Identity and Empire* (Princeton, NJ: Princeton University Press, 2006). Gaston and Wenger invite further research on race and Judeo-Christianity in *Imagining Judeo-Christian America* and *Religious Freedom*, 143–187.

7 Isaacs, *Inside Ocean Hill-Brownsville*; Lewis, *New York City Public Schools from Brownsville to Bloomberg*.

8 Murakawa, *The First Civil Right*, 9.

9 Bell, *Silent Covenants*; Lloyd, "Hope," in Dubler and Weiner, eds., *Religion, Law, USA*, 269–275.

10 Bell, *Silent Covenants*, 9, 29–48; George H. Taylor, "Racism as 'the National Crucial Sin': Theology and Derrick Bell," *Michigan Journal of Race and Law* 9 (2004): 269–322.

11 Flier Calling for Boycott, "February 3, 1964: New York City School Children Boycott Schools," *The Zinn Project*, www.zinnedproject.org.

12 Glaude, *African American Religions*; Barbara Dianne Savage, *Your Spirits Walk Beside Us: The Politics of Black Religion* (Cambridge, MA: Harvard University Press, 2012).

13 Dubler and Lloyd mirror this argument in "Mass Incarceration Is Religious (and So Is Abolition)."

14 Vincent Lloyd claims the figure of the child reveals "the precariousness of hope, the ever-present threat that hope is really just bloated optimism" in "Hope," 275. Even in the legal discussion of desegregation, the value of integration loomed.

15 Delmont, *Why Busing Failed*; Michael Glass, "From Sword to Shield to Myth: Facing the Facts of De Facto School Segregation," *Journal of Urban History* 44:6

(November 2018): 1197–1226; David Ment, "Racial Segregation in the Public Schools of New England and New York, 1840–1940," PhD diss. (Columbia University, 1975). "Toward the Integration of Our Schools: Final Report of the Commission on Integration," Folder 25, Box 13, Ella Baker Papers, Schomburg Center for Research in Black Culture, The New York Public Library (hereafter cited as Baker Papers).

16 Ella Baker and Ethel Schwaber, "Interim Report Sub-Commission on Zoning," Folder 25, Box 13, Baker Papers.

17 "Texts on the 1950–1951 Board of Education Approved Textbook List Containing Objectionable Material Against Minority Groups," Folder 32, Box 4, Series 261, NYCBER. Andrew Hartman discusses this document briefly to point out the Board's racism because "Some of the texts skewered by the report were authored by higher ups in the city's school administrative offices." Hartman, *Education and the Cold War*, 84.

18 "Texts on the 1950–1951 Board of Education Approved Textbook List Containing Objectionable Material Against Minority Groups."

19 "Analysis of the Insulting Anti-Negro, Anti-Semitic, Anti-Minority Group Book: 'Toaster's Handbook (Jokes, Stories, and Quotations),'" May 1951, Folder 32, Box 4, Series 261, NYCBER.

20 "Analysis of the Insulting Anti-Negro, Anti-Semitic, Anti-Minority Group Book."

21 See chapter 2 of this book.

22 "Toward the Integration of Our Schools."

23 Jennifer Goren, "Whatever Became of National Brotherhood Week?," *The World*, February 21, 2018, www.pri.org/stories. The Week officially ended in the 2000s, but popularity declined significantly after the 1960s. Although the NCCJ served the whole country, their 1958–1959 budget reflects that in general they put significantly more resources toward the Greater New York Area (without a breakdown of Brotherhood Week expenses); "The National Conference of Christians and Jews, Inc. Statement of Income and Expense Fiscal Years Ended September 30, 1958 and 1959 Final Report," February 1, 1960, Box 33, Finance and Budget Folder, NCCJR, 6 and 11.

24 It was first Brotherhood Day. Schultz, *Tri-Faith America*, 65–67.

25 Matthew Hedstrom discusses Brotherhood Week, but not in public schools, in *The Rise of Liberal Religion: Book Culture and American Spirituality in the Twentieth Century* (New York: Oxford University Press, 2012), 142–171. Also see NCCJR, Series 4.

26 Posters including "Lift Away!," "Good for What Ails You," "Forging: One Nation Under God," "Sometimes the Torch Needs a Shield," in Brotherhood Week 1955, Box 5, Series 4, NCCJR. For more on these posters, see Ribovich, "*Brown v. Board* and Religion and Law Beyond the First Amendment." Beyond the imagery, NCCJ founder Everett Clinchy believed that brotherhood had true medical effects. For Brotherhood Week in 1952, he reportedly said "'prejudices, animosities and hostilities lead in the direction of physical breakdown.'" In particular: "More attractive

personalities belong to people free of animosities, Dr. Clinchy maintains, because high blood pressure, heart diseases, glandular upsets, headaches and ulcers are correlated with hate." "Prejudice Leads to Bad Health Says Dr. Everett R. Clinchy, President of Nat'l Conference of Christians and Jews," *Jet Magazine*, February 28, 1952.

27 Kevin Kruse discusses the NCCJ's 1955 theme of "One Nation Under God" as exemplifying the relationship between businessmen and conservative clergy in his book *One Nation Under God*, 111.

28 "Brotherhood for College and Adult Groups," Brotherhood Week 1955, Box 5, Series 4, NCCJR.

29 "Brotherhood Nourished by PTA," Folder 93, Box 52, Subseries 8, Series 911, NYCBER. The article suggests that both parents and teachers were involved but someone in the archives has crossed out "PTA" and written "PA." "PA" is likely more accurate because many Parents Associations existed and not as many Parent Teacher Associations.

30 "Resource Units, Grade 4, 1956," Folder 45, Box 3, Series 550, NYCBER.

31 Hillary Kaell, *Christian Globalism at Home: Child Sponsorship in the United States* (Princeton, NJ: Princeton University Press, 2020), 94.

32 "Resource Units, Grade 4, 1956."

33 For example, "Resource Units, Grade 7," Folder 48, Box 3, Series 550, NYCBER. This may be drawing on the earlier cultural gifts movement, see Diana Selig, *Americans All: The Cultural Gifts Movement* (Cambridge, MA: Harvard University Press, 2008).

34 Genesis 4:1–18.

35 "Suggestions to Speakers," Brotherhood Week 1955, Box 5, Series 4, NCCJR.

36 "Suggestions to Speakers."

37 Carl M. Saunders, "And Who Was Cain?," Brotherhood Week 1955, Box 5, Series 4, NCCJR.

38 Ribovich, "*Brown v. Board* and Religion and Law Beyond the First Amendment."

39 "Rev. Clinchy Denounces Missionary Speech: Joins with Jewish Leaders in Condemning Address by Dr. John R. Mott," *The American Israelite*, January 22, 1931, 1.

40 "His Reply to Dr. Mott: The Rev. E. R. Clinchy Warned Against Mistrust and Hatred," *New York Times*, January 18, 1931, 36.

41 "Fact Sheet," Brotherhood Week 1955, Box 5, Series 4, NCCJR.

42 Murakawa, *The First Civil Right*, 9.

43 "Brotherhood Week Spots for Your . . . Weather Reporter," Brotherhood Week 1955, Box 5, Series 4, NCCJR. The phrasing "Americans All" may have referred to the 1938 and 1939 radio program "Americans All, Immigrants All," produced by "Federal officials at the Office of Education in Harold Ickes's Department of the Interior," which Barbara Dianne Savage says aimed to "create a state-sanctioned narrative of American history that made immigrants, African Americans, and Jews visible," but, "Built around an all-encompassing myth of success, this narrative construction ultimately failed to fit any of the groups it sought to represent."

Barbara Dianne Savage, *Broadcasting Freedom: Radio, War, and the Politics of Race, 1938–1948* (Chapel Hill: University of North Carolina Press, 1999), 21–22.

44 "Conference on Organization of Workshop in Puerto Rico, Summer 1957, February 7, 1957," Folder 12, Box 1, Series 550, NYCBER; Herbert L. Seamans, "Report on the 1957 Workshop," Folder 12, Box 1, Series 550, NYCBER.

45 "Guide to Curriculum Materials in the Records of the New York City Board of Education," Revised July 2018, accessed July 31, 2023, https://dorisarchive.blob.core.windows.net/finding-aids/FindingAidsPDFs/BOE_CurriculumMaterials-Guide-2018.pdf, 12.

46 "Not for Advance Publication, Release After Press Conference Monday April 6, 1959," Folder 8, Box 1, Series 550, NYCBER.

47 Class Report, May 1955, Folder 3, Box 1, Series 550, NYCBER. Original spelling. Name withheld to protect anonymity of minor.

48 Class Report.

49 Clare C. Baldwin, "The Education of Puerto Rican Children in the Schools of New York City," Folder 1, Box 1, Series 550, NYCBER.

50 Although Madeleine E. López argues that the PRS challenged social scientific racial stereotypes of Puerto Ricans rooted in the "cultural poverty thesis" by offering progressive bilingual education to Puerto Rican students in New York City, my research suggests that the PRS illuminates the Board's vision of assimilating Puerto Rican students into Judeo-Christian norms. Madeleine E. López, "Investigating the Investigators: An Analysis of the Puerto Rican Study," *Centro Journal* 19:2 (2007): 60–85.

51 "Puerto Rican Study Final Report, 1953–1957," Folder 67, Box 5, Series 550, NYCBER.

52 "Puerto Rico and the Puerto Ricans," Folder 66, Box 5, Series 550, NYCBER.

53 "Puerto Rico and the Puerto Ricans."

54 "Puerto Rico and the Puerto Ricans."

55 J. Cayce Morrison, *Character Building in New York Public Schools: An Analysis of Practices Reported by Teachers and Supervisory Officers for the School Year 1928–29* (Albany: University of the State of New York Press, 1931), 11.

56 Morrison, *Character Building in New York Public Schools*, 4.

57 Bellah, "Civil Religion in America," 7.

58 "Interviewing Puerto Rican Parents and Children in Spanish: A Guide for School Personnel," Board of Education of the City of New York, Folder 64, Box 5, Series 550, NYCBER.

59 "Interviewing Puerto Rican Parents and Children in Spanish."

60 "Resource Units, Grade 7."

61 "Resource Units, Grade 7."

62 "Resource Units, Grade 2, 1956–1957," Folder 42, Box 3, Series 550, NYCBER.

63 "Resource Units for Classes with Puerto Rican Pupils, Secondary School Orientation Stage." On reframing narratives about dirty neighborhoods and trash collection: Perry, *More Beautiful and More Terrible*, 46.

64 "Resource Units for Classes with Puerto Rican Pupils, Secondary School Orientation Stage."

65 See lists after resource unit publications in Boxes 3 and 4, Series 550, NYCBER.

66 "General Circular No. 27 1953–1954," Folder 6, Box 1, Series 550, NYCBER.

67 "Resource Units for Classes with Puerto Rican Pupils, Secondary School Orientation Stage."

68 "Resource Units Grade 1, 1956–1957," Folder 42, Box 3, Series 550, NYCBER.

69 "Joint Statement by Mr. Charles H. Silver, President of the Board of Education, and Dr. John J. Theobald, Superintendent of Schools."

70 "Joint Statement."

71 "Open Enrollment Program," Folder 4, Box 66, Subseries 10, Series 911, NYCBER.

72 Glaude, *African American Religion*, 11.

73 "Feb. 3, 1964: New York City School Children Boycott School," Zinn Education Project, www.zinnedproject.org.

74 Cone, *Black Theology and Black Power*, 22.

75 Cone, *Black Theology and Black Power*.

76 Sara Slack, "Reading Writing & Arithmetic: Mom Writes a Play," *New York Amsterdam News*, February 19, 1966, 13. Olatunji participated in what Ahmad Greene-Hayes calls "anti-commodified Black Studies" in "Anti-Commodified Black Studies and the Radical Roots of Black Christian Education."

77 Slack, "Reading Writing & Arithmetic."

78 Slack, "Reading Writing & Arithmetic."

79 Sorett, *Spirit in the Dark*, 17.

80 Wenger, *Religious Freedom*, 188–231.

81 Her approach differs from those described by Schultz, who argues that King was using the NCCJ's language in *Tri-Faith America*, 179–197, and Gaston, *Imagining Judeo-Christian America*, 205–206.

82 "Countee Cullen Branch," www.nyclgbtsites.org.

83 Michael Babatunde Olatunji, *Transcriptions of Ellis Island Oral Histories*. New York, New York: Ellis Island Immigration Museum, 2010, accessed through Ancestry Libraries. Hucks, *Yoruba Traditions and African American Religious Nationalism*, 115–117, places Michael Babatunde Olatunji in the Black Arts Movement, working at the intersection of Black Nationalism and Pan-Africanism. He participated in the Yoruba Temple Hucks describes in depth.

84 Bellah, "Civil Religion in America"; Herberg, *Protestant-Catholic-Jew*.

85 Glaude, *African American Religion*, 11–12.

86 Sorett, *Spirit in the Dark*, for more on spirit.

87 Leslie Etienne, "A Different Type of Summer Camp: SNCC, Freedom Summer, Freedom Schools, and the Development of African American Males in Mississippi," *Peabody Journal of Education* 88:4 (2013): 449–463, doi: 10.1080/0161956X.2013.821889; Jon N. Hale, *Freedom Schools Student Activists in the Mississippi Civil Rights Movement* (New York: Columbia University Press, 2016), "'The Student as a Force for Social Change': The Mississippi Freedom

Schools and Student Engagement," *Journal of African American History* 96:3 (2011): 325–347, doi: 10.5323/jafriamerhist.96.3.0325, and with William Sturkey, *To Write in the Light of Freedom: The Newspapers of the 1964 Mississippi Freedom School Movement* (Jackson: University of Mississippi Press, 2015).

88 "Summary of Freedom Schools Curriculum," Folder 2, Box 9, Baker Papers; "Harlem Parents Committee Freedom School Summer Program."

89 "Summary of Freedom Schools Curriculum."

90 Ribovich, "Saving Black Boys."

91 "Community Links Urged on Churches," *New York Times*, February 20, 1959, 13.

92 "East Harlem Protestant Parish Newsletter," Folder 49, Box 69, Subseries 10, Series 911, NYCBER.

93 "East Harlem Protestant Parish Newsletter."

94 "East Harlem Protestant Parish Newsletter." Given the newsletter's combination of general and male-specific language, the program was likely separated by boys and girls.

95 Hargraves, "The Local Church and Juvenile Delinquency," 180.

96 "East Harlem Protestant Parish Newsletter."

97 Ribovich, "Saving Black Boys."

CHAPTER 5. GOVERNMENT AID AND THE SCOPE OF PUBLIC EDUCATION

1 New York State Constitution, Article 19 § 2. See New York State Constitution [1938], Article 19 § 2, 243–244, https://history.nycourts.gov v. New York State Constitution [1894] with no such article, https://history.nycourts.gov.

2 At the time, the most recent convention had been held in 1938. Since then, New Yorkers had voted on around 100 amendments to the New York Constitution, adopting more than 80 amendments. Jim Hadjin, "'67 Delegates Can Rewrite Constitution," *Newsday*, November 8, 1965, 7.

3 Green, "The Insignificance of the Blaine Amendment," 297.

4 Homer Bigart, "Roosevelt Opposes Church School Aid," *New York Times*, October 18, 1966, 1; Bernie Bookbinder, "Candidates 2–1 for Parochial School Aid," *Newsday*, October 31, 1966, 15; Bernie Bookbinder, "Survey Indicates End of Blaine Amendment," *Newsday*, November 5, 1966, 11; "Write-In Votes Seen Winning Javits a Place at Convention," *Newsday*, November 19, 1966, 17; Richard L. Madden, "State Ban on Aid for Parochial Schools Is Debated Hotly at Charter Hearing," *New York Times*, October 5, 1966.

5 Richard Dougherty, "Something to Offend Everybody: N.Y. Constitution Battle Makes Strange Allies," *Los Angeles Times*, October 29, 1967, E1.

6 Herblock in the *Washington Post*, reprinted in *New York Times*, November 12, 1967, 211.

7 Dougherty, "Something to Offend Everybody."

8 For example, see Green, *The Bible, the School, and the Constitution* and Greenawalt, *Does God Belong in the Public Schools?*. This "duel" then results in one of the

Lemon test prongs of neither advancing nor inhibiting religion. For instance, see Hamburger, *Separation of Church and State*. Green challenges these arguments in his chapter on the Blaine Amendment in *The Bible, the School, and the Constitution*.

9 Balmer, *Bad Faith*; Kruse, *White Flight*; Lassiter, *The Silent Majority*.
10 Kruse, *White Flight*; Lassiter, *The Silent Majority*.
11 Ribovich, "Saving Black Boys."
12 Pluralism also circumscribed critical possibilities, as Lucia Hulsether argues in "The Grammar of Racism."
13 *Everson v. Board of Education*, 330 U.S. 1 (1947); Gordon, *The Spirit of the Law*.
14 First Amendment, US Constitution.
15 Some politicians, including Governor Nelson Rockefeller, thought that the government could now support nonreligious materials in denominational schools, and he wrote a law allowing for New York State to pay for textbooks. The law was being adjudicated in the highest state court and the US Supreme Court throughout the duration of the constitutional convention. "Excerpts From State Court Opinions," *New York Times*, June 2, 1967, 44; "Ask Ban on Tax Aid to Parochial Schools," *Chicago Tribune*, September 29, 1967, 2. After the convention ended, in 1968, the Supreme Court upheld the textbook loan law as constitutional in *Board of Education v. Allen*, 392 U.S. 236: "Textbook Loan to Parochial Schools in N.Y. Is Upheld," *Chicago Tribune*, June 11, 1968, 3. Among others, see: Rebecca E. Zietlow, "The Judicial Restraint of the Warren Court (and Why It Matters)," *Ohio State Law Journal* 69:2 (2008): 255–301.
16 *Brown v. Board of Education II* 349 U.S. 294 (1955) determined that desegregation should happen "with all deliberate speed," a vague phrase that led many districts to avoid applying *Brown*. Joel Spring, *Deculturalization and the Struggle for Equality: A Brief History of the Education of Dominated Cultures in the United States* (New York: Routledge, 2016, 8th ed.), 114–118.
17 Green, "The Insignificance of the Blaine Amendment," 297.
18 Green, "The Insignificance of the Blaine Amendment," 295n2.
19 Article XI, Section 3 (the "Blaine Amendment"), New York State Constitution.
20 Fessenden, *Culture and Redemption*; Hamburger, *Separation of Church and State*.
21 Fessenden, *Culture and Redemption*; Green, *The Bible, the School, and the Constitution*.
22 Bernie Bookbinder, "Catholics Start Aid Push," *Newsday*, October 4, 1966, 9.
23 Madden, "State Ban on Aid for Parochial Schools."
24 One could read the discussion here as an example of "the Catholic secular," if they find the phrasing useful.
25 "The State's Basic Law," *New York Times*, June 5, 1965, 30.
26 "'Modern' Constitution Urged," *New York Times*, November 12, 1965, 36.
27 "Statement of His Eminence, Francis Cardinal Spellman, On Federal Aid to Education," March 13, 1961, Folder 1, Box S/C-77, Cardinal Spellman Papers, Archives of the Archdiocese of New York (hereafter cited as Spellman Papers). Kennedy's

opposition to aid was complicated by his role as the first Catholic president of the United States. It followed from his position that one's own religion should be kept private, which he articulated in his famous 1960 campaign speech on religion. "Transcript: JFK's Speech on Religion," December 5, 2007, *National Public Radio*, www.npr.org. See also Randall Balmer, *God in the White House: A History: How Faith Shaped the Presidency from John F. Kennedy to George W. Bush* (New York: HarperCollins, 2008), 7–48.

28 Homer Bigart, "2 Candidates Give School-Aid Views," *New York Times*, October 19, 1966, 28; Homer Bigart, "Roosevelt Opposes Church School Aid," *New York Times*, October 18, 1966, 1; Homer Bigart, "Governor Wants Wider School Aid," *New York Times*, October 6, 1966, 42. Note: Folder 1, Box CH-30, Chancery Collection from the Archives of the Archdiocese (hereafter cited as Chancery Collection) offers quotations of Rockefeller later coming out in support of repeal; McCandlish Phillips, "Governor Scored on Aid to Schools," *New York Times*, October 22, 1966, 27.

29 Bernie Bookbinder, "Survey Indicates End of Blaine Amendment," *Newsday*, November 5, 1966, 11.

30 "For Immediate Release: The 'Blaine Amendment,'" April 6, Citizens for Educational Freedom, Folder 4, Box CH-30, Chancery Collection.

31 Bookbinder, "Survey Indicates End of Blaine Amendment," 11.

32 Bookbinder, "Survey Indicates End of Blaine Amendment."

33 Madden, "State Ban on Aid for Parochial Schools."

34 Madden, "State Ban on Aid for Parochial Schools."

35 Hamburger, *Separation of Church and State*, 470–472.

36 Mary Hornaday, "N.Y. Debates Church-School Proviso: Views Aired," *Christian Science Monitor*, October 12, 1966, 4.

37 Curtis J. Sitomer, "POAU Defends Church-State Wall," *Christian Science Monitor*, February 23, 1967, 7. For more on Archer, see Rob Boston, "Americans United's Founding Father: Meet Glenn L. Archer, AU's First Executive Director," *Church and State Magazine*, March 1, 2022, www.au.org.

38 Herberg, *Protestant-Catholic-Jew*, 89.

39 George H. Favre, "New York Scrap Due Over New Constitution," *Christian Science Monitor*, April 4, 1967, 4.

40 "Invocation and Excerpts from Speeches at Opening of Constitutional Convention," *New York Times*, April 5, 1967, 32.

41 "Statement of His Eminence, Francis Cardinal Spellman, On Federal Aid to Education," March 13, 1961, Folder 1, Box S/C-77, Spellman Papers.

42 "Invocation and Excerpts from Speeches at Opening of Constitutional Convention"; "Statement of His Eminence, Francis Cardinal Spellman on the Closing of the Constitutional Convention," September 26, 1967, Folder 1, Box CH-30, Chancery Collection.

43 Favre, "New York Scrap Due Over New Constitution," 4.

44 *The New York State Constitutional Convention Directory of Delegates and Staff* 1:90 (1967), 12 vols., *The Making of Modern Law: Primary Sources*, www.gale.com, March 12, 2017.

45 Maurice Carroll, "Democrats Favor Wider School Aid," *New York Times*, September 24, 1966, 18.

46 *The New York State Constitutional Convention Proceedings*, 1967, 12 vols., *The Making of Modern Law: Primary Sources*, www.gale.com, March 12, 2017, Vol. 2, 674.

47 *The New York State Constitutional Convention Proceedings*, 611, 674, 741.

48 1920; Census Place: Manhattan Assembly District 2, New York, New York; Roll: T625_1186; Page: 7A; Enumeration District: 138; Image: 791. Saxe's father's job industry was listed as "lunch room" on the 1920 census.

49 *The New York State Constitutional Convention Directory of Delegates and Staff*, Vol. 1, 90, 1967, 12 vols., *The Making of Modern Law: Primary Sources*, www.gale. com, March 12, 2017.

50 *The New York State Constitutional Convention Proceedings*, 763.

51 *The New York State Constitutional Convention Proceedings, 763.*

52 *The New York State Constitutional Convention Proceedings*, 763–764.

53 *The New York State Constitutional Convention Proceedings*, 763–764.

54 *The New York State Constitutional Convention Proceedings*, 763–764.

55 *The New York State Constitutional Convention Proceedings*, 763–764.

56 *The New York State Constitutional Convention Proceedings*, 763–764.

57 *The New York State Constitutional Convention Proceedings*, 830.

58 *The New York State Constitutional Convention Proceedings*, 830.

59 *The New York State Constitutional Convention Proceedings, 830.*

60 Milton A. Galamison, "If Blaine Is Repealed," *African-American Teachers Association Forum*, September–October 1967, Folder 11, Box 24, UFTR, and "Implications of 'Blaine Amendment,'" *New York Times*, October 21, 1967, 30.

61 *The New York State Constitutional Convention Directory of Delegates and Staff*, Vol. 1, 90, 1967, 12 vols., *The New York State Constitutional Convention Proceedings*, 802.

62 James Springer, "Pulse of New York: Letter to the Editor," *New York Times*, October 21, 1967, 16.

63 Marietta J. Tanner, "The Community Conscious," *New York Amsterdam News*, October 7, 1967, 6.

64 Tanner, "The Community Conscious."

65 Bernie Bookbinder, "Rocky Hits RFK Plan to Appoint Atty. Gen.," *Newsday*, June 22, 1967, 31.

66 PEARL, "Protecting Our Schools," Folder 26, Box 155, UFTR.

67 Wilkins shared her home with her husband, Roy Wilkins, executive director of the National Association for the Advancement of Colored People.

68 C. Gerald Fraser, "Negroes to Fight School-Aid Ban," *New York Times*, September 26, 1967.

69 Fraser, "Negroes to Fight School-Aid Ban."

70 On grassroots efforts, see Lewis, *New York City Public Schools from Brownsville to Bloomberg*.

71 Taylor, *Knocking at Our Own Door*, 196, 198–201, 205–206. He even later denied ever supporting community control.

72 Isaacs, *Inside Ocean Hill-Brownsville*, 110.

73 Milton A. Galamison, "Implications of 'Blaine Amendment,'" *New York Times*, October 21, 1967, 30.

CHAPTER 6. COMMUNITY CONTROL AS RELIGIOUS AND RACIAL WORLD-MAKING

1 See all issues of the *Negro Teachers Forum* and *African-American Teachers Association Forum* in Folder 11, Box 24, UFTR.

2 Milton A. Galamison, "If Blaine Is Repealed," *African-American Teachers Association Forum*, September–October 1967, Folder 11, Box 24, UFTR, and "Implications of 'Blaine Amendment,'" *New York Times*, October 21, 1967, 30. See Clarence Taylor on Galamison's positions in *Knocking at Our Own Door*, 206.

3 "Episode 3: Third Strike," *School Colors Podcast*.

4 Lewis, *New York City Public Schools from Brownsville to Bloomberg*, 55.

5 Lewis, *New York City Public Schools from Brownsville to Bloomberg*, 55–64.

6 "Episode 4: Agitate! Educate! Organize!," *School Colors Podcast*; Office of Education Affairs, "A Summary of the 1969 School Decentralization Law for New York City," 1969, https://files.eric.ed.gov.

7 Ravitch, *The Great School Wars*, 306.

8 Ravitch, *The Great School Wars*, 381.

9 Quoting Podair, Lewis, *New York City Public Schools from Brownsville to Bloomberg*, 10; Podair, *The Strike that Changed New York*, 212.

10 Isaacs, *Inside Ocean Hill-Brownsville*, 244, citing James Baldwin, Foreword to *The Chasm*, xvii.

11 Baldwin, Foreword, xvii.

12 Gordon, *Why They Couldn't Wait*; Lewis, *New York City Public Schools from Brownsville to Bloomberg*. Lewis does so by extending the timeline beyond community control's completion and the typical cast of characters, Gordon by exploring the underpinning political theory of democratic education.

13 Ravitch, *The Great School Wars*, 369.

14 Gordon, *Why They Couldn't Wait*; Lewis, *New York City Public Schools from Brownsville to Bloomberg*.

15 Maffly-Kipp, *Setting Down the Sacred Past*, 3.

16 Greene-Hayes, "Anti-Commodified Black Studies and the Radical Roots of Black Christian Education," 106.

17 Lewis, *New York City Public Schools from Brownsville to Bloomberg*, 44.

18 Chavers Johnson, "An Alternative to Miseducation for the Afro-American People," in *What Black Educators Are Saying*, edited by Nathan Wright, Jr. (New York: Hawthorn Books, 1970), 199.

19 Johnson, "An Alternative to Miseducation for the Afro-American People," 203.

20 Johnson, "An Alternative to Miseducation for the Afro-American People," 198.

21 Englewood High School 1936 Yearbook, Ancestry Library Edition, 27.

22 Maffly-Kipp, *Setting Down the Sacred Past*, 10; see discussion of "deprivation theory" in Sorett, "Secular Compared to What?," 57–65.

23 Chavers Johnson, "An Alternative to Miseducation for the Afro-American People," 200.

24 Maffly-Kipp, *Setting Down the Sacred Past*, 12.

25 Maffly-Kipp, *Setting Down the Sacred Past*, 3.

26 Edwina Chavers Johnson, "Teacher, Put Some Black on That Calendar!," *African-American Teachers Forum*, September 1969, Folder 11, Box 24, UFTR.

27 Albert J. Raboteau, *Slave Religion: The "Invisible Institution" of the American South* (New York: Oxford University Press, 1978, updated edition 2004), 8, 12, 30.

28 Maffly-Kipp and Lofton, *Women's Work*, 4.

29 Maffly-Kipp and Lofton, *Women's Work,* 4.

30 Maffly-Kipp, *Setting Down the Sacred Past*, 12.

31 Maffly-Kipp and Lofton, *Women's Work*, 11.

32 Chavers Johnson, "Teacher, Put Some Black on That Calendar!."

33 Chavers Johnson, "Teacher, Put Some Black on That Calendar!."

34 Her work continued into the 1990s. Board of Education of the City of New York, "DRAFT African-American Heritage: A Resource Guide for Teachers Grades 6–8," https://files.eric.ed.gov, 6, 8.

35 Chavers Johnson, "Teacher, Put Some Black on That Calendar!."

36 Edwina Chavers Johnson to Martin Luther King Jr., date unknown, The King Center, www.thekingcenter.org, accessed 2017, link now broken.

37 Maffly-Kipp, *Setting Down the Sacred Past*, 9.

38 Chavers Johnson, "Teacher, Put Some Black on That Calendar!."

39 Chavers Johnson, "Teacher, Put Some Black on That Calendar!."

40 Chavers Johnson, "Teacher, Put Some Black on That Calendar!."

41 Chavers Johnson, "Teacher, Put Some Black on That Calendar!." Italics in original. Original says September 1968, despite the article's September 1969 publication.

42 Chavers Johnson, "Teacher, Put Some Black on That Calendar!."

43 Chavers Johnson, "Teacher, Put Some Black on That Calendar!."

44 Dana Goldstein, "The Tough Lessons of the 1968 Teacher Strikes," *The Nation*, September 24, 2014, www.thenation.com; Alexander Russo, "New York City 1968 Was a Community Insurrection, Not a Teachers Strike," *Kappa Online*, September 26, 2018, www.kappanonline.org.

45 Tumblr Collection, accessed May 31, 2022, https://66.media.tumblr.com; Sam Roberts, "Rhody McCoy, Key Figure in New York's School Wars, Dies at 97," *New York Times*, May 21, 2020, www.nytimes.com.

46 Albert Raboteau, "African Americans, Exodus, and the American Israel," in *Religion and American Culture*, edited by David Hackett (New York: Routledge, 2003, 2nd ed.), 74–87.

47 "Episode 4: Agitate! Educate! Organize!," *School Colors Podcast*. Early on, the community seemed an ideal Pan-African utopia. However, some of the male leaders of The East and Uhuru Sasa Shule took an interest in polygamy to signal their "Africanness," which caused some of the women participants to leave. For more details, listen to the podcast.

48 Preston R. Wilcox, "Criteria for a Black Educational Methodology: A Think Piece," December 1971, Folder 23, Box 11, Preston Wilcox Papers, Schomburg Center for Research in Black Culture, The New York Public Library (hereafter cited as Wilcox Papers).

49 Baraka is also a complicated figure because of his comments about gay men and Israelis.

50 Imamu Amiri Baraka, *A Black Value System* (Newark, NJ: Jihad Productions, 1970), 5, accessed through Black Thought and Culture Database, https://alexanderstreet.com

51 Isaacs, *Inside Ocean Hill-Brownsville*; Lewis, *New York City Public Schools from Brownsville to Bloomberg*.

52 Lewis, *New York City Public Schools from Brownsville to Bloomberg*, 31n6. CUSA operated under the Brownsville Community Council's umbrella.

53 "Interview with Dolores Torres," October 31, 1988, Eyes on the Prize II Interviews, http://repository.wustl.edu.

54 Wilcox, "Education for Black Humanism," 11.

55 Preston R. Wilcox, "Discussion Stimulator: Some Thoughts on Black Humanism," July 26–27, 1969, Folder 30, Box 11, Wilcox Papers; and Wilcox, "Confronting White Institutional Racism," Folder 20, Box 11, Wilcox Papers.

56 Conroy-Krutz, *Christian Imperialism*; Kathryn Gin Lum, *Heathen: Religion and Race in American History* (Cambridge, MA: Harvard University Press, 2022); Sylvester Johnson, *The Myth of Ham in Nineteenth-Century America: Race, Heathens, and the People of God* (New York: Palgrave MacMillan, 2004); and Moss, "On Earth as It Is in Heaven."

57 Moss, *Schooling Citizens*, 10; Heather Andrea Williams, "'Clothing Themselves in Intelligence': The Freedpeople, Schooling, and Northern Teachers, 1861–1871," *Journal of African American History* 87 (2002): 372–389.

58 Moss, *Schooling Citizens*, 13.

59 See chapter 2 of this book.

60 Joseph Blankholm, "Secularism, Humanism, and Secular Humanism: Terms and Institutions," in *The Oxford Handbook of Secularism*, edited by Phil Zuckerman and John Shook (New York: Oxford University Press, 2017).

61 Wilcox, "Education for Black Humanism," 14.

62 Lewis, *New York City Public Schools from Brownsville to Bloomberg*, 28.

63 Taylor, *Knocking at Our Own Door*, 200.

64 Wilcox, "Education for Black Humanism," 8.

65 Wilcox, "Education for Black Humanism," 5.

66 Melissa Wilcox, *Queer Religiosities: An Introduction to Queer and Transgender Studies in Religion* (Lanham, MD: Rowman & Littlefield, 2020), 18.

67 Wilcox, "Education for Black Humanism," 14.

68 Wilcox, "Education for Black Humanism," 14.

69 Wilcox, "Education for Black Humanism," 14.

70 Wilcox, "Education for Black Humanism," 11.

71 Biondi, *To Stand and Fight*, 250; Robin D. G. Kelley, *Race Rebels: Culture, Politics, and the Black Working Class* (New York: Free Press, 1994), 22, elsewhere; Rolland Murray, *Our Living Manhood: Literature, Black Power, and Masculine Ideology* (Philadelphia: University of Pennsylvania Press, 2007); Sugrue, *Sweet Land of Liberty*, 317, 344, others.

72 Wilcox, "Education for Black Humanism," 4.

73 Wilcox, "Education for Black Humanism," 4.

74 John Kifner, "Eldridge Cleaver, Black Panther Who Became G.O.P. Conservative, Is Dead at 62," *New York Times*, May 2, 1998, www.nytimes.com; Dan Wells, "Born Again Black Panther: Race, Christian Conservatism, and the Remaking of Eldridge Cleaver," *Religion and American Culture* 30:3 (2020): 361–396.

75 Wilcox, "Education for Black Humanism," 14.

76 Wilcox, "Education for Black Humanism," 4–5.

77 Wilcox, "Black Control of Schools: Selected Viewpoints," Folder 13, Box 10, Wilcox Papers.

78 Preston R. Wilcox, "Black Power and Public Education," Folder 22, Box 10, Wilcox Papers.

79 Wilcox, "Black Control of Schools: Selected Viewpoints."

80 Kenneth Clark, "The Negro Protest: James Baldwin, Malcolm X and Martin Luther King Talk with Kenneth B. Clark" (Boston: Beacon Press, 1963), 22.

81 James Baldwin, "Negroes Are Anti-Semitic Because They Are Anti-White," *New York Times Magazine*, April 9, 1967, https://archive.nytimes.com; Ribovich and Rock-Singer, "Educating for the New Jerusalem."

82 Marc Dollinger, *Quest for Inclusion: Jews and Liberalism in Modern America* (Princeton, NJ: Princeton University Press, 2000); also see Beth Wenger, *History Lessons: The Creation of American Jewish Heritage* (Princeton, NJ: Princeton University Press, 2012). Calling Jews "white" is complicated yet illuminates the dynamics at play here. For more on the topic, see: Jonathan K. Crane, ed., *Judaism, Race, and Ethics: Conversations and Questions* (University Park, PA: Pennsylvania State Press, 2020); Jane Anna Gordon, "What Should Blacks Think When Jews Choose Whiteness?: An Ode to Baldwin," *Critical Philosophy of Race* 3:2 (2015): 227–258; Ribovich and Rock-Singer, "Educating for the New Jerusalem."

83 Wenger, *Religious Freedom*, 143–187.

84 Isaacs, *Inside Ocean Hill-Brownsville*, 185.

85 Isaacs, *Inside Ocean Hill-Brownsville*, 187.

86 Isaacs, *Inside Ocean Hill-Brownsville*, 186.

87 "The Unholy Sons of Shylock," Folder 9, Box 24, UFTR.

88 "The Unholy Sons of Shylock."

89 "Needed: A Responsible Jewish Voice," *African American Teachers Forum*, Folder 9, Box 24, UFTR; Preston R. Wilcox, "An Alternative to Black Educational Genocide," Folder 4, Box 10, Wilcox Papers.

90 Ravitch, *The Great School Wars*, 306.

91 John F. Hatchett, PS 68, "The Phenomenon of the Anti-Black Jews and the Black Anglo-Saxon," *African American Teachers Forum*, November–December 1967, 1 and 3, Folder 11, Box 24, UFTR.

92 Hatchett, "The Phenomenon of the Anti-Black Jews and the Black Anglo-Saxon." It is hard to identify the exact numbers since the Board of Education did not release statistical information about the religion of its employees.

93 Hatchett, "The Phenomenon of the Anti-Black Jews and the Black Anglo-Saxon."

94 Hatchett, "The Phenomenon of the Anti-Black Jews and the Black Anglo-Saxon."

95 Sorett, "Secular Compared to What?," 57–58.

96 Isaacs, *Inside Ocean Hill-Brownsville*, 132–134.

97 Taylor, *Knocking on Our Own Door*, 200.

98 Isaacs, *Inside Ocean Hill-Brownsville*, 133.

99 "Episode 3: Third Strike"; Leo Ferguson, "Ocean Hill-Brownsville and the Myth of 'Black Antisemitism,'" *Jewish Currents*, February 12, 2020, https://jewishcurrents.org; Isaacs, *Inside Ocean Hill-Brownsville*, 110, 132–138, 169–170; and Taylor, *Knocking on Our Own Door*, 200, 206.

100 Taylor, *Knocking on Our Own Door*, 200.

101 Isaacs, *Inside Ocean Hill-Brownsville*, 132.

102 "Episode 3: Third Strike."

103 "Interview with Dolores Torres"; "Episode 3: Third Strike." For a fascinating look at a theatrical attempt at interracial and interreligious harmony, see Alisa Solomon, *Wonder of Wonders: A Cultural History of* Fiddler on the Roof (New York: Picador, 2013), 258–290.

104 "Episode 3: Third Strike." The podcast hosts make this point.

105 Ironically given the arguably anti-Semitic origins of Christianity, see Carter, *Race*, 104.

106 James Baldwin, "A Talk to Teachers."

CONCLUSION

1 "Rulings Obeyed, Bible Reading in Assembly Ends," *The Public Schools of New York City*, Vol. II, No. 1, September 9, 1963, Box 3, Series 530, Staff Bulletin, 1962–1972, and Folder 354, Box 13, Subseries I: Subject Files, 1961–1964, Series 379, Max J. Rubin Files, NYCBER.

2 "Integration Plan Sets 4 Main Areas," *The Public Schools of New York City*, Vol. II, No. 1, September 9, 1963, emphasis in original.

3 On white "colorblindness" in education leading up to *Brown v. Board of Education*, see Zoe Burkholder, *Color in the Classroom: How American Schools Taught Race, 1900–1954* (New York: Oxford University Press, 2011).

4 Sullivan, *Church State Corporation*, 10, 160–179.

5 Amy Hollywood, "Performativity, Citationality, Ritualization," *History of Religions* 42 (2002): 93–115. Each performance of a ritual differs, yet the ritual continues, according to Hollywood. Rituals, and therefore power relations, contain the possibility for change.

6 Balmer, *Bad Faith*; Cooper, *Family Values*; Hartman, *A War for the Soul of America*; Kruse, *White Flight*; Lassiter, *The Silent Majority*; Petrzela, *Classroom Wars*; Zimmerman, *Whose America?*.

7 Charles McCrary and Leslie Ribovich, "The Supreme Court's Holy War Against Public Schools," *New Republic*, July 5, 2022, https://newrepublic.com.

SELECTED BIBLIOGRAPHY

ARCHIVAL COLLECTIONS

Archives of the Archdiocese of New York, St. Joseph's Seminary, Dunwoodie.
  Francis Cardinal Spellman Collection, Collection 007.
  Chancery Office, Collection 021.
George Washington University, Special Collections Research Center.
  Educational Policies Commission Series, National Education Association Records.
New York City Municipal Archives.
  New York City Board of Education Records.
New York City Public Library, Manuscripts and Archives Division.
  David Spitz Papers.
New York State Archives.
  New York State Education Department Commissioner Lewis A. Wilson Subject Files.
  Subseries 2: Deputy Commissioner James E. Allen's Subject Files.
  New York State Education Department Commissioner's Interim Subject Files.
  New York State Education Department Commissioner James E. Allen Subject Files.
New York University, Tamiment Library/Robert F. Wagner Labor Archives.
  United Federation of Teachers Records, WAG 022.
Schomburg Center for Research in Black Culture, The New York Public Library.
  Ella Baker Papers.
  Preston Wilcox Papers.
Social Welfare History Archives, University of Minnesota Libraries.
  National Conference of Christians and Jews Records.

SELECTED SOURCES

Agyepong, Tera Eva. *The Criminalization of Black Children: Race, Gender, and Delinquency in Chicago's Juvenile Justice System, 1899–1945*. Chapel Hill: University of North Carolina Press, 2018.
Baldwin, James. "A Talk to Teachers." *The Saturday Review*. December 21, 1963. Delivered as "The Negro Child—His Self-Image." PS 180. Harlem, October 16, 1963. www.zinnedproject.org.
———. Foreword to Robert Campbell, *The Chasm: The Life and Death of a Great Experiment in Ghetto Education*. Boston: Houghton Mifflin, 1974.
Balmer, Randall. *Bad Faith: Race and the Rise of the Religious Right*. Grand Rapids, MI: Wm. B. Eerdmans Publishing, 2021.

Bell, Derrick. *Silent Covenants: Brown v. Board of Education and the Unfulfilled Hopes for Racial Reform.* New York: Oxford University Press, 2005.

Bellah, Robert N. "Civil Religion in America." *Daedalus* 96:1 (1967): 1–21. doi: www.jstor.org/stable/20027022.

Bender, Courtney and Pamela Klassen, eds. *After Pluralism: Reimagining Religious Engagement.* New York: Columbia University Press, 2010.

Benedek, Laslo. *Boy with a Knife.* Film. 1956. New York: Dudley Pictures Corporation.

Biondi, Martha. *To Stand and Fight: The Struggle for Civil Rights in Postwar New York City.* Cambridge, MA: Harvard University Press, 2006.

Boyarin, Daniel. *Intertextuality and the Reading of Midrash.* Bloomington: Indiana University Press, 1990.

Carter, J. Kameron. *Race: A Theological Account.* New York: Oxford University Press, 2008.

Cone, James. *Black Theology and Black Power.* New York: Harper & Row, 1969.

Conroy-Krutz, Emily. *Christian Imperialism: Converting the World in the Early American Republic.* Ithaca, NY: Cornell University Press, 2015.

Cooper, Melinda. *Family Values: Between Neoliberalism and the New Social Conservatism.* Princeton, NJ: Princeton University Press, 2017.

Crane, Jonathan K., ed. *Judaism, Race, and Ethics: Conversations and Questions.* University Park: Pennsylvania State University Press, 2020.

Delmont, Matthew F. *Why Busing Failed: Race, Media, and the National Resistance to School Desegregation.* Oakland: University of California Press, 2016.

Dubler, Joshua and Vincent Lloyd. "Mass Incarceration Is Religious (and So Is Abolition): A Provocation." *Abolition Journal.* August 18, 2016. https://abolitionjournal.org.

Dubler, Joshua and Isaac Weiner, eds. *Religion, Law, USA.* New York: New York University Press, 2019.

Fessenden, Tracy. *Culture and Redemption: Religion, the Secular, and American Literature.* Princeton, NJ: Princeton University Press, 2007.

Gaston, K. Healan. "Interpreting Judeo-Christianity in America." *Relegere* 2:2 (2012): 291–304. doi: 10.11157/rsrr2-2-505.

———. *Imagining Judeo-Christian America: Religion, Secularism, and the Redefinition of Democracy.* Chicago: Chicago University Press, 2019.

Gin Lum, Kathryn. "The Historyless Heathen and the Stagnating Pagan." *Religion and American Culture* 28:1 (2018): 52–91. doi: 10.1525/rac.2018.28.1.52.

Glaude Jr., Eddie S. *African American Religions: A Very Short Introduction.* New York: Oxford University Press, 2014.

Glueck, Sheldon and Eleanor Glueck. *Unraveling Juvenile Delinquency.* New York: The Commonwealth Fund, 1950.

Gordon, Jane Anna. *Why They Couldn't Wait: A Critique of the Black-Jewish Conflict Over Community Control in Ocean-Hill Brownsville, 1967–1971.* New York: Routledge, 2001.

Gordon, Sarah Barringer. *The Spirit of the Law: Religious Voices and the Constitution in Modern America.* Cambridge, MA: Belknap Press, 2010.

Green, Steven K. "The Insignificance of the Blaine Amendment." *Brigham Young University Law Review* 2 (2008): 295–333.

——. *The Bible, the School, and the Constitution: The Clash that Shaped Modern Church-State Doctrine.* New York: Oxford University Press, 2012.

——. *The Third Disestablishment: Church, State, and American Culture, 1940–1975.* New York: Oxford University Press, 2019.

Greenawalt, Kent. *Does God Belong in Public Schools?* Princeton, NJ: Princeton University Press, 2005.

Greene-Hayes, Ahmad. "Anti-Commodified Black Studies and the Radical Roots of Black Christian Education." *Souls: A Critical Journal of Black Politics, Culture, and Society* 22:1 (2020): 104–117. doi: 10.1080/10999949.2020.1804802.

Hamburger, Philip. *Separation of Church and State.* Cambridge, MA: Harvard University Press, 2002.

Hargraves, J. Archie. "The Local Church and Juvenile Delinquency." *Christianity and Crisis* 17:28 (January 1958): 180–183.

Hartman, Andrew. *Education and the Cold War: The Battle for the American School.* New York: Palgrave Macmillan, 2008.

——. *A War for the Soul of America: A History of the Culture Wars.* Chicago: University of Chicago Press, 2015.

"Hebrew Culture Contest." WNYC. June 4, 1952. www.wnyc.org/. Accessed August 21, 2020.

Herberg, Will. *Protestant-Catholic-Jew: An Essay in American Religious Sociology.* New York: Doubleday, 1955.

Herzog, Jonathan P. *The Spiritual-Industrial Complex: America's Religious Battle Against Communism in the Early Cold War.* New York: Oxford University Press, 2011.

Holscher, Kathleen. *Religious Lessons: Catholic Sisters and the Captured Schools Crisis in New Mexico.* New York: Oxford University Press, 2012.

Hucks, Tracey. *Yoruba Traditions and African American Religious Nationalism.* Albuquerque: University of New Mexico Press, 2012.

Hulsether, Lucia. "The Grammar of Racism: Religious Pluralism and the Birth of the Interdisciplines." *Journal of the American Academy of Religion* 86:1 (March 2018): 1–41. doi: 10.1093/jaarel/lfx049.

"Interview with Dolores Torres." October 31, 1988. Eyes on the Prize II Interviews. http://repository.wustl.edu.

Isaacs, Charles S. *Inside Ocean Hill-Brownsville: A Teacher's Education, 1968–69.* Albany: State University of New York Press, 2014.

Jansen, William and Nellie B. Allen. *Distant Lands: Part Two.* Boston: Ginn and Company, 1931.

Juvenile Delinquency Evaluation Project of the City of New York: Final Report No. I: The Planning of Delinquency Prevention and Control. February 1961. https://babel.hathitrust.org.

Juvenile Delinquency Evaluation Project of the City of New York: Final Report No. II: Delinquency in the Great City. Princeton University Library, Public Administration Collection. July 17, 1961.

Kruse, Kevin M. *White Flight: Atlanta and the Making of Modern Conservatism*. Princeton, NJ: Princeton University Press, 2005.

———. *One Nation Under God: How Corporate America Invented Christian America*. New York: Basic Books, 2015.

Lassiter, Matthew. *The Silent Majority: Suburban Politics in the Sunbelt South*. Princeton, NJ: Princeton University Press, 2006.

Lee, Robert. "Delinquent Youth in a Normless Time." *The Christian Century* 79:49 (December 1962): 1475–1478.

Lewis, Heather. *New York City Public Schools from Brownsville to Bloomberg: Community Control and Its Legacy*. New York: Teachers College Press, 2013.

MacIver, Robert. "The City of New York Juvenile Delinquency Evaluation Project: A Progress Report." January 1958. https://babel.hathitrust.org.

Maffly-Kipp, Laurie. *Setting Down the Sacred Past: African-American Race Histories*. Cambridge, MA: Harvard University Press, 2010.

Maffly-Kipp, Laurie and Kathryn Lofton. *Women's Work: An Anthology of African-American Women's Historical Writings from Antebellum America to the Harlem Renaissance*. New York: Oxford University Press, 2010.

Masuzawa, Tomoko. *The Invention of World Religions: Or, How European Universalism Was Preserved in the Language of Pluralism*. Chicago: University of Chicago Press, 2005.

McCrary, Charles. *Sincerely Held: American Secularism and Its Believers*. Chicago: University of Chicago Press, 2022.

McLaren, Norman. *Neighbours*. Film. 1952. Montreal: National Film Board of Canada. www.nfb.ca.

Meyer, Birgit. "Medium." *Material Religion* 7:1 (2011): 58–64. doi: 10.2752/175183411X12968355482015.

Moss, Hilary J. *Schooling Citizens: The African American Struggle for Education in Antebellum America*. Chicago: University of Chicago Press, 2009.

Moss, Kelsey. "On Earth as It Is in Heaven: Spiritual Racialization and the Atlantic World Economy of Salvation in the Colonial Americas." PhD diss., Princeton University, 2018.

Muhammad, Khalil Gibran. *The Condemnation of Blackness: Race, Crime, and the Making of Modern Urban America*. Cambridge, MA: Harvard University Press, 2010.

Murakawa, Naomi. *The First Civil Right: How Liberals Built Prison America*. New York: Oxford University Press, 2014.

The New York State Constitutional Convention Proceedings. 1967. 12 vols. *The Making of Modern Law: Primary Sources*. www.gale.com

Perry, Imani. *More Beautiful and More Terrible: The Embrace and Transcendence of Racial Inequality in the United States*. New York: New York University Press, 2011.

Petrzela, Natalia Mehlman. *Classroom Wars: Language, Sex, and the Making of Modern Political Culture*. New York: Oxford University Press, 2015.

Podair, Jerald. *The Strike that Changed New York*. New Haven, CT: Yale University Press, 2004.

Ravitch, Diane. *The Great School Wars: A History of the New York City Public Schools.* Baltimore, MD: Johns Hopkins University Press, 2000 [1978].

Ribovich, Leslie. "Saving Black Boys: Delinquency, Race, and the Institutionalization of Religious Practice at the Wiltwyck School for Boys, 1937–1942." *American Religion* 2:1 (2020): 101–130. doi: 10.2979/amerreli.2.1.10.

———. "*Brown v. Board* and Religion and Law Beyond the First Amendment." In *Bloomsbury Religion in North America: Religion and Law*, edited by Mona Oraby. London: Bloomsbury Publishing, forthcoming.

Ribovich, Leslie and Cara Rock-Singer. "Educating for the New Jerusalem to Deliver the Messianic Age: Imagining Friendship for Other Futures with Louis Finkelstein and James Baldwin." *Jewish Quarterly Review* (forthcoming).

Rock-Singer, Cara. "A Prophetic Guide for a Perplexed World: Louis Finkelstein and the 1940 Conference on Science, Philosophy and Religion." *Religion and American Culture* 29:2 (2019): 179–215. doi: 10.1017/rac.2019.2.

"School Colors." 2019. Podcast. From "Brooklyn Deep," Mark Winston Griffith and Max Freedman, creators/hosts. www.schoolcolorspodcast.com/episodes.

Schultz, Kevin. *Tri-Faith America: How Catholics and Jews Held Postwar America to Its Protestant Promise.* New York: Oxford University Press, 2011.

Smith, Carol Cordes. "Using Films in Group Guidance with Emotionally Disturbed Socially Maladjusted Boys." *Exceptional Children* 24:5 (1958), doi: 10.1177/001440295802400503.

Sorett, Josef. "Secular Compared to What?: Toward a History of the Trope of Black Sacred/Secular Fluidity." In *Race and Secularism in America*, edited by Jonathon Kahn and Vincent Lloyd. New York: Columbia University Press, 2016.

———. *Spirit in the Dark: A Religious History of Racial Aesthetics.* New York: Oxford University Press, 2016.

Strub, Whitney. *Perversion for Profit: The Politics of Pornography and the Rise of the New Right.* New York: Columbia University Press, 2011.

Sugrue, Thomas. *Sweet Land of Liberty: The Forgotten Struggle for Civil Rights in the North.* New York: Random House, 2008.

Sullivan, Winnifred Fallers. *Church State Corporation: Construing Religion in U.S. Law.* Chicago: University of Chicago Press, 2020.

Taylor, Clarence. *Knocking at Our Own Door: Milton A. Galamison and the Struggle to Integrate New York City Schools.* New York: Columbia University Press, 1997.

———. *Reds at the Blackboard: Communism, Civil Rights, and the New York City Teachers Union.* New York: Columbia University Press, 2011.

Vertinsky, Patricia. "Physique as Destiny: William H. Sheldon, Barbara Honeyman Heath and the Struggle for Hegemony in the Science of Somatotyping." *Canadian Bulletin of Medical History* 24:2 (2007): 291–316. doi: 10.3138/cbmh.24.2.291.

Weiner, Melissa. *Power, Protest, and the Public Schools: Jewish and African American Struggles in New York City.* New Brunswick, NJ: Rutgers University Press, 2010.

Weisenfeld, Judith. *New World A-Coming: Black Religion and Racial Identity during the Great Migration.* New York: New York University Press, 2017.

Weissman Joselit, Jenna. *Set in Stone: America's Embrace of the Ten Commandments.* New York: Oxford University Press, 2017.

Wenger, Tisa. *Religious Freedom: The Contested History of an American Ideal.* Chapel Hill: University of North Carolina Press, 2017.

Wilkerson, David. *The Cross and the Switchblade.* New York: Penguin, 1962.

Wright, Jr., Nathan, ed. *What Black Educators Are Saying.* New York: Hawthorn Books, 1970.

Zimmerman, Jonathan. *Whose America?: Culture Wars in the Public Schools.* Cambridge, MA: Harvard University Press, 2002.

INDEX

Pages numbers in italics indicate Figures

ABOUT THE AUTHOR

LESLIE BETH RIBOVICH is Director of the Greenberg Center for the Study of Religion in Public Life and Associate Professor of Religious Studies and Public Policy and Law at Trinity College in Hartford, CT. She is part of the Young Scholars in American Religion 2020–2023 cohort. Her work has been published in *American Religion*, *Religion & Politics*, and *The New Republic*.